An Introduction to the Criminology of Genocide

William R. Pruitt

An Introduction to the Criminology of Genocide

palgrave
macmillan

William R. Pruitt
Endicott College
Beverly, MA, USA

ISBN 978-3-030-65210-4 ISBN 978-3-030-65211-1 (eBook)
https://doi.org/10.1007/978-3-030-65211-1

Cover illustration: Sudarsani Ida Ayu Putu/Shutterstock

This Palgrave Macmillan imprint is published by the registered company Springer Nature Switzerland AG.
The registered company address is: Gewerbestrasse 11, 6330 Cham, Switzerland

I dedicate this book to all those who have suffered through genocide,
the most heinous crime on earth—those who survived,
those who we lost, their friends and their families.
It is my hope and desire that one day
we may eradicate this scourge from the world.

Preface

This project began over a decade ago. I have long wondered about genocide as a crime and what we can do about it. As a graduate student I created a course on the criminology of genocide not only to educate others about genocide but also to help myself deal with what seemed like an insurmountable problem. That first class turned into teaching that course several times over the years.

Each time I taught this course I would learn something new to add to my expanding understanding of genocide. I was able to combine much of that information into this book. I have little doubt that once I submit this manuscript I will learn something new and desire to add more to what is already here. But I do believe what is in this book is a good start to processing genocide as a crime.

While genocide cannot be limited to one category like crime, it has been called the "crime of crimes" and we cannot address it fully without an understanding of the act as a crime. I hope this book can serve to fill in the gap in knowledge about criminology and genocide. I make no claim that this is all there is to the criminology of genocide and any errors are mine.

Chapter 1 explains the evolution of the concept of genocide and the definitional issues that exist in determining what acts qualify as genocide. A discussion of the work of Raphael Lemkin includes highlighting his early work on the subject, his development of the word, and his original definition of the crime. This includes exploring Lemkin's methodology of genocide—how genocide could occur.

After exploring Lemkin's original definition of genocide, there is a discussion of how the concept of genocide was officially codified by the United Nations. After exploring the UN official definition of genocide, it can be compared with Lemkin's original concept for similarities and differences. Then alternative definitions of genocide will be explored.

In Chap. 2, it is shown that understanding why genocide occurs is crucial to a full understanding of the crime and hopefully its prevention. There is no single reason why genocide might occur; there are many reasons and many possible explanations for it. This chapter looks at the different academic explanations for genocide from a variety of disciplines. Ideally, after exploring the myriad theories one can look for common factors among the disciplines that might help explain how we understand genocide.

These understandings come from different disciplines but feed into the recent criminological theories of genocide. Since criminology is an interdisciplinary field it is easy to connect these diverse fields to criminology and explain what aspects of these fields could be incorporated into a general criminological theory of genocide.

Chapter 3 recognizes that genocide is a topic crossing many academic disciplines and that there is no single theoretical explanation for why genocide occurs. The many different disciplines examining genocide have offered many different theories of genocide. These theories though can be categorized and grouped together in certain ways.

The purpose of this chapter is to explore in more depth specific theories that explain why genocide might occur. Tying these theories back to the previous chapter will allow students to make connections between the material in Chap. 2 and how they are used in theoretical work.

Then Chap. 4 explores the question of who commits genocide. It may not seem obvious that the "state" in many cases is committing the act. To understand this concept, it is presented by showing that the "state" does not exist by itself, it is a collection of individuals. When their work turns to crime or genocide, the state is responsible for the action.

Essentially, this chapter is looking at how perpetrators can be at the macro-level (state) and the micro-level (individuals). At the micro-level, there are many reasons people commit genocide from ideology to fear to duress. These motivations also affect their personal liability for the crime. Who commits genocide is more than just "crazy" murderers; it includes the state itself and otherwise rational individuals.

Chapter 5 is designed to be a brief history of the concept of genocide. This chapter is designed to introduce students to critical thinking about cases of genocide that might have occurred before the word/crime existed.

Case studies include the Herero genocide, the Armenian genocide, the Bangladesh genocide, Darfur, and the Rohingya genocide. The case studies are designed to explore the history that led to the genocide. In this way similarities and differences can be analyzed in order to create potential warning signs of impending genocide.

The next chapter is designed to explain the methods available to respond to genocide. This can include military or political intervention during an ongoing genocide or a legal response after a genocide has occurred. By exploring the Rwandan and Kosovo situations we understand that the UN response to genocide is not enough to prevent its occurrence. Following the disastrous response to the Rwandan genocide much work was put into what became known as R2P—the responsibility to protect.

A discussion of how individuals can respond to genocide includes simple actions one can take when confronted with genocide. The goal of this chapter is to explore how to respond to genocide and not whether we should respond.

The final chapter deals with genocide denial. Denial is a way in to diminish the atrocities that have occurred and forget about the victims. This behavior has been hypothesized to lead to reoccurrence of genocide. Denial permits people to forget and when no survivors are left all that remains is memory. When memory is attacked and denied, the possibility of reoccurrence emerges.

As a criminal aspect, many European countries have criminalized genocide denial. The reasoning for this is to protect memory and honor the victims. These reasons counteract the goal of denial which is usually to forget. As such these laws have a place in our understanding of genocide denial.

Throughout the book, readers should see and make connections among the various chapters. The purpose of using thematic questions is to recognize that all of these questions are intertwined.

Beverly, MA William R. Pruitt
September 2020

Acknowledgments

There are many people to thank for getting me to this place. No man is an island, and writing a book is no better place to discover the truth of that statement. This project has undergone many changes in both direction and structure, all for the better I believe. This would not have been possible without the wonderful advice and contributions from many people including the early reviewers.

A manuscript is nothing if not an exercise in mental strength and ability, but it takes a strain on much more than the mind. I would not be where I am today without my amazing family and their undying support. I cannot thank them enough for their understanding and compassion throughout this project and throughout my life.

A thank you is not enough, but I must say thank you, thank you, thank you to my amazing parents—my mother, Patricia Pruitt, and my father, William Pruitt. I only wish they were here with us now to see this completed project. I must thank my wonderful sister, Jennifer Roberts, for all she has given and sacrificed so that I might be where I am today.

Finally, there are many others who lent an ear and a pat on the back when needed, especially my dear friends Drs Emme and LaToya Colm, Brian Roberts, and Dr. Taryn Myers. Thank you to all the terrific people who have lifted me up when I was down and showed me the way to succeed. As trite as it may sound, I would not be here today without your support and kind words. To anyone I forgot to thank, I ask for your forgiveness and say thank you.

Contents

List of Tables

What Is Genocide?

1

In April 1994, the small country of Rwanda in central Africa devolved into mass violence and slaughter. By the time the violence ended in July over 500,000 people would be dead. For months during that summer the United States government struggled to find a word to attach to these killings. The United Nations determined that the killings were a coordinated effort to exterminate an ethnic group—the Tutsis.[1] *This finding should have paved the way for labeling this crisis genocide.*

However, on May 20, 1994 the United States government met to determine what label to place on this event. The Department of State agreed to say that "acts of genocide" had occurred.[2] *At a news conference on June 10, 1994 State Department spokeswoman Christine Shelly said, "We have every reason to believe acts of genocide have occurred."*

One reporter asked, "How many acts of genocide does it take to make genocide?" Shelly responded, "Um…that's just not a question that I'm in a position to answer."[3]

While the reasons why the United States was loath to call the killings in Rwanda genocide can be debated, the ultimate question was: what is genocide? Are there specific requirements of genocide? Can any event be labeled genocide?

In this chapter we will discover what defines genocide. While many definitions exist, only one refers to the act as an international crime.

W. R. Pruitt, *An Introduction to the Criminology of Genocide*,
https://doi.org/10.1007/978-3-030-65211-1_1

Pre-genocide

"Genocide is a new word, but the evil it describes is old. It is as old as the history of mankind."[4] The act of genocide has been around for generations. Examples of genocide have been found to date back to Melos in 416 B.C.E. and the fall of Carthage in 150 B.C.E.[5] Genocide can be found in the Bible—the rape of the Sabine women. In the twelfth century, the Mongols became victims of the Huns.[6] From the fifteenth to the eighteenth centuries, native populations were often exterminated in the name of progress.[7]

MELOS AND CARTHAGE

When Melos refused to assist in Athens's Peloponnesian War, Athens attacked. All the men on the island were killed and the women and children enslaved.

The Romans seized Carthage and in doing so estimates of 150,000 (out of 200,000) Carthaginians were killed. ◄

The twentieth century has been referred to as the century of genocide due to the many cases during the century. The twenty-first century has also started with a few cases of genocide of its own. So, while the action has been a plague on the world for millennia, the word genocide is a relatively recent addition to the lexicon.

The word genocide dates back to 1942. In order to discuss where the word genocide came from we must introduce Raphael Lemkin. Raphael Lemkin was a Polish Jewish lawyer born in 1900 and grew up on a farm called Ozerisko.[8] In 1915, during World War I, the Russians occupied Lemkin's hometown. Under occupation, Lemkin began to study history and explore how other minority groups were being treated.

When the war ended, Lemkin learned of how Ottoman Turks had killed and expelled the Armenians for no other reason than their religion. Lemkin, and the world, watched as those accused of the murder of one million Armenians were never held accountable for their actions. Lemkin wondered, "Why is a man punished when he kills another man, yet the killing of a million is a lessor crime than the killing of an individual?"[9] This question would haunt him for many years.

Lemkin pursued an education in law, ultimately becoming a deputy prosecutor in Warsaw, Poland in 1929. By 1933 Adolf Hitler had been appointed Chancellor of Germany and Lemkin saw dark clouds on the horizon. In October 1933 Lemkin planned on attending an international legal conference to be held in Madrid. He intended to present a new crime to the conference in response to both Hitler's ascent to power and the Armenian tragedy.[10]

Lemkin formulated two crimes which he thought could curb the attacks on groups based on their identity. He called the first one—the crime of barbarity. The second he called the crime of vandalism. Barbarity was defined as destroying a national or religious collectivity.[11] Vandalism included the destruction of culture of a collectivity (such as destroying works of art or literature).[12]

Sadly, Lemkin never made it to Madrid. The government of Poland refused to allow Lemkin to travel to Spain for the conference. What the government may not have known was that Lemkin had already sent his proposal to the conference ahead of time. After Lemkin discovered he could not travel to Madrid he contacted friends in Western Europe asking them to share and support his proposal.[13] This made it impossible for the conference to ignore his proposal.

Lemkin's proposal was discussed at the Madrid conference. There was not much support for it though. The proposal was tabled meaning no vote was taken.[14] Lemkin saw this action as a success saying, "They would not say yes, but they could not say no."[15] Even though Lemkin's proposal was not acted upon, he did not stop his fight to have the law and the world pay attention.

By 1939, Lemkin was facing a difficult decision. Germany had invaded Poland soon followed by the Russians. Having experienced Russian occupation during World War I and having studied what happened to the Armenians and other minority groups, Lemkin made the decision to leave Poland. He tried to get his family to leave with him, but most of them just could not see how they were in danger.

After several weeks of arduous travel, Lemkin made his way to Sweden. His ultimate goal was to reach the United States. He accomplished this goal by obtaining a teaching position at Duke University in North Carolina. Following several boat, plane, and train rides (totaling over 14,000 miles) he arrived in North Carolina in 1941.[16]

Lemkin in the United States Lemkin arrived in the United States on April 18, 1941. Lemkin fled Poland in 1939 and took refuge in Lithuania. When that country was seized by the Russians he fled to Sweden. From Sweden Lemkin arrived on the west coast of the United States by traveling the Siberian route across Russia, through Japan and across the Pacific Ocean (Biographical Reference Collection, Box 17, "Raphael Lemkin," David M. Rubenstein Rare Book & Manuscript Library, Duke University). Lemkin then took a train across the United States to arrive in North Carolina. His journey would have encompassed over 12,500 miles.

Lemkin's first position was at Duke University Law School in Durham, North Carolina as a special lecturer in comparative law. In 1942, Lemkin was invited by the Board of Economic Warfare in Washington D.C. to become the chief consultant for the board. Lemkin accepted and arrived in Washington at a crucial time in US history. Lemkin saw this as an opportunity to encourage the US government to pay attention to the crime of genocide as it was currently being executed by Germany.

In order to promote his work on genocide, Lemkin wrote to President Roosevelt encouraging him to act. The president responded that he was aware of the issue but time and patience was needed. Lemkin found this response unsatisfactory and decided that he needed to reach out to more than just politicians if he was to see action taken (Frieze, Donna-Lee (ed.) (2013) *Totally unofficial: The autobiography of Raphael Lemkin*, New Haven: Yale University Press).

It was then that Lemkin began work on what would become his magnum opus. In 1944, he published *Axis Rule in Occupied Europe*—a 700+ page volume analyzing the laws with which Nazi Germany governed its occupied territories. Chapter IX was devoted to genocide. Lemkin again reiterated his previous work on the subject explaining how he created the word and how he defined its acts.

After the end of World War II Lemkin spent most of his time at the United Nations seeking an international law against the crime of genocide. Up until his death at age 59, Lemkin worked to see the UN Convention on Genocide ratified by as many nations as possible. Unfortunately, Lemkin did not live long enough to see his adopted country of the United States ratify the Convention. Lemkin is buried in Mount Hebron Cemetery in Queens, New York.

A few years later in 1944 Lemkin published *Axis Rule in Occupied Europe* and revealed to the world the word genocide. Lemkin had combined the Greek word *genos* (meaning tribe/race) and the Latin word *cide* (meaning killing) to create a new word that described age-old action: "the crime of destroying national, racial, or religious groups."[17]

Genocide According to Lemkin

As the creator of the word genocide Lemkin gave us the first definition of the act. Lemkin said that genocide was a coordinated plan with the aim of destroying the essential foundations of the life of national groups so that these groups wither and die.[18] The killings may be directed at individuals, but the broader purpose is to eliminate the entire group to which that person belongs.[19]

Lemkin believed that this destruction could occur in many different ways. He labeled these techniques of genocide and explained how they could attack the life of a group. Lemkin considered murder the most direct and drastic technique.[20] Murder and other physical attacks on the group would bring about its end. When most people think of genocide they think of mass murder. Lemkin cautioned that there were many other ways to eliminate a group.

The political technique of genocide involved preventing communication and mutual assistance by a group.[21] A country may also recast the legal system to ostracize the minority group. Lemkin saw this occur to the Armenians in World War I and the Jews in World War II. In both cases, the law made it legal to discriminate against a certain group. This then justified the horrible conditions of the group. These minorities were also excluded from the political life of their country and thus could not effectively argue for fairer treatment.

The social technique of genocide includes attacking the intelligentsia of a group.[22] This subset is attacked because they often act as leadership for the larger group. By removing leadership and potential leaders, it becomes easier to marginalize the group. Marginalization can lead to greater subjugation of the out-group. Losing the intelligentsia of the group may mean that there are no leaders to help champion their rights.

The cultural technique according to Lemkin focused on destroying the unique culture of a group.[23] Culture could include language, art, books, sculpture, and any special cultural icon associated with the targeted group. Again, Lemkin saw this happen to the Jews and other groups. Refusing to allow Yiddish to be used in Germany could potentially erase the language as it is no longer taught or heard. This cultural attack weakens the group.

The religious/moral technique occurred when the power of the church was undermined.[24] By undermining a group's faith, the moral standards also weaken. Weakened morals may contribute to the overall weakening of the group and its willingness to fight. Burning synagogues was a common tool used in Germany. As we will see, burning of churches and mosques is a common way to target religious groups.

The economic technique involved lowering the standards of living for the group.[25] A lower standard of living creates pressures of its own. Survival becomes paramount and little energy is left to maintain a cultural or national existence. By taking away the possibility to work or earn money to buy food, the group must spend its time on finding ways to survive. This technique undercuts the group's solidarity by forcing them to focus on survival and not resistance.

The biological technique involved decreased birth rates and excluding inferiors.[26] This technique combines with other techniques to accomplish its goals. If a group is focused on survival, reproduction may not be a priority. And even if the group reproduces the issue may become whether the children will survive. Poor health conditions combined with a lack of food and vitamins will slowly eliminate the group and also effect the likelihood of young children surviving to adulthood. The **Holodomor** (Ukrainian famine) is an example of how creating a famine nearly killed an entire population.

HOLODOMOR

The Holodomor was a famine created by the government of the USSR targeting Ukraine in 1932–1933. The famine was created by the government in order to stop independence movements in Ukraine. Estimates of the dead from the famine are in the millions. Lemkin would have no issue calling this genocide as it attacked the biological well-beings of an entire people. ◄

Lemkin's original concept of genocide was expansive and included many techniques that targeted a group for maltreatment with an ultimate goal of eradication. This broad definition was never adopted by others. Part of the reason may be because it is harder to "see" genocide when it is accomplished through methods other than murder. As Lemkin sought for genocide to become a crime, he had to make some sacrifices in his definition to win support. As a lawyer, Lemkin likely knew he would have to make concessions at some point.

Genocide According to the United Nations

Lemkin spent many years guiding the United Nations in defining and outlawing genocide. His goal was to see an international law against genocide. Lemkin desired an international law because he believed that genocide affects the vital interests of *all* people. The consequences of genocide cannot be limited in scope. Lemkin believed that if one group is eliminated the entire world suffers because we lose the art, literature, science, etc. that the group would have contributed to society.

Further, calling genocide a national crime would not be sufficient because the state is usually involved in the act and is not going to hold itself accountable. An international law would be needed to hold states liable for their criminal behavior. To reach an international law meant Lemkin must get many nations to agree to a single definition.

This process was not easy as some countries wanted to avoid being charged with genocide, so they fought against an expansive definition. Political groups were excluded from the final definition because the Soviet Union and other nations were repressing political groups inside their borders. After years of work, the United Nations settled on a definition incorporating many of Lemkin's ideas.

The official definition of genocide according to the United Nations Convention on the Prevention and Punishment of Genocide:

> Genocide means any of the following acts committed with intent to destroy, in whole or in part, a national, ethnical, racial, or religious group, as such:

(a) Killing members of the group;
(b) Causing serious bodily or mental harm to members of the group;
(c) Deliberately inflicting on the group conditions of life calculated to bring about its physical destruction in whole or in part;
(d) Imposing measures intended to prevent births within the group;
(e) Forcibly transferring children of the group to another group.

This definition is narrower than Lemkin's original concept. First, there must be intent to destroy. All criminal acts require an intent in order to be considered a crime. Second, the intent must be to destroy in whole or in part. This wording has been argued over for many years. What is a part of a group? Is a minimum number required?

There is still no consensus on what "in part" means but when the United States ratified the Convention, they included an interpretation that "in part" meant "substantial part." Other nations have agreed to this understanding. The UN has called the murder of 8000 Bosniak men as genocide. So while no minimum number exists there is no officially labeled genocide with a lower death count.

Perhaps most importantly, the UN definition of genocide is limited to a list of specific groups. In order to be genocide, the attack must be on a national, ethnic, racial, or religious group. If an attack occurs on a group not listed, it is not genocide. Therefore, attacks on political groups, gender, or social groups do not qualify legally as genocide. This exclusion of groups has been contentious from the beginning. As we explore other definitions of genocide, this limitation often disappears.

The list of prohibited acts includes killing and causing serious bodily or mental harm. This accords with Lemkin's original techniques of genocide (biological, economic). Other prohibited acts include the broader notion of inflicting conditions of life designed to bring about the group's destruction. This might coincide with Lemkin's techniques of genocide including social, political, and cultural. Though there have been no known criminal prosecutions for this aspect of genocide.

The final two acts refer to the erasure of a group by preventing births and forcibly removing children from one group to another. This technique has been seen in Darfur where soldiers raped women with the intent that they would bear children of the father's ethnicity, not the mother's. In these cases, the children were removed from their mother's ethnic group and placed in one that was not the free choice of the mother.

The UN definition is the official legal definition of genocide that is being applied in the International Criminal Tribunal for Yugoslavia (ICTY) and the International Criminal Tribunal for Rwanda (ICTR). This definition has been attacked almost from its inception as being too weak and requiring too strict of an intent requirement in order for genocide to have been committed legally. The main attack on the UN definition is the exclusion of political groups and social groups. By excluding political groups from the UN definition several episodes of mass violence cannot be considered genocide. The exclusion of social groups means that the elimination of homosexuals, the mentally ill, and the mentally challenged by the Germans would not be punishable as genocide.

Other Definitions of Genocide

In order to correct what some people saw as the flaws of the UN Convention definition of genocide, scholars began writing their own definitions. These definitions change the legal meaning but may better reflect what Lemkin had in mind when he created the term.

Frank Chalk and Kurt Jonassohn were interested in studying genocide in a broader way than the UN definition would allow. They argued that the legal definition was inadequate.[27] The exclusion of political and social groups would mean that many episodes of mass violence would have to be overlooked. While these crimes would qualify as **crimes against humanity**, labeling an action genocide carries more weight and condemnation.

CRIMES AGAINST HUMANITY

Crimes against humanity are defined as widespread and systematic attacks on a vulnerable group. ◄

In order to address what they saw as the deficiencies of the UN definition, Chalk and Jonassohn wrote their own definition of genocide. They defined genocide as:

> *A form of one-sided mass killing in which a state or other authority intends to destroy a group, as that group and membership in it are defined by the perpetrators.*[28]

Let's break this definition down into its component parts: (1) a form of one-sided (2) mass killing in which (3) a state or other authority (4) intends to destroy a group (5) as that group and membership in it are defined by the perpetrators.

If the violence must be one-sided, does that mean that the victims cannot resist or fight back? Many times genocide is committed against those without power but these groups often still attempt to resist. In Ottoman Turkey, a group of Armenians held off the Turks for several days before being caught and killed. Would this act not be genocide simply because the Armenians resisted? It is unlikely Chalk and Jonassohn intended that but definitions are by design supposed to tell us what falls into the definition and what is excluded.

Second, the definition calls for mass killing. As Lemkin was quick to point out, a group can be destroyed without ever having to kill anyone. In this way, the definition is narrower than Lemkin would have wanted. They choose to focus only on mass killing and not on destruction of culture, art, literature, serious bodily or mental harm, preventing births, or transferring children.

The third element of the definition is that the state or other authority is involved. Most genocides do involve the state but by including other authority they cover those rare cases where the genocide is executed by non-state militias. Arguably militias could be considered an "other authority" though it is not clear what is meant by authority. We will see how these militias have been used by states trying to hide its culpability in later chapters.

The intent element here seems to be the same as the UN definition. There is intent to destroy a group. Though this definition avoids the confusing language of "in whole or in part" and simply calls for an intent to destroy. Success of the elimination is irrelevant; the entire group need not be exterminated for it to be called genocide.

Finally, this definition covers any group—race, religion, political, social, etc. This fixes the problem of the UN definition that limits genocide to four groups. In this way, the definition better represents what Lemkin wanted—protection for all groups.

Israel Charny has argued for a more generic definition of genocide without some of the limitations found in other definitions. His generic definition states:

> *Genocide in the generic sense is the (1) mass killing of (2) substantial numbers of human beings, when (3) not in the course of military action against the military forces of an avowed enemy, under (4) conditions of the essential defenselessness and helplessness of the victims.*[29]

Again we can break this definition down to analyze its effectiveness. First, Charny, like Chalk and Jonassohn, limits genocide to mass killing. This excludes actions that fall short of killing but are still designed to destroy the group. The focus on murder offends Lemkin's original concept and ultimate goal to protect all people from any attempt to eradicate them or their culture.

Second, Charny's definition calls for substantial numbers to be killed. This is in some ways similar to the UN definition of "in part." How many people killed make a substantial number? Can a numerical value be placed on the definition? Like the UN definition, Charny does not provide guidance on what qualifies as a substantial number.

In part three, Charny seems to carve out an exception for genocide when committed during war against the military of an enemy. His attempt may be to exclude war deaths, but if the intent is to destroy a group and you start with the military, should that not be considered genocide? Finally, the victims are assumed to be helpless. If the victims have the capability to fight back, is it not genocide? This is similar to Chalk and Jonassohn's idea of the killing being one-sided.

Many questions remain with this definition and their resolution will impact what events qualify as genocide and which ones do not. Such a generic definition is not likely to be useful when trying to determine what cases qualify as genocide and what cases do not qualify.

Martin Shaw defined genocide in a way that addresses some of the problems with the above definitions. He said genocide is:

> *A form of violent social conflict, or war, between armed power organizations that aim to destroy civilian social groups and those groups and other actors who resist this destruction.*[30]

Shaw does not limit his definition to killing but includes violent conflict which could cover many aspects included in the UN definition. He also recognizes that genocide could occur during war, unlike Charny.

But this definition is not free from problems. Shaw says that conflict occurs between armed power organizations. What if the victim group is not an armed power? In many cases of genocide, the perpetrators have made it impossible for the victims to defend themselves with arms. This ensures less resistance and greater likelihood of success. Would those cases still be considered genocide?

QUESTION

Can you think of an example where a victim group may not be helpless? Consider what it means to be helpless—lack of resources, lack of power, etc. ◄

The intent here is to destroy a group much like the other definitions of genocide. By using the term social groups though Shaw is broadening the scope of who would be covered. A social group could include political groups, sexual orientation, or other groups not mentioned in the UN. Shaw also includes destruction of those who resist the violence even if not part of the targeted group. In Rwanda, the main target of the genocide was the Tutsis but many Hutus who refused to participate were also killed. Shaw would include this in his definition of genocide.

The sociologist Helen Fein defined genocide as:

> *Sustained purposeful action by a perpetrator to physically destroy a collectivity directly or indirectly though interdiction of the biological and social reproduction of group members, sustained regardless of the surrender of lack of threat offered by the victim.*[31]

As a sociologist, Fein was interested in understanding how a society can commit genocide. Her definition mirrors much of the UN definition. She refers to physically destroying a collectivity directly or indirectly. Unlike the UN definition, Fein does not limit what groups would qualify as a collectivity. But similar to the UN, Fein mentions destroying a group directly (murder) or indirectly (physical and mental harm, conditions of life). She also includes biological destruction which is included in the legal definition.

Sociologist Leo Kuper wrote about genocide in the early 1980s He initially accepted the UN definition because of its international recognition. However, Kuper was not willing to overlook instances of mass violence that might technically fall outside of UN protection. Kuper argued that there were two categories of genocide—those occurring as a result of internal fighting and those occurring during international war. While internal strife or war is often conducive to genocide, there is no limitation in the UN that genocide must occur during wartime. So while Kuper was willing to accept the UN definition his interpretation of it modified the

Table 1.1 The many definitions of genocide

Author	Field of study	Definition of genocide	Use of definition
Raphael Lemkin	Law	"[A] coordinated plan of different actions aiming at the destruction of essential foundations of the life of national groups, with the aim of annihilating the groups themselves" (Power 2002: 43).	This definition was used prior to the UN Convention.
United Nations	Law	Genocide means any of the following acts committed with intent to destroy, in whole or in part, a national, ethnical, racial or religious group, as such: (a) Killing members of the group; (b) Causing serious bodily or mental harm to members of the group; (c) Deliberately inflicting on the group conditions of life calculated to bring about its physical destruction in whole or in part; (d) Imposing measures intended to prevent births within the group; (e) Forcibly transferring children of the group to another group.	This definition is used for prosecution of genocide perpetrators. Currently being used by the ICTY and ICTR.
Chalk/ Jonassohn	History/ sociology	"A form of one-sided mass killing in which a state or other authority intends to destroy a group, as that group and membership in it are defined by the perpetrators"	This definition was used in Chalk & Jonassohn's historical study.
Israel Charny	Sociology	"Genocide in the generic sense is the mass killing of substantial numbers of human beings, when not in the course of military action against the military forces of an avowed enemy, under conditions of the essential defenselessness and helplessness of the victims"	This definition has been called too broad and is used only by Charny.
Martin Shaw	International Relations/ Politics	Genocide is "a form of violent social conflict, or war, between armed power organizations that aim to destroy civilian social groups and those groups and other actors who resist this destruction"	This definition has not been adopted by anyone at this point.

(continued)

Table 1.1 (continued)

Author	Field of study	Definition of genocide	Use of definition
Helen Fein	Sociology	"Genocide is sustained purposeful action by a perpetrator to physically destroy a collectivity directly or indirectly, through interdiction of the biological and social reproduction of group members, sustained regardless of the surrender or lack of threat offered by the victim"	This definition is prominent in sociological studies of genocide because of Fein's prominence in the field.
Leo Kuper	Sociology	Adopts UN definition but adds political groups and recognizes a nexus between war and genocide.	Used by Kuper but acknowledged as reasonable extension.

definition to include political groups and highlight a connection between war and genocide.

As you can see, there is much debate over how to define genocide (Table 1.1). This definitional debate is not unique to the study of genocide. Since we are concerned with genocide as a crime, it seems appropriate to point out that crime is often defined in different ways by different cultures. Emile Durkheim, a French sociologist, defined crime as an action that "shocks the collective consciousness of a community by violating some widely and strongly held societal value."[32]

Since Durkheim defined crime in 1895 societal values have changed. This means that what is considered crime has also changed. The definition of what acts qualify as criminal is always evolving. In this way, the definition of crime changes regularly.

CRITICAL THINKING

Can you think of a behavior that was once considered criminal but is now not considered to be a crime? How about the reverse—is there a criminal behavior today that was not considered criminal in the past? ◄

So while it can seem overwhelming to have to consider so many different definitions of genocide, the important thing to remember is that it is more crucial that we act when we see genocide occurring rather than argue over whether an act qualifies as genocide under a certain definition. For purposes of considering genocide as a crime it seems most appropriate to use the United Nations definition because it is the only definition that addresses genocide as a criminal act. We can recognize the flaws of the UN definition while at the same time using it as a guide to build upon in the future.

Genocide as a Crime

Regardless of the definition we use to identify genocide, here we must understand how genocide became an international crime. The origins of genocide firmly root the act as a crime. Lemkin originally saw genocide in broad terms, but always as an international crime worthy of condemnation. In 1946, Lemkin wrote in *The American Scholar* about how genocide needs to be criminalized internationally because of its global effects on humanity.[33]

THE AMERICAN SCHOLAR

The American Scholar is a magazine published by the Phi Beta Kappa society. The Phi Beta Kappa society is the oldest academic honor society in the United States. Lemkin's article in this magazine would be aimed at those with some power to affect his goals and spread the knowledge of genocide to other academics. ◄

Lemkin began by pointing out the many examples of genocide from history. He of course refers to the extermination of the Jewish population in Germany, but he also points to the Crusades, the Albigenses, and the Armenians.[34] Lemkin then highlights the problem here which is that "there has been no serious endeavor hitherto to prevent and punish the murder and destruction of millions."[35]

DELICTA JURIS GENTIUM

"Wrong against the law of nations."

Many activities have qualified as crimes against the law of nations. Piracy and drug trafficking have been called international crimes against the interest of humanity. Can you think of any other crimes that might qualify as delicta juris gentium? ◄

After explaining how he created the word genocide he defines the term as "the *crime* of destroying national, racial, or religious groups."[36] At this early stage, the creator of the word defined these actions as a crime. In fact, Lemkin wrote that it had to be considered an international crime because of its legal, moral, and humanitarian nature.[37] The severity of genocide ranked the crime among those that affect the common good of mankind. Crimes that affect mankind (or humanity) have been considered international crimes by the law of nations.[38]

In just four pages Lemkin set out the history, development, and future of genocide. He concluded his piece by setting forth seven propositions for creating an international treaty against the crime of genocide. While these were not the only aspects Lemkin thought important to a treaty, these are the crucial aspects that Lemkin believed would make the treaty strong enough to have an effect.

According to Lemkin, an international treaty on genocide should include:[39]

1. The crime of genocide may be defined as: "Whoever, while participating in a conspiracy to destroy a national, racial or religious group, undertakes an attack against life, liberty or property of members of such groups is guilty of the crime genocide."
2. Genocide should be written into every nation's criminal code. Perpetrators may be prosecuted by the country where the crime occurred or where the perpetrator is apprehended.
3. Perpetrators should not be considered political criminal for extradition purposes.
4. Liability for genocide should fall on those who gave and executed the orders, those who incited the crime, and those who organized the genocide.
5. In addition to individual responsibility for the crime of genocide, the state should be held accountable by the United Nations Security Council.
6. During war, international organizations should have the right to supervise the treatment of civilian populations in order to be able to determine whether genocide is occurring.
7. An international treaty does not preclude nations creating bilateral treaties (treaties creating obligations between two countries) to provide more protection against genocide.

In order to promote his international law proposal Lemkin arrived at the newly formed United Nations at the end of October 1946. He brought with him a resolution condemning genocide that he wanted the UN General Assembly to pass. Lemkin spent most his time at the UN soliciting support for his resolution. On December 11, 1946, after about six weeks of lobbying, the General Assembly passed Resolution 96(I) condemning genocide as "the denial of the right of existence of entire human groups."[40]

After the UN showed support for outlawing the crime of genocide by passing Lemkin's resolution, he began work on the first draft of what would become the United Nations Convention on the Prevention and Punishment of the Crime of Genocide. Writing the Convention took several months as Lemkin's broad definition of genocide was not favored by all nations. In order to see the Convention become law Lemkin had to make compromises. There was so much debate about the Convention that the drafting ultimately limited genocide to racial, national, ethnic, or religious groups even though Lemkin would have gone for protection of more groups.

Finally, on December 9, 1948 the UN was set to vote on the Convention after it had gone through several drafts. Lemkin stood in the press gallery as the nations voted.[41] It passed by a vote of 55 to 0.[42] After years of work to alert the world to the crime of genocide, Lemkin had achieved passage of one of the first international treaties on a matter of global concern. The Convention became effective on January 12, 1951, after 20 countries ratified it in their national legislatures.

The United Nations Convention contains 19 articles of which the first nine set out the definition of genocide and the applicable punishment. Take a minute to read through the Convention paying attention to what qualifies as genocide and what punishments are available.[43]

> Convention on the Prevention and Punishment of the Crime of Geno cide
>
> The Contracting Parties,
>
> Having considered the declaration made by the General Assembly of the United Nations in its resolution 96 (I) dated 11 December 1946 that genocide is a crime under international law, contrary to the spirit and aims of the United Nations and condemned by the civilized world,
>
> Recognizing that at all periods of history genocide has inflicted great losses on humanity, and
>
> Being convinced that, in order to liberate mankind from such an odious scourge, international co-operation is required,
>
> Hereby agree as hereinafter provided:
>
> Article I
>
> The Contracting Parties confirm that genocide, whether committed in time of peace or in time of war, is a crime under international law which they undertake to prevent and to punish.
>
> Article II
>
> In the present Convention, genocide means any of the following acts committed with intent to destroy, in whole or in part, a national, ethnical, racial or religious group, as such:
>
> (a) Killing members of the group;
> (b) Causing serious bodily or mental harm to members of the group;

(c) Deliberately inflicting on the group conditions of life calculated to bring about its physical destruction in whole or in part;
(d) Imposing measures intended to prevent births within the group;
(e) Forcibly transferring children of the group to another group.

Article III

The following acts shall be punishable:

(a) Conspiracy to commit genocide;
(b) Genocide;
(c) Direct and public incitement to commit genocide;
(d) Attempt to commit genocide;
(e) Complicity in genocide.

Article IV

Persons committing genocide or any of the other acts enumerated in article III shall be punished, whether they are constitutionally responsible rulers, public officials or private individuals.

Article V

The Contracting Parties undertake to enact, in accordance with their respective Constitutions, the necessary legislation to give effect to the provisions of the present Convention, and, in particular, to provide effective penalties for persons guilty of genocide or any of the other acts enumerated in article III.

Article VI

Persons charged with genocide or any of the other acts enumerated in article III shall be tried by a competent tribunal of the State in the territory of which the act was committed, or by such international penal tribunal as may have jurisdiction with respect to those Contracting Parties which shall have accepted its jurisdiction.

Article VII

Genocide and the other acts enumerated in article III shall not be considered as political crimes for the purpose of extradition. The Contracting Parties pledge themselves in such cases to grant extradition in accordance with their laws and treaties in force.

Article VIII

Any Contracting Party may call upon the competent organs of the United Nations to take such action under the Charter of the United Nations as they consider appropriate for the prevention and suppression of acts of genocide or any of the other acts enumerated in article III.

Article IX

Disputes between the Contracting Parties relating to the interpretation, application or fulfilment of the present Convention, including those relating to the responsibility of a State for genocide or for any of the other acts enumerated in article III, shall be submitted to the International Court of Justice at the request of any of the parties to the dispute.

Article X

The present Convention, of which the Chinese, English, French, Russian and Spanish texts are equally authentic, shall bear the date of 9 December 1948.

Article XI

The present Convention shall be open until 31 December 1949 for signature on behalf of any Member of the United Nations and of any non-member State to which an invitation to sign has been addressed by the General Assembly.

The present Convention shall be ratified, and the instruments of ratification shall be deposited with the Secretary-General of the United Nations. After 1 January 1950, the present Convention may be acceded to on behalf of any Member of the United Nations and of any non-member State which has received an invitation as aforesaid. Instruments of accession shall be deposited with the Secretary-General of the United Nations.

Article XII

Any Contracting Party may at any time, by notification addressed to the Secretary-General of the United Nations, extend the application of the present Convention to all or any of the territories for the conduct of whose foreign relations that Contracting Party is responsible.

Article XIII

On the day when the first twenty instruments of ratification or accession have been deposited, the Secretary-General shall draw up a procès-verbal and transmit a copy thereof to each Member of the United Nations and to each of the non-member States contemplated in Article XI. The present Convention shall come into force on the ninetieth day following the date of deposit of the twentieth instrument of ratification or accession. Any ratification or accession effected subsequent to the latter date shall become effective on the ninetieth day following the deposit of the instrument of ratification or accession.

Article XIV

The present Convention shall remain in effect for a period of ten years as from the date of its coming into force. It shall thereafter remain in force for successive periods of five years for such Contracting Parties as have not denounced it at least six months before the expiration of the current period. Denunciation shall be affected by a written notification addressed to the Secretary-General of the United Nations.

Article XV

If, as a result of denunciations, the number of Parties to the present Convention should become less than sixteen, the Convention shall cease to be in force as from the date on which the last of these denunciations shall become effective.

Article XVI

A request for the revision of the present Convention may be made at any time by any Contracting Party by means of a notification in writing addressed to the Secretary-General. The General Assembly shall decide upon the steps, if any, to be taken in respect of such request.

Article XVII

The Secretary-General of the United Nations shall notify all Members of the United Nations and the non-member States contemplated in article XI of the following: (a) Signatures, ratifications and accessions received in accordance with article XI; (b) Notifications received in accordance with article XII; (c) The date upon which the present Convention comes into force in accordance with article XIII; (d) Denunciations received in accordance with article XIV; (e) The abrogation of the Convention in accordance with article XV; (f) Notifications received in accordance with article XVI.

Article XVIII

The original of the present Convention shall be deposited in the archives of the United Nations. A certified copy of the Convention shall be transmitted to each Member of the United Nations and to each of the non-member States contemplated in article XI.

Article XIX

The present Convention shall be registered by the Secretary-General of the United Nations on the date of its coming into force.

After reading the Convention, go back to Lemkin's seven elements to his treaty proposal. Did Lemkin get everything he wanted in an international treaty? If not, what is missing? If you were in Lemkin's place would you have been satisfied with the Convention?

The UN Convention on Genocide is the official legal document criminalizing genocide and setting out the elements of the crime. Article I clearly states that genocide is an international crime whether committed during peace or war time. This statement ensures that a genocide cannot be ignored merely because it occurred during broader wartime fighting.

Article II establishes the intent of genocide; a special intent to destroy in whole or in part. There are four protected groups—nationality, ethnicity, race, and religion—under the Convention. The rest of Article II establishes the acts prohibited including murder, mental harm, preventing births, and transferring children.

Article III sets out the numerous offenses criminalized by the Convention. In addition to committing genocide, conspiracy to commit genocide is also prohibited. Conspiracy occurs when two or more people agree to commit a crime—in this case genocide. Incitement to commit genocide is also outlawed. Encouraging others to commit genocide occurred in Rwanda where radio broadcasts read lists of names for killers to target and encouraged violence.

The crime of attempt occurs when one has the intent to commit a crime, tries to do so, and then fails. So genocide need not be successful in order to prosecute. If one tries to destroy a group and fails to do so, the crime of attempted genocide has occurred. Finally, complicity in genocide is when people may not engage in action but help others to do so. These five crimes all relate to the goal of genocide to eliminate a group, but it expands liability to hold more people culpable for their behavior.

Article IV says that state leaders can be held liable for genocide. This was important as sovereign immunity often protected heads of state from being held culpable. Article VI is the first to mention punishing the offense of genocide. The Article mentions an international court which did not exist at the time and did not come into existence until 2002. Lemkin thought an international court was necessary to prosecute those responsible for genocide. He believed that national courts were not adequate as they might favor their own citizens and allow individuals to escape justice.

Article VIII allows any UN state to ask the **Security Council** to take action to prevent genocide. Further liability can be found under Article IX. This allows one state to take another state to the UN Court of Justice for violating the Convention. While not often used, in 2019, The Gambia took Bangladesh to the court for committing genocide against the Rohingya (a Muslim minority).

UN Security Council

The UN Security Council is a principle organ of the UN charged with ensuring international peace and security. Most issues related to genocide are discussed in the Security Council where action can be taken to intervene. ◄

Articles X–XIX explain how the UN member states must go about signing, ratifying, and enforcing the Convention. Before the Convention could go into force, 20 nations had to ratify it. Ratification is the formal validation of a proposed law. In many countries this occurs via a vote in their national legislature. The Convention went into full force on January 12, 1951, after receiving the twentieth ratification.

- The first 21 countries to ratify the Convention were:
- Australia, Cambodia, Costa Rica, Ecuador, El Salvador, Ethiopia, France, Guatemala, Haiti, Iceland, Israel, Jordan, Liberia, Monaco, Norway, Panama, Republic of Korea, Saudi Arabia, Sri Lanka, Turkey, and Yugoslavia.
- Consider the list of countries that were first to formally bind themselves to the Genocide Convention. Can you think of any reasons these nations were the first to ratify? You may have to look at the history of these nations and remember that ratification occurred between 1948 and 1951.

Conclusion

The seemingly easy question of "what is genocide?" has many different answers. How you view genocide probably depends on what perspective you take. Is genocide a crime? A social act? A political act? Your viewpoint here will impact what definition you believe to be best suited to explain the complex phenomenon that is genocide. In some ways there is no single right or wrong answer to "what is genocide?"

But there must be an official definition for legal purposes. In order for a law to exist the prohibited action must be defined so that the public knows what is and is not allowed. So the UN definition of genocide has stood as the official legal definition for over 70 years. In that way it is crucial to understand the UN definition and its flaws. These flaws have been fixed by other scholars defining genocide in broader terms.

The father of genocide, Raphael Lemkin, would likely agree that the UN definition is flawed and incomplete. But the other option would have been for the UN to ignore the devastation caused by genocide. When faced with that stark consequence, it seems tolerable to accept a flawed definition in order to prevent mass destruction of human lives.

Further, Lemkin's goal had always been to achieve an international law criminalizing genocide and holding perpetrators accountable. Therefore, the legal definition of the crime of genocide must take prominence over other definitions. Genocide began as a new crime; it has evolved into a social and political act that can be explained from many different disciplines (more on this in Chap. 2). But it has always been grounded as a crime against world humanity.

Moving forward it is important to remember that any definition of genocide is incomplete and flawed in some way. In order to keep Lemkin's overall goal of eliminating genocide a possibility is to bring attention to the act whenever and wherever it occurs. We can and will argue over what qualifies as genocide but so long as attention is being paid there is a greater likelihood of prevention and punishment.

So what is genocide? It is a scourge on humanity, it is an attack on our brothers and sisters, it is demoralizing and dehumanizing. Genocide is many things. But as Lemkin told the world more than half a century ago: Genocide is "a coordinated plan aimed at destruction of the essential foundations of the life of national groups so that these groups wither and die like plants that have suffered a blight."[44]

Discussion Questions

1. Should political groups be protected against genocide in the UN Convention? Explain why or why not? Consider what makes a political group the same/different from groups based on race or religion.
2. Go back to the scenario that opened this chapter on the US State Department's hesitancy to call that the acts in Rwanda genocide. If you were at that press conference, what would you have said when faced with such uncertainty?
3. Can you construct a definition of genocide that addresses the issues raised in this chapter by Lemkin, the United Nations, and others seeking a comprehensive definition? What would you include? Or more importantly what would you exclude?

Notes

1. Jehljune, D. (1994, June 10). Officials told to avoid calling Rwanda killings 'genocide.' *The New York Times*, p. 8.
2. United States Department of State. (1994). *Action memorandum from Assistant Secretary of State for African Affairs George E. Moose to Secretary of State Warren Christopher, "Has genocide occurred in Rwanda?"* George Washington University: The National Security Archive.
3. TheHistoryTV. (2016, March 23). *Genocide and the world response (State Department Rwanda 1994)*. Retrieved from https://www.youtube.com/watch?v=DFgLA2tE7_o
4. Lemkin, Raphael (2012). *Lemkin on genocide*. Steven L. Jacobs (Ed.). Lanham, MD: Lexington Books, 20.
5. Chalk, Frank & Jonassohn, Kurt (1990). *The history and sociology of genocide: Analyses and case studies*. New Haven: Yale University Press.
6. Supra note 4.
7. Rubinstein, William D. (2004). *Genocide: A history*. Harlow, England: Pearson.
8. Lemkin, Raphael (2013). *Totally unofficial: The autobiography of Raphael Lemkin*. Donna-Lee Frieze (Ed.). New Haven: Yale University Press.
9. Ibid., at 19.
10. Power, Samantha (2002). *"A problem from hell": America and the age of genocide*. New York: Harper Perennial.
11. Ibid., at 20–22; Supra note 8 at 22.
12. Ibid.
13. Supra note 8 at 23.
14. Supra note 10 at 22.
15. Supra note 8 at 24.
16. Supra note 10 at 25–26.

17. Lemkin, Raphael (1946). Genocide. *American Scholar,* 15(2), 227–230: 227.
18. Lemkin, Raphael (1945). Genocide—A modern crime. *Free World*, 4, 39–43.
19. Supra note 17.
20. Supra note 18.
21. Ibid.
22. Ibid.
23. Ibid.
24. Ibid.
25. Ibid.
26. Ibid.
27. Supra note 5.
28. Ibid., at 23.
29. Charny, Israel (1994). "Toward a generic definition of genocide." In G.A. Andreopoulous (Ed.), *Genocide: Conceptual and historical dimensions* (pp. 64–94). Philadelphia: University of Pennsylvania Press.
30. Shaw, Martin (2007). *What is genocide?* Cambridge: Polity Press: 154.
31. Fein, Helen (1990). "Genocide: A sociological perspective." *Current Sociology*, 38(1): 24.
32. Durkheim, Emile ([1895] 1982). *The rules of the sociological method.* Steven Lukes (Ed.) (W.D. Halls, Trans.). New York: Free Press, 67–68.
33. Supra note 17.
34. Ibid.
35. Ibid., at 227.
36. Ibid., at 228 (emphasis added).
37. Ibid.
38. Ibid.
39. Ibid., at 230.
40. Supra note 10 at 54.
41. Ibid.
42. Ibid.
43. United Nations (1948). Convention on the Prevention and Punishment of the Crime of Genocide. Available at: https://www.un.org/en/genocideprevention/documents/atrocity-crimes/Doc.1_Convention%20on%20the%20Prevention%20and%20Punishment%20of%20the%20Crime%20of%20Genocide.pdf
44. Supra note 18 at 39.

Further Reading

You can read Raphael Lemkin's original piece on genocide available online:

Lemkin, R. (1946). Genocide. *American Scholar, 15*(2), 227–230 Available at http://pscourses.ucsd.edu/poli120n/Lemkin1946.pdf.

Samantha Power provides a detailed description of Lemkin and his quest to see an international law against genocide achieved: Power, S. (2002). *"A problem from hell": America and the age of genocide.* New York: Harper Perennial. See chapters 2, 3, and 4.

Useful Websites

United States Holocaust Memorial Museum: www.ushmm.org

United Nations Office on Genocide Prevention: https://www.un.org/en/genocideprevention/index.shtml

2 How Can We Understand Genocide?

In June 1987, [during Iraq's attack on its Kurdish population, a] process of drawing irreversible boundaries—the red line between "us" and "them"—was legalized by issuing two sets of standing orders, which were based on a simple axiom with a result few, if any, of the Kurds could comprehend: in the "prohibited" rural areas, all Kurdish residents were coterminous with the peshmerga insurgents (Kurdish guerrilla), and they would be dealt with accordingly.

Through a policy of shoot-to-kill, the first of al-Majid's directives was to ban all human existence in the "prohibited areas." The second constitutes an unmistakable inducement to mass murder, spelled out in a chilling clear language. In clause 4, army commanders are ordered "to carry out random bombardments, using artillery, helicopters and aircraft, at all times of the day or night, in order to ***kill the largest number of persons*** *present in these prohibited zones."*

In clause 5, al-Majid ordered that "All persons captured in those villages shall be detained and interrogated by the security services and ***those between the ages of 15 to 70*** *shall be executed after any useful information has been obtained from them, of which we should be duly notified."*[1]

These types of orders are used to show the intent to destroy a group. But at that same time we need to explore why and how these orders are developed. By doing so, we can better understand the process of genocide.

W. R. Pruitt, *An Introduction to the Criminology of Genocide*, https://doi.org/10.1007/978-3-030-65211-1_2

Introduction

Genocide is an act that has many dimensions. Genocide is a criminal act. Genocide is also often a political act. Genocide could be an economic act. Genocide is a social action. Since genocide has many different aspects, it makes sense that many different academic disciplines examine genocide in an attempt to understand it. The way a lawyer, a political scientist, an economist, and a sociologist look at genocide will vary. Scholars from all of these fields have contributed to the understanding of genocide.

Due to the complexity of genocide, perhaps we can take a partial understanding from all of these disciplines. In that way we become interdisciplinary. Interdisciplinary means that we examine actions from a variety of knowledge branches. We cannot become experts in all fields, but we can learn from those who have put the work in to understand genocide from their specific viewpoint and then we may be able to create a common knowledge of genocide.

In this chapter we look at how different disciplines have studied genocide and what information we can take away from those studies. Each of these various fields offer distinct views of genocide as a phenomenon. The legal field is concerned with the legal challenges involved in the enforcement of the United Nations Convention on Genocide and finding justice after genocide. Law is where Lemkin grounded genocide initially so understanding genocide from the legal perspective is crucial for achieving the goal of eliminating genocide from the world.

Psychologists are interested in understanding the mindset of genocide perpetrators. Are all perpetrators insane or is there a more nuanced explanation?[2] So psychology uses individual-based variables such as personality traits and disorders and cognitive characteristics to analyze individual behavior during genocide. If perpetrators can be identified by traits or disorders, could we prevent genocide by targeting potential perpetrators before they commit genocide?

Political scientists are concerned with the effect of genocide on a state's political structure and how a political elite might execute genocide. In several cases, genocide is committed with a political goal in mind. Those in charge may be seeking a way to solidify their position or eliminate opposition groups. If the state holds all of the power, then understanding how they wield that power in genocide becomes important.

Sociologists analyze genocide as a social event and aim to understand the structural and cultural factors involved. Genocide is unlikely to succeed without support from society either explicitly or through silence. Could genocide ever be considered a natural aspect of human society? Emile Durkheim considered deviance and crime to be a natural part of society.[3] If crime is a natural aspect of society, is genocide just an extreme form of that natural phenomena?

While deviance is a natural part of society, extreme deviance resulting in the eradication of a group of people is not what Durkheim had in mind. Most scholars dismiss the idea that genocide is simply a naturally occurring event—there needs to be a setup before genocide can begin. We will see this in Chap. 5 when we examine different episodes of genocide through time.

Finally, of interest to us is how criminologists examine genocide. Unfortunately, for a long time criminology ignored genocide and allowed other disciplines to be primary investigators. But recently some criminologists have entered the realm of genocide and produced new insights on genocide specifically as a crime. These involve some already established criminological theories (like techniques or neutralization or general theory of crime) and new ways to examine the crime of genocide.

As you can see, no single field can claim dominion over genocide; there are too many prisms that can be used to study the topic. Taken separately these fields offer useful information on a single dimension of genocide. However, taken together these studies greatly expand the understanding and possible response to genocide. This chapter focuses on the different disciplinary approaches to the study of genocide with a hope to show that there is room for the field of criminology to add more of its own unique contribution to the field of genocide study.

> *Critical Thinking Exercise* Recall the legal definition of genocide from the United Nations. If you were a judge faced with deciding if the defendant in front of you has committed genocide, what would you want to know before making your decision?

Law

The United Nations Convention on the Prevention and Punishment of the Crime of Genocide created a legal responsibility to prevent and to punish genocide. Since the passage of the UN Convention there have been only three courts to ever consider genocide cases. In the mid-1990s the United Nations established the International Criminal Tribunal for the former Yugoslavia (ICTY) and the International Criminal Tribunal for Rwanda (ICTR). The International Criminal Court (ICC) was established in 2002. These courts have been tasked with interpreting the Convention and applying it in prosecutions of **génocidaires**. Several legal scholars have tried to assist these courts by offering their interpretation of the Genocide Convention.

GÉNOCIDAIRE

Génocidaire is the French word for a person who commits genocide. There is no equivalent English translation. ◄

Lawyers and legal scholars see genocide as a violation of international law. The signatories to the UN Convention agreed to prevent genocide when possible and to punish those responsible for committing genocide. As part of adopting the UN Convention, each nation had to add genocide as a criminal offense in their national legal codes. The United States law against genocide can be found in 18 U.S.C. §1091. The definition of genocide mirrors that used by the United Nations, though it does indicate that the intent must be to destroy in whole or in *substantial* part. This is used to further clarify the UN definition of "in part." Unlike some countries, notably Canada and Belgium, the United States has never had a trial under its genocide law.

By requiring nations that joined the UN Convention to pass a local law against genocide, an international prohibition against the act emerged rather quickly. Unfortunately, in most instances of genocide there has been no punishment for the atrocity. Legal scholars have focused their research on three main issues in the prosecution and enforcement of genocide statutes—intent, sovereign immunity, and universal jurisdiction. These issues tend to take prominence because they act as barriers to prosecution which may allow some génocidaires to escape punishment.

Like many crimes, the UN Convention requires that genocide be committed with intent, not through negligence or recklessness. It has been argued that requiring **specific intent** for genocide is too strict. Replacing specific intent with a general knowledge requirement has been suggested.[4] Legal scholar Caroline Fournet has said that if the perpetrators have knowledge that their act is in pursuit of genocide as a whole then criminal liability should attach. The reason for replacing specific intent is to ensure that génocidaires will not be able to avoid punishment by claiming that they did not have the intent to destroy an entire group. While it would be possible to make a defense of lack of intent, there is no assurance that it would be successful.

SPECIFIC INTENT

Recall from the United Nations definition of genocide that the crime must be committed "with intent to destroy in whole or in part." This is referred to as specific intent because the intent to destroy is specific toward the targeted group. ◄

The ICTR has stated that "intent can be inferred from a certain number of presumptions of fact."[5] The court explained that intent can be inferred from words and actions. Evidence to be considered in proving specific intent includes the physical targeting of a specific group or their property; the use of derogatory language toward members of the target group; the weapons used and the extent of bodily injury inflicted; the methodical planning; and systematic manner of the killing. Finally, the number of victims from the targeted group can also be considered. In many cases, evidence such as this would make it difficult for defendants to claim a lack of intent because their actions may speak louder than words.

On the other hand, the ICTY abandoned most of these considerations and applied a definition of intent based solely on the number of victims killed. The court stated that the "ordinary meaning" of "in part" in the UN Convention requires that "a reasonably significant number, relative to the total of the group as a whole, or else a significant section of a group as its leadership" be killed before intent for genocide can be satisfied.[6] The court failed to articulate any specific number of victims where intent can be reasonably inferred.

There is reason to believe that the ICTR's definition and inference standard is considered a more accurate interpretation of the UN Convention than the ICTY analysis. The ICC defined intent in its **founding document**. The Court defines intent as either meaning to engage in the prohibited behavior or meaning to cause the outcome (genocide) or being aware that the outcome will occur.[7] This definition of intent is closer to the idea of knowledge proposed by many legal scholars. Combining this definition with the ICTR's inference standard should make it more difficult for perpetrators to claim a lack of intent since there is no requirement that they say out loud their intent.

ROME STATUTE

The founding document of the International Criminal Court is the Rome Statute developed over many years by the countries of the United Nations. The Rome Statute sets out the controlling law at the ICC including the legal definition of genocide. You can explore how the ICC works by visiting https://www.icc-cpi.int/. ◄

The Genocide Convention was passed upon the idea that the destruction of any group harms humanity as a whole. Therefore, it is irrelevant if genocide is part of a larger plan (i.e., war strategy), perpetrated by the state or private individuals, whether it is successful or not, or how large in scope it is. With these guiding principles our goal should be to punish those responsible for genocide regardless of their personal standing or failure to make a statement of their intent. This will also hopefully put more potential perpetrators on notice that their actions can be used against them to prove intent. Maybe then they will think twice before acting out their violence against others.

Another perceived problem with enforcing the Genocide Convention was the concept of sovereign immunity. Prior to 1945 the notion of **sovereign immunity** was very powerful. There was an unspoken agreement that one nation would not intervene into another nation's domestic affairs. Since most genocides occur within the borders of one nation, it could be considered a domestic affair.

SOVEREIGN IMMUNITY

The concept of sovereign immunity developed from the British idea that the King could do no wrong. Therefore no one could hold the government accountable without the government giving its permission first. ◄

The shield of sovereign immunity was an obstacle to the Nuremberg trials following World War II. The lack of response to the Armenian genocide during World War I was based on sovereign immunity.[8] Other nations believed that they could not intervene even if they desired to do so because domestic affairs must be handled by the home nation. Only when the world saw the horrific atrocities committed by Germany during the World War II and believed that the perpetrators might not be punished for their acts did the doctrine of sovereign immunity come under serious attack.

A well-known criminologist at the time, Sheldon Glueck, attacked the doctrine of sovereign immunity and quickly dismissed it. Sovereign immunity is based on the idea of national comity and courtesy with the expectation that the sovereign will act in a law-abiding and trustworthy manner.[9] If a sovereign nation violates these expectations it has forfeited its immunity. When a sovereign willfully orders his people to commit flagrant violations of law, he has clearly voided his immunity and made himself liable.[10] Some sovereigns may still claim immunity but no court is willing to accept that defense anymore for the crime of genocide.

But that does not mean that sovereign immunity for genocide is non-existent. The International Criminal Court issued an arrest warrant in 2009 for the president of Sudan, Omar al-Bashir, for his involvement in the genocide in Darfur. However, the ICC does not have a law enforcement capability to make an arrest. The Court relies on member states to make the arrest. But many countries have refused to arrest al-Bashir for various reasons but sovereign immunity has been cited.

Legal scholars examining genocide are also concerned with the concept of universal jurisdiction. The UN Convention says that génocidaires can be tried by any nation regardless of where the actual acts occurred. Universal jurisdiction is assumed. The idea of universal jurisdiction is that there are some crimes so harmful and dangerous that perpetrators should be subject to prosecution in any country. Normally the nation where the act occurred would have jurisdiction. Universal jurisdiction allows other nations to prosecute for the crime of genocide if the perpetrator is found within their borders.

The United Nations has relied on universal jurisdiction for the ICTY and ICTR. The International Criminal Tribunal for the genocidal crimes in Yugoslavia sits in the Netherlands (thousands of miles away from the scene of the crime), and the ICT for the Rwandan genocide meets in Tanzania (hundreds of miles from the fighting). Even though the Nuremberg trial and the International Criminal Tribunals are based on universal jurisdiction, there are still arguments raised against the practice.

The history of international crime has no basis for universal jurisdiction. Early treaties recognized that there should be international cooperation for the punishment of criminals—mostly pirates.[11] These treaties though were entered into by independent nations who agreed to prosecute pirates on behalf of each other. These treaties did not advocate universal jurisdiction. Currently, one of the complaints that the United States has against the International Criminal Court (ICC) is the universal jurisdiction that the ICC can exercise. The United States has raised the issue of universal jurisdiction again making it a possible argument against international courts prosecuting genocide.

The legal dimension of genocide focuses on the appropriate response following genocide as defined by the UN. Legal scholars are not necessarily concerned with the causes of genocide, but instead with the legal response to address genocide and punish génocidaires. While law has a prevention aspect in that laws are designed to inform the public as to what they cannot do, the law by itself does not stop crime from occurring. Genocide is outlawed at the national and international level, but it still occurs. The law can help us recognize when genocide is occurring though by examining intent and other legal requirements.

▶ *Critical Thinking Exercise* In order to commit a crime as heinous as genocide does a person need to suffer from some psychological abnormality? Could it be possible for "regular" people to commit genocide? If so, what might be the motivations for these individuals?

Psychology

Psychology—the study of human thought and behavior—has a role to play in the study of genocide and the field has produced several works on genocide. Ervin Staub has studied genocide for several years. In his 1989 book *The Roots of Evil*, he proposed a basis for the origins of genocide. He stated that genocide was more likely to occur when a person or society was faced with difficult life conditions and adhered to certain cultural characteristics that generated psychological processes that led to one group turning against another group.[12] More simply—a person may be susceptible to supporting genocide because of his/her own personal characteristics and cultural beliefs.

Some psychologists root their analysis of genocide in the studies of **Stanley Milgram**. In the 1950s Milgram conducted studies where one person was asked to deliver what they believed to be electric shocks to another person. There was an authority figure with the person asking them to do the shocking who would have no response when participants began to express pain from the shocks.

STANLEY MILGRAM

Have you ever done something because someone asked you to even if you were not entirely comfortable with it?

Milgram asked people to deliver electric shocks to strangers and many did so because there was an authority figure telling them to do it. Do you think you would shock the stranger or stand up against the order? ◄

Milgram found that people were willing to override their inhibition to harm others when there was an authority figure present. Obedience to power had a strong influence on people's behavior. This obedience to authority left little room for a person to oppose what they believed to be legitimate orders. These findings have been used to evaluate the events of the Holocaust.[13]

It appears plausible that some people may have participated in the Holocaust because of orders they perceived to be legitimate. But this does not explain why some people waited several months before participating. Also, fear or obedience to authority does not explain those perpetrators who clearly enjoyed their work. So this is an incomplete explanation of genocide.

Another application of Milgram's study to genocide found that obedience to authority fit well with the banality of evil argument. The banality of evil argument was developed by Hannah Arendt in her study of the **Adolf Eichmann** trial in Israel.[14] She found Eichmann to be relatively free of hatred, but an obedient soldier in following orders.

ADOLF EICHMANN

Adolf Eichmann was a senior leader in Nazi Germany responsible for organizing the deportation of Jewish people to concentration camps. He was captured in Argentina in 1960 and sent to Israel to stand trial. He was convicted and executed in 1962. ◄

Arendt claimed that genocide was perpetrated, not by hate-filled evil monsters, but by the average German. The obedience to orders claim has also been made by génocidaires in Cambodia, Rwanda, and Bosnia.[15] But genocide is rarely successful without the participation of the average person or at least their willingness to ignore what was happening. Some perpetrators may be doing so simply out of obedience to authority but there are others who commit genocide for other reasons. This is the complexity of trying to understand the brain of the génocidaire.

We should also consider that there is some evidence to suggest that obedience to authority is not truly what Milgram found in his study. People may choose to obey an order for any variety of reasons including fear, hatred of the victim, desire for promotion, or agreement with the order. Milgram never examined these external forces in his studies. While the obedience to authority claim may explain the involvement in genocide of some individuals, it fails to offer a significant reason for the resort to genocide as a policy.

Other psychologists have turned to the psychology of hate as the basis for studying genocide. Hatred of an out-group can arise rationally if that group is seen as taking resources away from the in-group.[16] In Rwanda, the Hutu represented a numerical majority of the populations but the minority Tutsi were in charge of the government. This was seen as an attack on the Hutu because they lacked political power to make changes that would benefit their group. During World War I the Ottomans believed that the Armenian population was working with Russia to undermine Turkey and lead to its defeat. These perceived abuses by a minority group may allow hatred to develop and be rationally explained as self-defense.

Hatred can also arise irrationally based on long-lasting prejudices against the out-group. In Germany the Jewish population was less than 3% of the total population. However, many Germans were convinced that the Jewish population was exercising too much control in finance and other areas. Realistically this was not possible because of their small numbers, but truth did not matter once hatred began to evolve.

If hate leads to distancing and dehumanization of the out-group, then genocide is much more likely to occur. Hatred of a certain group often leads to an us-versus-them mentality. In these situations, the "us" is usually deemed to be good or right and "them" is wrong or bad. Once society is divided into "us" and "them" it becomes easier to create more distance between the groups. Interaction between the groups begins to fade and there may be expectations that the groups will not interact. After distancing the out-group, dehumanization can occur.

Dehumanization occurs when the out-group begins to be seen as animals or disease and not as human beings. In Rwanda, the Tutsi were called cockroaches and snakes. In Germany, the Jewish population was called a disease on society. Once a group is dehumanized it is easier to kill. It is easier to kill a bug than it is to kill a human. When hatred evolves into dehumanization, the groundwork for genocide has occurred.

Even when hatred is irrational, individuals can have their feelings of hate validated. The government may validate your feelings of hatred which can then lead you to believe your actions are justified. This occurs when the out-group is labeled as a legitimate enemy by superiors. This leads the individual members of the in-group to believe that their feelings of hate and animosity are right and the only response one can have toward the out-group.[17] Once these feelings have been justified, it becomes easier to use violence against the out-group because they "deserve" such treatment.

Political Science

Many genocides are acts of political oppression. In most genocides the state is committing the crime or complicit in its commission. As such political scientists have attempted to understand the political aspects of genocide. The political scientist **R.J. Rummel** hypothesized that democide (his word for any state-sponsored mass killing) was less likely to occur in a democratic state.[18] Essentially, while power kills, absolute power kills absolutely. In his analysis of democide and political structure, he found that as one progresses from a democratic state to a totalitarian state, the likelihood of democide increases rapidly.

R.J. RUMMEL

Rummel has analyzed many cases of genocide and other mass killings to determine how these events share certain characteristics. You can explore his work here: https://www.hawaii.edu/powerkills/NOTE1.HTM

There are many tables and charts that highlight the similarities among genocide cases. ◄

The more a nation has complete control over the social, economic, and cultural groups and institutions within their borders, the greater the ability to rule arbitrarily. An arbitrary government accounted for the magnitude and intensity of genocide. The nature of power becomes the explanation of genocide.

Ernesto Verdeja has offered five factors that contribute to genocide; these factors revolve around the government and its structure.[19] First, a segmented society can more easily accept an "us-versus-them" ideology (see above). Totalitarian governments can create and maintain a segmented society through their complete control over all state institutions. Rapid and profound social change is the second factor. Many times totalitarian governments have ascended to power through war or are facing a threat from other political powers. This creates a scenario where social change is possible depending on how the people respond to the government.

Thirdly, an exclusionist political ideology that reinforces the social differences between groups can lead to genocide. Most totalitarian governments will not share power with "others" and will promote the causes of their own people over others. The state's capacity to organize and carry out mass atrocities will directly affect the success of genocide. A totalitarian regime controls all social institutions within the state easily adapting the state's existing structure to the evil ends of genocide.

The final causal factor of genocide is an international component that affects the duration of the genocide. This factor recognizes that genocide is only stopped by some form of international response (more on this in Chap. 6). This last factor has less of an effect on the process leading to genocide and more on the ability of the international community to stop the killing once it has begun. The international community usually chooses not to intervene for many reasons, but the power of the perpetrators' government is a concern. For example, it has been claimed that the United States has refused to end the genocide in Darfur because the government in Sudan has offered some useful information on the "war on terror."[20] In this way, political relationships can have a negative effect for the victims of genocide.

In 2003, Barbara Harff made a complete list of all genocides since 1945.[21] Based on her findings, she believed that genocide was more probable during or after an internal war, regime collapse, or revolution—all political events.[22] She focused on the ideology of the regimes involved and found that they tended to have an exclusive ideology that justified their elimination of the out-group. These leaders also tended to be from isolated nations with little international trade or responsibilities. This may have led some leaders to feel insulated from any international repercussions for their actions.

Analyzing the episodes of genocide since 1945 and the state in which they occurred, Harff calculated the probability of genocide. If a state had none of the risk factors (internal war, regime collapse, revolution, past genocide, exclusive ideology) the probability of genocide was 0.028 (just 2.8% chance). An autocratic nation with no other risk factors had a 0.090 probability of genocide (a 9% chance). If all risk factors were present in a state, there was a 0.90 probability of genocide (a 90% chance of genocide!). This work is one of the few empirical studies of genocide suggesting that genocide can be predicted before it occurs.

Not all political scientists agree that totalitarian governments are the only states that will resort to genocide. For many years in the field of political science there was the democratic peace theory, which states that "democracies rarely fight one another because they share common norms of live-and-let-live and domestic institutions that constrain the recourse to war."[23] When applied to genocide studies, many scholars focused solely on totalitarian states ignoring democratic regimes. There is reason to doubt the democratic peace theory in genocide study.

If absolute power kills absolutely, the only response to that is democracy. On the other hand, some believe that democracy will not stop genocide, but can actually encourage it. There is some support for the idea that genocide has its roots in failed democratization or in the face of increasing political parties attempting to create democracy. If true, then we must focus not just on authoritarian states, but also on democratic nations.

Yugoslavia disintegrated into genocide after the fall of communism and the beginning of a more democratic government. Rwanda became enveloped in genocide soon after a power-sharing treaty was signed whereby the controlling elites were required to share power with the minority Tutsis. In both cases, it can be argued that these states were in a process of becoming more democratic when genocide occurred.

A state engaged in genocide is actually engaged in being a dual state.[24] A dual state consists of two parts, one which functions to perform the necessary conditions for maintaining the social order, and the other part is genocidal in purpose targeting the victim group and eliminating them. This state within a state theory poses that warfare has been part of the creation of the state for centuries and thus using genocide to retain power is not unusual.

Political science studies genocide to answer the question why some states resort to genocide and others do not. Political scientists have analyzed and supported the idea that genocide is a crime committed by the state. The political structure of the state is a contributing factor to genocide worldwide; the political nature of genocide cannot be ignored. In fact, "violence is a core element of state ideology, serving to make mass violence the means of socializing a majority to live in a culture of violence."[25]

Sociology

The field of sociology has studied genocide as a **social fact** produced by the particular cultural and structural composition of society. Genocide sociologists have focused their attention on the concepts of ethnic conflict and the social norm of violence (including groupthink).

SOCIAL FACT

Emile Durkheim, a French sociologist, defined social fact as "the beliefs, tendencies, and practices of the group taken collectivity" ([1895] 1982: 54). ◄

Ethnic conflicts can lead to collective violence expressed as terrorism, civil war, or genocide. Since the end of World War II, the number of ethnic conflicts has been increasing due to new multi-ethnic states, nation building activities, and the spread of new ideology.[26] Robin Williams found that the level of division between ethnic groups, their concentration in one geographic location, inequality, and fear of exclusion all increased the possibility of ethnic conflict.[27]

Another crucial element in ethnic conflicts is the relationship between the ethnic groups and the state. This relationship becomes even more important if the state claims sole sovereignty over all ethnicities within their borders. If there is disagreement concerning collective goods of society, including language, religion, political rights, and parity in the economy, the likelihood of ethnic conflict increases. If an ethnic group challenges the state on these grounds, the state may feel force is an appropriate response, including elimination of the group in severe cases.

Aside from ethnic strife, other sociologists have attempted to explain why genocide flourishes as a social norm. Once genocide, or any group behavior, has begun society tends to develop an acceptance of the violence.[28] Society and its institutions begin to change in a manner that supports the violence; violence breeds more violence in societies like this. Eventually, killing and participation in genocide becomes the "right" thing to do.

Societies may then become involved in "**groupthink**."[29] Groupthink can create an illusion of invincibility, which often leads to excessive optimism and risk-taking behavior. Groupthink also allows the society to rationalize their actions and their position on violence. Since groupthink creates a shared illusion of unanimity, it becomes even more difficult to dissent. Once the ability to dissent is silenced there is little hope of stopping the violence.

GROUPTHINK

Groupthink occurs when decisions are made with the goal of achieving consensus not based on critical reasoning or recognizing the possible negative outcomes. ◄

Once critical reasoning and dissent are eliminated, violence of any kind, including genocide, may be seen as a social norm in society.[30] This norm can be manipulated and mobilized under certain circumstances. If violence is a norm, then the truly deviant behavior is not committing violence. By a society transgressing in this manner, a so-called ecstatic community is formed where perpetrators feel a heightened sense of belonging to society since everyone has transgressed together.[31]

The ecstatic community creates a new level of bonding among society members. From this solidarity can emerge personal release and a social revival. This social revival allows people to participate in acts that they otherwise would have considered wrong. When genocide becomes normalized in society we see that génocidaires are more often than not, regular citizens—"all civilized men are capable of savagery."[32]

While some sociologists have focused on the social causes of genocide, the genocidal event itself has also been the object of sociological investigation. For sociologists, the concept of genocide includes more than the mass murder of an entire population. Sociologist Vahakn Dadrian has offered several different types of genocide categorized based on three factors: the intent of the perpetrator; the level of victimization; and the scale of the casualties.[33]

The four types of genocide that he distinguishes are cultural genocide, latent genocide, retributive genocide, and optimal genocide. Cultural genocide occurs when assimilation has been taken to the extreme.[34] Often the victim group is excluded from the power structure and violence is used to secure compliance. Cultural genocide seeks to eradicate the unique identity of the victim group while at the same time reinforcing the culture of the dominant group. Destruction of culture is something that Raphael Lemkin would consider genocide as it could destroy the identity of a group and have permanent consequences.

Latent genocide is an unintended consequence of the pursuit of certain goals.[35] When the government does not stop the unintended consequences, then the actions could become genocidal in nature. The perpetrators here focus not only on the target group but specifically the power base of that group. Latent genocide can include the forceful removal of a group with the final result being the extermination of the group. When the Ottomans moved the Armenian population to the Syrian desert during World War I the expressed goal was to prevent Armenians from undermining the war effort, but the result was the extermination of over one million Armenians.

Retributive genocide is a limited form of genocide with the objective of meting out punishment to a minority population that is challenging the dominant group.[36] As the name suggests, the goal here is to obtain retribution. Retribution can be seen as a statement that the victim deserves what is happening to them because of their actions.

Optimal genocide is massive in scope and indiscriminate in application. Optimal genocide has the goal of the complete obliteration of the target group.[37] The victim group is viewed as a threat to the dominant party and the power to destroy the group lies in the hand of the dominant group. The Holocaust is an example of optimal genocide because it was widespread with the goal of total elimination of the Jewish people and the power to do this rested with the German government.

Bradley Campbell believes that certain societies are more predisposed to genocide than others. Genocide occurs in a society that is both overly diverse and understratified.[38] Overdiversity means that a society is ethnically divided or that previously separate ethnic groups are now in contact.[39] Understratification means a high-status ethnic group's position is threatened or in fact declines.[40] Societies fitting this overdiversity and understratification model include Rwanda where the Tutsis and Hutus were divided on ethnic lines and the powerful Hutus were threatened by power sharing with the Tutsis.

As we move on to how criminology examines genocide it must be noted that there is much overlap between the sociological perspective on genocide and that of criminology. Criminology is a sub-field within the field of sociology. But it is also more than that. Criminology, as we will see, is a multi-disciplinary area which includes elements of sociology in its foundation as well as several other disciplines. From this criminological approach a theoretical framework for studying genocide can be developed.

▶ *Critical Thinking Exercise* Criminologists study crime, so what happens when they ignore genocide—the crime of crimes. Can you think of reasons why someone would not study genocide?

Criminology

At its core, according to Edwin Sutherland, criminology is concerned with the study of law-making, law-breaking, and law enforcement.[41] As a field, criminology is different from the previously examined academic arenas. Criminology is an interdisciplinary field by design. From its inception, criminology in the United States has been very closely linked with sociology, while criminology in Europe maintains closer ties with law. While criminology has benefited greatly from its close relationship with sociology, the field touches on many other disciplines as well. Criminology is where scholars from diverse backgrounds can come together to study a single, yet important, social phenomenon—criminal behavior.

This diverse background should encourage the study of genocide from an interdisciplinary approach. However, as a discipline, criminology has ignored genocide as an area of study until recently. This seems patently contradictory when genocide has been called "the crime of crimes." The lack of criminological attention to genocide has been noted by several scholars in the field.[42] George Yacoubian looked at the number of articles published on genocide in several mainstream criminology journals. He found only one article on genocide out of 3138 articles published between 1990 and 1998. As will be seen, this acts as only one internal barrier to the study of genocide within criminology.

In a comparable study, Dawn Rothe and Jeffrey Ross examined the coverage of state crime in popular undergraduate criminology textbooks. Genocide is an act of a state and would appear under state crime when and if covered. However, of the eight most popular criminology textbooks, three texts did not cover state crime at all and two texts gave only brief coverage under the topic of state-sponsored terrorism. Only one text covered state crime as an act of a nation and not as a political action or as occupational crime (like white-collar crime). None of the textbooks offered a comprehensive review of the literature on state crime or a theory of state crime. The absence of state crime from criminology textbooks is another barrier within the field to the study of non-traditional crime.

Internal barriers to the study of genocide in criminology begin with the marginalization of the topic at the undergraduate level. This marginalization continues into the graduate level of criminology and beyond. It is difficult to obtain funding in the United States to study a topic that occurs mostly outside of the country.[43] In order to survive in academia, one needs to avoid the study of genocide because of its more qualitative methodology and difficulties in publishing in major journals. As a result of these barriers the field of criminology has suffered from a paucity of literature and theory on genocide.

In order to reverse this course, it must become more acceptable for genocide to be viewed and analyzed as a crime. Scholars (like you) must pay heed to the gap that currently exists, not only in criminology, but in the study of genocide as a whole. You can help fill the gap by sharing your knowledge of genocide with others; you can also conduct your own research on genocide and share that as well. We all play a role in raising awareness of genocide in criminology.

Fortunately, the last few years have seen an increase in attention paid by criminology to the crime of genocide. Alexander Alvarez applied the techniques of neutralization to the Holocaust as an explanation for individuals' involvement.[44] The techniques of neutralization is a criminological tool explaining how people neutralize their feelings in order to commit crime; its application by Alvarez to the Holocaust appears to support the idea that the techniques are more of a psychological explanation of genocide.

The Holocaust was bureaucratized in many ways and participation was so pervasive that it would not be considered deviant to participate. Before the Holocaust began and after the Holocaust ended, many perpetrators lived law-abiding lives. There is some evidence from perpetrators that they viewed their "work" as unpleasant and traumatic. If the perpetrators of the Holocaust were not inhuman, there must be an explanation for why they participated in such atrocities.

Applying the techniques of neutralization, Alvarez examines the psychological process that may have contributed to some génocidaires participation. First, denial of responsibility allows the perpetrator to believe that their actions are outside of their own control. They are not responsible; there is a greater force at work. Denial of injury allows the perpetrator to classify their behavior in a more socially acceptable manner. They claim no one was really hurt by their actions—killing was referred to as "special treatment" or "cleansing."

Denial of victim occurs when the perpetrator is able to claim that the victim is responsible for their situation. The victim is to blame for their own victimization. By casting the Jews as the enemy, the Germans were allowed to make a claim of self-defense and attempt to place their actions in a more tolerable position. Condemning the condemners eases moral responsibility by stating that everyone is corrupt and they have no right to pass judgment on us. During the Holocaust, no major Western power allowed an increase in immigration quotas to accept more Jews, nor did they attempt to stop the killings by bombing the concentration camps. The Germans could cite this lack of action as wrong in its own right, thereby reducing any moral superiority that the Western nations claimed to have over Germany.

The final technique, that of appeal to higher loyalty, permits the génocidaire to claim that they are not acting selfishly, but to please a higher power. That power can be human or supernatural. Hitler used devotion to patriotism to claim that the génocidaires were supporting Germany by their actions. The techniques of neutralization seem to offer an explanation for why people participated and how they were able to justify their behavior.

One of the publications on genocide in criminology is Augustine Brannigan and Kelly Hardwick's analysis of genocide using Gottfredson and Hirschi's **general theory of crime**. Brannigan and Hardwick attempt to structure genocide as a crime that can fit within the general theory of crime.[45] While the rationalization of genocide under the general theory of crime is difficult to accept fully, it is a first step toward criminological theorizing about genocide. In fact, the authors themselves note that the general theory of crime is not truly appropriate for genocide, but they believe it is the only current criminological theory that could be applied to genocide.

GENERAL THEORY OF CRIME

The general theory of crime (GTC) says that crime is the result of low self-control. Individuals with low self-control tend to be more impulsive. ◄

In 2002, John Hagan and Scott Greer wrote an article explaining the important roles played by criminologists in developing international law. In an analysis of the International Criminal Tribunal for Yugoslavia, John Hagan and Ron Levi explained how interest in international law is growing within criminology and the effects that has on the understanding of crime.[46] Hagan then began to study the genocide in Darfur in depth. In 2006, Hagan, Heather Schoenfeld, and Alberto Palloni examined how crime victimization surveys can affect the work of humanitarian agencies during emergencies.[47] Hagan and Wenona Rymond-Richmond used survey data from the United States government to detail how the government of Sudan contributed to the racial division that led to genocide in Darfur.[48]

Hagan and Rymond-Richmond use quantitative analysis to suggest that the genocide in Darfur is based on race and encouraged by the government. Utilizing the work on collective action and collective efficacy, the authors devise a collective action theory of genocide. The theory explains that macro-level constructs of competition and ideology led to the creation of micro-level interest groups (Arabs and black Africans). Then individuals in the Arab group, having internalized racial ideology, began violent acts rising to the level of genocide against black Africans.

While Hagan and Rymond-Richmond's work is exceptional and definitely a step forward in the criminology of genocide, their theory appears so narrow that it may only apply to genocide based on racial divides. Hagan and Rymond-Richmond posit that the genocidal state is the result of a progression from state-level ideology to individual racial distrust. Then this individual racial animosity causes a collectivized racial intent which then leads to the execution of genocide at the state level. This approach begins at the state level but the ultimate genocide is the result of individual action.

While it is true that individuals commit genocide, the state plays a crucial role. Hagan and Rymond-Richmond acknowledge the importance of the state as the initiator of the racial animosity but the actual genocidal events—in their theory—seem to be the result of individual hatred. The link between the state and the individual in initiating genocide is vital. Hagan and Rymond-Richmond posit that this link is collective racial animosity; yet there may be a stronger meso-level link between the state and the individual. So there still exists a need for a theory incorporating criminological and other disciplinary ideas to assist us in understanding genocide in all locations.

Following Hagan and Rymond-Richmond, Alvarez (who used the techniques of neutralization on the Holocaust) published his book *Genocidal Crimes*.[49] In this volume, he explores the role of the perpetrators of genocide and how they may have been able to commit such crimes. Using a criminological viewpoint, he highlights the role of the state in committing genocide and how we can understand crime committed by large entities. He explores the idea of states of exception. A state of exception is when there is a legal no-man's-land which suspends the law and allows individuals to act outside of what would normally be legal. Genocide may flourish when these states of exception exist.

Recent work on combining criminology and genocide studies have shown overlap. While the language of criminologists and genocide scholars may differ, their meaning is often quite similar. Criminology is concerned with how culture can impact crime and genocide scholars are concerned with how cultural expressions (like anti-Semitism) affect the likelihood of genocide.[50] Criminologists explore social disorganization and anomie while genocide scholars look at war and crises, which often lead to social disorganization and anomie.[51]

Savelsberg points out that criminologists tend to work deductively testing theories with data and genocide scholars tend to work inductively going from gathering facts to arrive at an explanation.[52] While these approaches are different, elements of both deductive and inductive reasoning can further strengthen each other. These differences are by no means insurmountable. In fact, both criminology and genocide studies would benefit from borrowing from each other's methodologies.

Augustine Brannigan (who had explored the general theory of crime and genocide) also produced more research on genocide. In his analysis he addresses three paradoxes when examining genocide in criminology.[53] The first paradox is how to understand the voluntary nature of ordinary people engaging in violent murderous activity. This speaks to criminology's ability to understand violent behavior and motivations behind criminal activity.

The second paradox is how large-scale crimes can go unpunished. If the law is not enforced, the field of criminology can feel irrelevant. So we must recognize that even when the law fails, criminology can still provide explanations for these most heinous crimes. The final paradox is how genocide has gone unnoticed by criminology for so long. Legal immunity and holding political elites responsible are very difficult so it often goes unexamined. Brannigan argues that criminology should address these paradoxes and not ignore them.

Nicole Rafter published a comprehensive review of genocide from a criminological standpoint.[54] She examined the multiple layers of genocide from the big picture state-level activity to the individual-level participants. In doing so she was able to draw together many criminological ideas to propose the construct of genocidal propensity. Genocidal propensity exists when a state suffers from several large-scale issues like war, instability, or polarization. These countries then have a greater chance of falling into genocide than countries without these issues. Genocidal propensity allows for an opportunity to prevent genocide if we watch for the warning signs.

In addition to genocidal propensity, Rafter brings forth the issue of gender and genocide. Rafter argued that men accomplish extreme forms of masculinity through murder and rape.[55] Women, on the other hand, avoided violence or became victims by doing gender.[56] Doing gender refers to following the stereotypes of being a woman—frail, kind, and gentle. In Rwanda, rape was a tool of genocide used to subjugate and harm the Tutsis as a whole.[57]

Other research has shown that women in Rwanda served as perpetrators, victims, and rescuers.[58] Brown found that participation was limited by the role of womanhood as it was in Rwanda. A woman's loyalty to her ethnic group overrode any sense of solidarity of sisterhood.[59] Fox and Brehm explored why women acted to save others finding that socialization and context were important to decision-making on whether to rescue.[60] Understanding the role of gender in genocide is another area explored by criminology in addition to why genocide occurs.

The study of genocide in criminology has been growing. We will see more criminological theory and genocide in the next chapter. Since Lemkin proposed the idea of genocide as a crime, it is only fitting that the field of study which examines crime should pay attention. Ideally, criminology could offer ideas to predict genocide and if early warning signs are heeded then perhaps we may even prevent genocide in the future.

Conclusion

Genocide is a topic that has numerous angles from which one can approach it. Each field offers its own theories and explanations of genocide. Here we argue that criminology is best suited to integrate these diverse fields of study and their contributions on genocide into a coherent theoretical perspective on the crime of genocide.

Each discipline we discussed can be integrated into a criminological understanding of genocide. The important part to remember is that no one field can dominate the study of genocide. It will take many different perspectives to fully understand the complex nature of genocide.

In the next chapter, we examine the several different theories of genocide and the contributions they make to our understanding of the phenomenon. We will explore theories from several fields of study that can give us a better understanding of what causes genocide to occur. We will find that there are many causal factors leading to the crime of genocide. It becomes our next responsibility to analyze these factors to decide which ones are most crucial.

Discussion Questions

1. Which field do you think best understands genocide? Why?
2. Make a chart detailing the fields and their respective understandings of genocide. Do you see any way for these different fields to combine their understandings to better address genocide?
3. Which of the disciplines do you think best address Lemkin's original concept of genocide?

Notes

1. Salih, Khaled. (1995). Anfal: The Kurdish genocide in Iraq. *Digest of Middle East Studies*, 4(2), 24–39: 26–27.
2. See Goldensohn, Leon (2004). *The Nuremberg interviews: An American psychiatrist's conversations with the defendants and witnesses.* New York: Knopf.
3. Durkheim, Emile (1938). "The normal and the pathological," in *Rules of Sociological Method.* New York: The Free Press.
4. Fournet, Caroline (2007). *The crime of destruction and the law of genocide: Their impact on collective memory.* Hampshire, UK: Ashgate.
5. Alonzo-Maizlish, David (2002). "In whole or in part: Group rights, the intent element of genocide, and the 'quantitative criterion'." *New York University Law Review*, 77, 1369–1403: 1373.

6. Ibid., at 1395.
7. Rome Statute of the International Criminal Court, Article 30(2), available at https://www.icc-cpi.int/resource-library/Documents/RS-Eng.pdf
8. Power, Samantha (2002). *"A problem from hell": America and the age of genocide.* New York: Harper Perennial.
9. Glueck, Sheldon (1944). *War criminals: Their prosecution and punishment.* New York: Knopf.
10. Glueck, Sheldon (1946). *The Nuremberg trial and aggressive war.* New York: Knopf.
11. Clark, Roger S. (2001). "Countering transnational and international crime: Defining the agenda." *Hume Papers on Public Policy*, 6, 20–29.
12. Staub, Ervin (1989). *The roots of evil: The origins of genocide and other group violence.* Cambridge: Cambridge University Press: 13.
13. Brannigan, Augustine (1998). "Criminology and the Holocaust: Xenophobia, evolution and genocide." *Crime and Delinquency*, 44(2), 257–277.
14. Kressel, Neil J. (2002). *Mass hate: The global rise of genocide and terror.* New York: Westview Press.
15. Ibid.
16. Sternberg, Robert J. (2003). "A duplex theory of hate: Development and application to terrorism, massacres, and genocide." *Review of General Psychology*, 7(3), 299–328.
17. Ibid.
18. Rummel, R. J. (1995). "Democracy, power, genocide, and mass murder." *Journal of Conflict Resolution*, 39(1), 3–26.
19. Verdeja, Ernesto (2002). "On genocide: Five contributing factors." *Contemporary Politics*, 8(1), 37–54.
20. Savelsberg, Joachim J. (2009). "Genocide, criminology, and Darfur." *Theoretical Criminology,* 13(4), 477–480.
21. Harff, Barbara (2003). "No lessons learned from the Holocaust? Assessing risks of genocide and political mass murder since 1945." *American Political Science Review*, 97(1), 57–73.
22. Ibid.
23. Conversi, Daniele (2006). "Demo-skepticism and Genocide." *Political Studies Review*, 4, 247–262: 247.
24. Kolin, Andrew (2008). *State structure and genocide.* Lanham, MD: University Press of America.
25. Ibid., at 67.
26. Williams, Jr., Robin W. (1994). "The sociology of ethnic conflicts: Comparative international perspectives." *Annual Review of Sociology*, 20, 49–79.
27. Ibid.
28. Dutton, Donald G., Boyanowsky, Ehor O. & Bond, Michael H. (2005). "Extreme mass homicide: From military massacre to genocide." *Aggression and Violent Behavior*, 10, 437–473.
29. Ibid.
30. Stone, Dan (2004). "Genocide as transgression." *European Journal of Social Theory*, 7(1), 45–65.
31. Ibid.
32. Ibid., at 59.

33. Dadrian, Vahakn N. (1975). "A typology of genocide." *International Review of Modern Sociology*, 5, 201–212.
34. Ibid.
35. Ibid.
36. Ibid.
37. Ibid.
38. Campbell, Bradley (2015). *The geometry of genocide: A study in pure sociology.* Charlottesville, VA: University of Virginia Press.
39. Ibid.
40. Ibid.
41. Sutherland, Edwin H. (1947). *Principles of Criminology* (4th Ed.). Philadelphia: J.B. Lippincott.
42. Day, L. Edward & Margaret Vandiver (2000). "Criminology and genocide studies: Notes on what might have been and what still could be." *Crime, Law, & Social Change*, 34, 43–59; Yacoubian, Jr. George S. (2000). "The (in)significance of genocidal behavior to the discipline of criminology." *Crime, Law, & Social Change*, 34, 7–19; Rothe, Dawn L. & Ross, Jeffrey I. (2008). "The marginalization of state crime in introductory textbooks on criminology." *Critical Sociology*, 34(5), 741–752; Laufer, William S. (1999). "The forgotten criminology of genocide" In Freda Adler and Gerhard O. W. Mueller (eds.), *The criminology of criminal law* (pp. 71–82). New Brunswick, NJ: Transaction Publishers; Maier-Kitkan, Daniel, Mears, Daniel P. and Bernard, Thomas J. (2009). "Towards a criminology of crimes against humanity." *Theoretical Criminology*, 13(2), 227–255.
43. Rothe, Dawn L. & Friedrichs, David O. (2006). "The state of the criminology of crimes of the state." *Social Justice*, 33(1), 147–161.
44. Alvarez, Alexander (1997). "Adjusting to genocide: The techniques of neutralization and the Holocaust." *Social Science History*, 21(2), 139–178.
45. Brannigan, Augustine & Hardwick, Kelly H. (2003). "Genocide and general theory." In Chester L. Britt & Michael R. Gottfredson (Eds.), *Control Theories of Crime and Delinquency* (109–131). New Brunswick, New Jersey: Transaction.
46. Hagan, John & Levi, Ron (2005). "Crimes of war and the force of law." *Social Forces*, 83(4), 1499–1534.
47. Hagan, John, Schoenfled, Heather, & Palloni, Alberto (2006). "The science of human rights, war crimes, and humanitarian emergencies." *Annual Review of Sociology*, 32(3), 29–49.
48. Hagan, John & Rymond-Richmond, Wenona (2008). "The collective dynamics of racial dehumanization and genocidal victimization in Darfur." *American Sociological Review*, 73, 875–902.
49. Alvarez, Alex (2010). *Genocidal Crimes.* New York: Routledge.
50. Savelsberg, Joachim J. (2010). *Crime and human rights.* Los Angeles, CA: Sage
51. Ibid.
52. Ibid.
53. Brannigan, Augustine (2013). *Beyond the banality of evil: Criminology and genocide.* Oxford: Oxford University Press.
54. Rafter, Nicole (2016). *The crime of all crimes: Toward a criminology of genocide.* New York: New York University Press.

55. Ibid.
56. Ibid.
57. Fox, Nicole (2019). Rwanda, genocide, and gender-based violence. *Contexts: Sociology for the public*. Available at: https://contexts.org/blog/rwanda-genocide-and-gender-based-violence/
58. Brown, Sara E. (2018). *Gender and the genocide in Rwanda: Women as rescuers and perpetrators*. New York: Routledge; Fox, Nicole, and Brehm, Hollie Nyseth (2018). "I decided to save them": Factors that shaped participation in rescue efforts during genocide in Rwanda. *Social Forces*, 96(4), 1625–1648.
59. Brown, *Gender and genocide in Rwanda*, 40.
60. Fox, Nicole, and Brehm, Hollie Nyseth (2018). "I decided to save them": Factors that shaped participation in rescue efforts during genocide in Rwanda. *Social Forces*, 96(4), 1625–1648.

Further Reading

You can read more about Stanley Milgram's experiment and new thoughts about it here: https://www.theatlantic.com/health/archive/2015/01/rethinking-one-of-psychologys-most-infamous-experiments/384913/

You can read more about the Stanford prison experiment about how people react to power dynamics here: https://www.newyorker.com/science/maria-konnikova/the-real-lesson-of-the-stanford-prison-experiment

Useful Websites

Genocide Watch: www.genocidewatch.com

You should explore the ten stages of genocide outlined here.

NPR: Is genocide predictable? Researchers say absolutely. You can listen to a short story here about predicting genocide: https://www.npr.org/sections/goatsandsoda/2018/12/20/675582639/is-genocide-predictable-researchers-say-absolutely

3 Why Does Genocide Occur?

Bosnia and Herzegovina was one of the most ethnically diverse portions of the former Yugoslavia. By population, Bosniacs (Bosnian Muslims) represented 44% of the population, Serbs constituted 31%, and Croats represented 17%.

The Bosniacs had lived among these other ethnic groups for many decades under the communist rule of Yugoslavia. As the nation began to separate and divide by ethnic lines, the idea of a Muslim section of the land ignited deep-seated racist notions.

Early Muslim beliefs concerning food, the celebration of holidays, and clothing were the only visible differences between the Bosniacs and their neighbors. It was once said that the only difference between the Muslim and non-Muslim population was the way that the Muslims pray and what they eat.

The Bosniacs ultimately became the target of genocide.

One perpetrator of the massacres has said, "I was sorry for those people simply. I had no reason to shoot at those people. They had done nothing to me."

Another witness to the aftermath reported, "I went into several...houses...after they had been destroyed, and what I noticed was that they'd actually taken time to desecrate certain things that were central to Muslim identity."[2]

It is this disconnect that we must try to understand when examining genocide. The perpetrator states that the Bosniacs had done nothing to him, but he and others still destroyed and desecrated relics of Muslim faith. How can we comprehend why this happens when perpetrators themselves acknowledge the victim's innocence?

W. R. Pruitt, *An Introduction to the Criminology of Genocide*,
https://doi.org/10.1007/978-3-030-65211-1_3

Introduction

Genocide has myriad causes and no single theory may ever be able to encompass all of the elements. However, theory was never meant to explain every instance. When looking at crime in general there are many theories that try to explain why people resort to criminal behavior. No theory has explained every criminal and why s/he acts in that way. But we continue to test theories and refine them to better understand the phenomena of crime.

Theorizing genocide comes with the same caveat. No theory will be able to explain every instance of genocide. But we should still try to better understand the underlying causes in order to respond and perhaps even prevent genocide. But we should never try to force a genocide to fit in a specific theory when a new theory may be appropriate.

Theorizing involves creating generalizations to be tested and modified by research. If a theory of genocide fails to account for certain episodes then the theory should be re-examined. However, true social scientists should have no qualms about disposing of a theory that does not work and creating a new theory that does work. The rigor of the scientific method should prevent the forcing of theory to fit genocide or vice versa.

There are several theories of genocide and its causes. Most of these theories are based on **qualitative data**. Few empirical studies have been done due to the difficulty of obtaining accurate information during and after genocide has occurred. The lack of **quantitative studies** has been seen as a weakness in genocide studies.

Qualitative data is gathered via observation in non-numerical form. Qualitative data is descriptive in nature. ◀

Quantitative data is counted, measured, and expressed in numerical form. ◀

Not surprisingly, an overview of genocide theory will show areas of agreement as well as disagreement. We should seek to answer some of the remaining questions about the phenomenon and address the gaps in the current theories. Following the structure set out by Maureen Hiebert in her analysis of genocide theories,[3] this chapter identifies how current theories overlap and strengthen each other.

▶ Can genocide be blamed all on the perpetrators? While there may be other causes, understanding perpetrators is important. The following theories address the role of individuals in genocide. As you read them, ask whether they make sense of the violence.

Agency-Oriented Theories

The agency-oriented theories are concerned primarily with the behavior of the perpetrators either individually or acting in groups. Agency-oriented theories of genocide focus on the decision-making and perpetrators of the event.[4] Agency-oriented approaches include the role of the elites, the frontline killers, and the role that society plays as a cause of genocide.

When looking at genocide perpetrators, there are often multiple layers. The high-ranking elites may never physically harm anyone but they are responsible for the planning and encouragement of the genocide. The frontline killers tend to be individuals who either agree to participate or are forced to do so. These perpetrators tend to be the ones inflicting death and serious injury. At the end of the genocide, we then have to decide how to hold these offenders accountable. Do those who planned the genocide deserve more or less punishment than those who executed it?

The following theories explore how these different perpetrators might end up at the same place on genocide. We should be aware that these decisions could go toward explaining the intent of the offenders.

Elites

Theories that focus on the elite state that senior government decision-makers decide to eliminate a group of people.[5] The motivation for this decision could be personal (hatred or fear), psychological (irrational belief), or ideological (the group is subhuman). Most states are essentially concerned with only their own needs and the best way to achieve those needs.[6] By focusing on their desires a state tends to become indifferent to the needs or desires of other states. When the state feels that their power is beginning to wane, the elites may decide that genocide is the best way to maintain their control. The use of genocide will often instill fear in the general public undermining any will to oppose the government for fear of being the next target.

Research has found that control over the state machinery is critical to genocide.[7] The government elites who have control over every state institution are more likely to resort to genocide because control of the state means genocide is more likely to be successful. In many cases of genocide there is an authoritarian government in place beforehand. This style of government can then control the military, the police, the media, and almost every agency of the government. This total control will facilitate the execution of genocide because there will be little room for dissent.

In an analysis of colonial and modern genocide, the role of the state's elites was crucial.[8] The decision-makers had to be certain that genocide was necessary to be victorious. Also, the state's leaders were likely to choose genocide when they based their decision on predetermination. When one group is perceived to be standing in the way of another group, elimination may appear to be a resolution to the problem. In these cases, the elite may believe themselves to be superior based on religion, race, or history.

To many people genocide may seem irrational, but there may be times when the ruling elites believe genocide to be a rational choice to deal with a perceived problem. During World War I, Turkey claimed that the genocide of the Armenians was actually a military decision to prevent the Armenians from helping Russia and undermining Turkey's war effort. To solve this perceived problem, the government resorted to genocide—the solution seemed rational to them at the time.

Frontline Killers

Theories that focus on frontline killers are asking why individuals participate in genocide. Much of the work done in the area of frontline killers is psychological in nature because the focus is on how individuals come to decide to participate in mass violence. Alexander Alvarez proposed a comprehensive explanation of how ordinary people become involved in genocide. By applying the techniques of neutralization to the individual's decision to participate, Alvarez showed the process that some people might undergo in their transformation to génocidaire (see Chap. 2).

In a similar vein, Augustine Brannigan approaches genocide looking for an individual-level explanation behind the thought process of génocidaires.[9] Brannigan desires an individualistic approach because of the varying degrees of participation of the German people during the Holocaust. In order to explain why some people took to their role in the genocide with vigor and others refused to participate, one must understand the psychology of the individual. Only by understanding these "frontline killers" can genocide be fully explained. However, fully understanding an individual's choice to commit genocide is difficult, in some cases the perpetrators themselves cannot fully explain it.

One overview of the current theories of genocide highlighted the absence of individual-level theories.[10] Most theories of genocide are state-centered because of the involvement of the state in all episodes of genocide. In response, it is suggested that theorists need to focus on the individual involved in genocide because it is the individual who commits the killings. Here is a place where criminology could be beneficial as we have many individual-level theories of crime.

Individual-level theories of crime include strain theory which posits that a person who lacks legal-coping mechanism may resort to crime when faced with serious strains or stressors. In learning theory, individuals learn to commit crime through interactions with others. Control theories believe that individuals would commit crime but for being stopped by outside people/mechanisms which control their behavior. Could genocide be caused by strain? Or learned behavior? Or the result of a lack of control in a person's life? These areas require more research to fully understand.

> Recall the role of sociology in studying genocide. Can you think of how society plays a role in genocide? The next theories borrow heavily from sociology to explain the crime of genocide.

Society

The role that society plays in genocide includes bystanders and others who tacitly permit genocide to flourish. One theory states that the structure of a society, combined with difficult life events and social disorganization, leads to genocide. Social disorganization is used in criminology to explain how neighborhood structure may influence people to commit crime. A disorganized community often lacks the power to organize and act uniformly. This possibility should be explored more in the field to better understand whether a disorganized social structure might predict genocide.

If societal structure does lead to genocide, then intervention by bystanders—either internal or external—can affect the likelihood and success of genocide. Other countries can act as bystanders and their intervention, or lack thereof, affects the course of genocide in the perpetrator state. In many cases it would be easier for the international community to intervene than it would for the bystanders trapped inside the country where genocide occurs. The failure of the international community to act in these situations exacerbates the genocide.

Genocide is a social process that is initiated and implemented by social agents.[11] A common indication of impending genocide is societal crisis; this crisis will alter the way in which society reacts to problems that arise. Genocide may become a more feasible option when society agrees that it is the appropriate response. There is a lack of theories analyzing the role of society. Those few studies that do exist should be reinforced with research.

Structural Theories

Structural theories of genocide focus on the organization of the perpetrator state. These theories differ from the above agency-oriented approach of society because these structural theories are macro-level—the state as an institution. Structural theories include an analysis of culture, regime type, crisis, and modernity. Below, we will briefly discuss each of these structurally based themes.

Culture

Utilizing culture to explain genocide is difficult because of the lack of a unifying definition of culture. Nonetheless, culture does have a role in genocide. Some believe that genocide is the result of cultural aspects within the state.[12] The two main cultural aspects that lead to genocide are ethnicity and colonization.

Ethnicization of the state is considered one of the dominant forces behind genocide. Ethnicization can occur when a dominant power ascribes ethnic or racial identities to a group that does not identify as such. In Rwanda, the ethnic identities of Hutu and Tutsi were passed down by the child's father. After centuries of intermarriage, by the time of the genocide in 1994 it was almost impossible to identify ethnicity by sight.

To further its genocidal ideology the state issued ethnic identity cards that labeled each person regardless of whether they agreed with the designation. These cards were used to identity Tutsis during the genocide and became death warrants for many Tutsi.

This example of ethnicization is tied to colonization as well. Colonization began in Rwanda with the Germans. Following World War I, the Belgians came in as colonial powers and separated the population into Hutus and Tutsis. The original identification was based on the Belgian belief that Tutsis "looked" more European.

In many ways the Rwandan genocide can be tied back to colonization, but as we will see in later chapters, there have been genocides co-occurring with colonization. The Germans colonizing of South-West Africa (today Namibia) led to the genocide of the Herero (more on this in Chap. 5). The forced relocation and deaths of Native Americans in the United States, Canada, and Australia are also examples of colonization genocides.

If genocide has a cultural dimension then it becomes crucial to understand cultures effect on the phenomenon of genocide. Cultural characteristics may predispose some states to committing genocide. Some cultures may feel a sense of superiority over others in their community and if faced with losing that control, genocide may result. The divisive nature of the culture might influence the policy choice of the state.

Regime Type

This typology is concerned with how the structure of political regimes determines the adoption, or not, of genocide. The main focus has been on totalitarian states versus democratic nations. The main weakness in these theories tends to be the fact that even though non-democratic states have more instances of genocide, it has not been possible to establish a cause-and-effect relationship.

In one quantitative study of genocide since 1945, it was found that totalitarian regimes were more likely to experience genocide.[13] Totalitarian states can readily target one group as the enemy because the government is capable of isolating and highlighting the minority without concern of repercussion. Also, most non-democratic nations are based on military rule making the resort to violence easier. However, while it appears that genocide has occurred more in totalitarian states than in democratic nations, there has been little research to confirm these observations.

Others have explored the idea that there are two types of states that become involved in genocide—weak states and strong states.[14] Weak states are less likely to resort to genocide because a weak state cannot sustain continued violence. A strong state, though, is able to support genocide and implement it successfully. Strong states also have the ability to execute genocide quicker and in a more brutal manner. Totalitarian regimes tend to be strong states in the sense that they have control over all state institutions and apparatuses. While the analysis that weak and strong states affect the success of genocide is plausible, we lack strong empirical evidence that such association exists.

One critique of totalitarian theory is that its focus is too centered on totalitarian regimes at the expense of neglecting other nations.[15] In order to break away from the strictures of the totalitarian theory, genocide studies must embrace a critical theory that looks beyond the single episode of genocide and its attendant circumstances. An example includes the hypothesis that the more democratic a nation is, the less likely they are to commit democide. Democide encompasses all state-sponsored mass killings. The conclusion was that the extent to which a state controls all social, economic, and cultural institutions partially accounts for the intensity of genocide.

The degree to which the elite can rule arbitrarily may account for the magnitude of genocide. For domestic episodes of democide, political power, measured as democratic or totalitarian, was the single explanatory variable.[16] This analysis shows that democratic states do not commit democide on the same scale as non-democratic nations, but there does exist the possibility for democide in democracies. Theories of genocide that focus on regime types miss those episodes of genocide that do occur in democratic nations.

Divided Society

Theories of genocide that concentrate on divided societies examine the ethnic, religious, and socioeconomic breaks within the society. The belief is that society may become vulnerable to genocide along these cleavages. A society that imposes inequalities upon its minority population is more likely to experience genocide. A fractured society may not have far to go before genocide appears to be the appropriate solution to these differences.

Sociologist Helen Fein expected that if ethnic stratification was present then genocide would be more likely to result because the minority group will rebel against the dominant power structure. In order to maintain their power, the dominant group will use genocide to stop the rebellion. Research has shown that rebellion does increase when faced with ethnic stratification. If the likelihood of rebellion is high, then the possibility of genocide increases if those in power believe that eliminating the minority group is the only way to end the rebellion.

Unfortunately, it is not possible to evaluate whether ethnic stratification led directly to genocide or if it was moderated by the presence of rebellion. In a similar study, it was hypothesized that an exclusionist culture is likely to lead to genocide. An exclusionist ideology is "a belief system that identifies some overriding purpose or principle that justifies efforts to restrict, persecute, or eliminate certain categories of people."[17] This ideology can be based on race, religion, or any other categorization. Here it was found that countries that expressed an exclusionist ideology were more likely to experience genocide.

Analyzing the onset and the severity of genocide and other instances of state-sponsored mass violence, research has found that ethnic stratification did not have a significant effect on the onset of such violence.[18] In addition, ethnic stratification did not have a significant effect on the severity of the mass violence. These conclusions raise questions over the actual importance of a divided society in the occurrence of genocide. If a society has a division between a majority and minority group, genocide may be utilized against the minority group not because the division led to the violence, but because other stresses led to the use of violence and the government can place blame on the minority group.

The idea that a society will be divided prior to genocide has been taken up by several theorists. During and after genocide, the divisions within society become obvious; however, prior to genocide these divisions are often not as intense or clear. The weakness of these theories is they ignore the fact that genocide exacerbates divisions that may be difficult to identify before the conflict.

Modernity

Modernization theories of genocide argue that the material structure of the modern state facilitates genocide. It could be argued that modernization is a process that occurs through choice or evolution; thus the inevitableness of modernization would seem to lessen the responsibility of the state. The weakness of these theories is that they fail to explain why states choose to perpetuate genocide in the first place.

Two parallel elements have been identified to have occurred during the twentieth century.[19] First, the twentieth century has been marked by rapid progress in modernization and second, the twentieth century has seen more episodes of genocide than any other time period. The fact that these two factors have occurred simultaneously is not coincidence. Aspects of modern society—such as instantaneous communication, numerous intellectuals, newer and more sophisticated weapons, and greater international political negotiations—have led to the facilitation of genocide. These same elements, though, can be used to prevent genocide; unfortunately, they have not been utilized toward that end.

There are two ways to view the impact of modernity on genocide.[20] First, modernity can be seen as a progression of liberty, reason, and progress; if true, then genocide is a perversion of modernity. Second, modernity can be viewed as a radically fractured and unbalanced program. In this case, genocide can be an inherent possibility because of the uncertainty that modernity carries with it. If genocide is viewed in a modernity rubric, then there is little that the field can do to study genocide.

Arguably, though, all crime can be seen as inevitable. Crime has existed for the known existence of the world and studying it has not erased it, but it has raised consciousness to the subject. In fact, French sociologist **Emile Durkheim** argued that crime is inevitable and necessary in society.[21] But this did not mean it was not worthy of study and explanation, so too can the study of genocide within criminology raise the awareness of scholars and others concerned with mass atrocities in our world.

EMILE DURKHEIM

Emile Durkheim (1858–1917) was one of the founders and leading figure in modern sociology. He served as professor of philosophy at the University of Bordeaux. ◄

Currently, modernization has taken on a global significance. Globalization may require some states to accelerate their modernization in order to remain competitive. If the state is forced to increase the rate of modernization there may be direct conflict with groups in society who are not prepared for such changes. When the state is faced with such obstruction, genocide may seem to be the politically expedient option. In the end, though, modernity and modernization may indeed be an indicator that genocide is possible, but these theories cannot explain the decision to resort to genocide and why other modernized nations did not experience genocide.

Crisis, Revolution, War

There has been an assumption within genocide studies that there is a link between crises, revolutions, war, and genocide. Empirical analyses have shown some positive relationships between these two variables. In one comprehensive examination of genocide, it was acknowledged that there is a complex link between genocide and war.[22] Both genocide and war are acts of aggression and war can lead to genocide as well as genocide leading to war. The more aggression is used in these scenarios, the more it will be continued to be used going forward.

War is criminogenic, meaning that it can lead to other crime. Even for those who do not engage in war fighting, they can be pushed into committing other crime due to the breakdown of social norms during war/crisis. Those involved in the fighting can be pushed to commit other offenses during the war due to societal breakdown. War allows for people to steal and kill because in war it becomes expected to act in ways that would normally be considered criminal.

War can also be used to cover the existence of genocide and hide the actions taken as well as the number of victims. During World War I, the destruction of the Armenians was accomplished under the cover of war-time resettlement. The Holocaust was also initially hidden by the fog of war. War can also destabilize a government leading to the rise of opposition and conflict. This could be a predictor of genocide since opposition can turn violent.

Similarly, research has found that societal crisis is a common precipitant to genocide. When crisis weakens a nation, the struggle over power increases and may end in genocide. A failing nation that had previous internal wars or regime crises was more likely to experience genocide. If a failing state had instances of prior genocide, these states were more likely to resort to genocide again (perhaps because it was seen as successful previously).

One study found that civil war was the best predictor for the onset of genocide.[23] Internal and international war increased the possibility of the onset of genocide. When decolonization and civil war occurred together, there was a large effect on the onset of genocide. Passionate war may disguise a state that tries to implement genocide. War may actually make genocide a practical choice to win and the results of war may be the loss of protection for the victim group.

Others observed that genocides tend to occur during war or crises within a state.[24] Every genocide has to be analyzed separately to determine what historical and regional characteristics have led to that instance of genocide. This type of analysis, however, looks at genocide after it has occurred and does not seek to understand how to prevent the event. In one theory of genocide, profound social change was seen as a precondition to genocide.[25] These structural changes can include war, revolution, coups, or any major social transformation.

The connection between war, revolution, crisis, and genocide seems natural. Genocide is the ultimate war on people. Genocide is a crisis of immeasurable proportions. Empirical analyses have shown that there is a connection between war/crisis destructive events and genocide.

> Part of criminology is to understand victims in addition to perpetrators. While genocide is never the fault of the victim group, the following theories help explain how they may be victimized. These theories borrow from criminology and might help explain other types of crime in society.

Victim-Group Construction Theories

Genocide theories based on the construction of the victim group differ from the other theories of genocide because of the focus on victims and not perpetrators. These theories have been divided into three categories—the victim as the "other," victim dehumanization, and victim as threat to the state. In some ways, these theories are not concerned with the explanation of the onset of genocide, but with the targeting of the group victims.

Trying to understand why victims are targeted is not blaming them for their victimization. This is something we must be careful to never do. But if we better understand how victims become targets we could prevent genocide by looking for warning signs. Prior to the genocide of the Kurds in Iraq, they were excluded from the census count which implied that they were not truly citizens of the country. This is a warning sign related to targeting a victim prior to the genocide. If international will had existed then perhaps we could have seen what was about to befall the Kurds and intervene. Our goal should be to protect the vulnerable so understanding how they become vulnerable can assist in that outcome.

The Victim as the "Other"

When groups of people are classified in in-group and out-group terms (us v. them), it becomes easy to label one group as the "other." Once a group has been identified as the "other" it becomes possible to remove that group from the realm of obligation. If a specified group of people are removed from the state's sense of obligation, then there is no barrier to eliminating the group.

In many cases of genocide, the victims are not seen as full members of society. In Myanmar, the Rohingya are not officially counted in the population. This exclusion pushes the Rohingya out of the state's responsibility because essentially they do not exist to the state. Being denied recognition as people further excludes the "other" from society.

Using the techniques of neutralization, génocidaires can deny the victim and their suffering. Denial of victim and denial of injury are two techniques of neutralization used to make criminal behavior possible. Denying the victim implies that they deserve what is happening to them. In Rwanda, the Tutsis were blamed for their victimization because the Hutu believed that if they did not kill Tutsi, they would take over the country. This myth was stoked by the government to identify Tutsi as "other" and deny that they were victims. Instead the Tutsis were seen as bringing the violence on themselves.

Denying injury implies that there is no suffering because any injury is self-inflicted. Here the offender does not believe that their behavior causes any great harm. While it may seem hard to deny genocide causes injury, imagine a case of self-defense. When a person responds to an attack with justified force, there is injury but it is justified. In genocide, perpetrators often feel that their violence is justified and not really an injury to anyone (who doesn't deserve it). When the group is seen as the "other" then this denial is simpler and the elimination of those people is less disturbing.

In one study, it was found that exclusion of the group was present in all episodes of genocide analyzed.[26] Colonial genocides involved groups that were not well integrated within the larger community before the genocide. A classic example of colonial genocide is the Herero of South-West Africa (we will see more on this in Chap 5). Other poorly integrated groups include the Kurdish population in Iraq/Iran and the Rohingya of Myanmar. Both of these groups were denied full citizenship prior to the genocide.

The genocides of the Jewish people and the Armenians involved groups that were better integrated into their community. However, before the genocide against these groups they were deemed to be the "other" and not welcomed among the broader society. It was more difficult to exclude these groups from the community, but they were successfully excluded prior to the instigation of genocide. In both cases, difference in religious belief became a dividing point that was exaggerated to push the minority out of the state's responsibility.

Identifying the victim group as the "other" also fits theoretical models of genocide because it is difficult to kill your neighbors, but it is not so difficult to kill a stranger. Recall the role of culture and divided society from above, the "othering" process helps widen the gap in divided societies. Othering also often targets the culture of the "other" as weird or unacceptable to the majority of society, which can then help encourage genocidal action.

Dehumanization

The process of dehumanization occurs when people are redefined as not being part of the human species meaning there is no need to protect them or save them if they are in danger. Similar to identifying victims as the "other" dehumanization lessens the barrier to commit genocide. The moral compunction to kill is overcome by the dehumanization process and perpetrators can act guilt-free.

The process of dehumanization includes different actions. The out-group is often assigned derogatory, degrading, and subhuman characteristics. The murder of an animal is much less stigmatizing than that of a human being. In Rwanda, the Hutu majority would call the minority Tutsis cockroaches or snakes. During the genocide, radio broadcasts would encourage people to hunt down the snakes in the grass. Murdering a snake is much easier for people than murdering a human; dehumanization allows for increased likelihood of participation in genocidal killing.

Ervin Staub's theory of genocide includes an element of devaluation—a widespread human tendency that serves a psychological basis as a precondition to doing harm. The roles among which dehumanization occurs most often include race

(Hereros were called barbarians), religion (the Jewish population in Germany were called bacteria and germs), status, wealth, power (Tutsis were seen as power hungry), and politics. This devaluation leads to viewing people as objects upon which you can act with little risk of retaliation.

The criminological theory of techniques of neutralization may help explain how dehumanization works in genocide. There are five techniques of neutralization by which someone might overcome their natural inhibition to commit crime. The techniques include denial of injury; denial of victim; denial of responsibility; condemning the condemners; and appeal to higher loyalties.

As discussed above, denial of victim involves the claim that no one was hurt by your actions or that the victim deserved what happened. If the Tutsis are snakes then there is no human victim to be concerned with and as snakes could kill you first, your actions have become justified.

It is important to recognize that exclusion of the "other" does not have to occur via dehumanization.[27] Criminologist Nicole Rafter points to the Katyn massacre as an example of genocide lacking dehumanization. The Katyn massacre was the execution of Polish military officers by the Soviet Union during World War II. Dehumanization did not occur in this case prior to the execution of the officers. However, they were still seen as the "other" mostly based on their military affiliation.

While dehumanization did not occur here, under the United Nations definition, the Katyn massacre is not legally genocide. The targeted groups were military and perhaps political identities not covered by the UN Convention on Genocide.

Dehumanization may not be a prerequisite for genocide, but we can see that it has been present in many cases. One study analyzing ten episodes of genocide found that "othering" occurred in all cases but at different levels.[28] Identifying "othering" as either low or high, roughly 60% of the genocides studied experienced low "othering."[29] This could indicate that dehumanization was not part of the "othering" process, or not as prevalent as in other genocides.

Dehumanization has occurred in many episodes of genocide, though not all. But that does not mean that we should ignore its importance in explaining how genocide can occur.

Threat to State

The labeling of the victim as a threat to the state makes destruction of the group plausible—genocide may be seen as the option to eradicating the threat. When faced with a threat, the people of the state will most likely fear those identified as the threat. This fear can become anger and even hatred resulting in the twisted logical position that genocide is the only way to save their nation.

By isolating the victim group as a threat to the state, the citizenry is more likely to accept the punishment meted out to the threatening group, even if the threat is imagined. Through exaggeration and hyperbole, Hitler saw the Jews as a literal disease that could kill Germany if not eradicated. The Holocaust eventually grew out of Hitler's devotion to "save" Germany from death by eliminating the disease.[30]

German chair of propaganda **Joseph Goebbels** noted in his diary that the Holocaust was barbaric but required because there was a "life-and-death struggle between the Aryan race and the Jewish bacillus."[31]

JOSEPH GOEBBELS

Paul Joseph Goebbels was born on October 29, 1897. Under Hitler, he became minister of propaganda. He is credited with presenting a favorable image of the Nazi regime to the German people. Goebbels served as chancellor of Germany for one day following Hitler's suicide before Goebbels himself committed suicide alongside his wife.

For more on Joseph Goebbels see: https://www.britannica.com/biography/Joseph-Goebbels ◄

When a state faces some threat to its existence, its citizens readily come together to eliminate the threat. During World War II, the United States isolated Americans of Japanese descent for "security purposes." The US Supreme Court upheld this isolation as constitutional holding that the need to protect against espionage outweighed an individual's right to be free.[32]

The solidification of people in response to danger still occurs. This solidarity is easily seen even in today's international community. Following the terrorist attacks on the United States of September 11, 2001, the people of the United States quickly and resolutely proclaimed their unified desire to eradicate the threat. This call to nationalism is a natural response to a threat. If that fervor is used negatively, and the threat is identified as an internal threat, genocide may result.

Hiebert's comprehensive overview of genocide theory offers several categories in which to place theories of genocide. But there are many other theories that do not fit into these categories. This merely shows the great diversity and complexity among the many theories of genocide. There are biological and some criminological theories of genocide that do not fit into Hiebert's analytic structure. These theories are no less important to the study of genocide and provide crucial insights from different viewpoints.

> Early theories of crime relied on biological factors to explain why people committed crime. This meant that people were born criminal. While these theories have been debunked today, the following section examines how criminology and biology failed to prevent Nazi Germany's genocidal behavior.

Biological Theories

Biological theories of crime were prominent until the 1960s when sociological theories became the dominant influence.[33] Biological and biosocial theories of crime are now on the rise again. In application to genocide, biological factors may play some part in understanding the complexity. The idea of a biological basis for genocide can be traced to Charles Darwin.[34] During his research, Darwin was a witness to several tragedies, which would today be called genocide. To Darwin, the evolution of a higher humanity could not occur without the demise of the lower. Darwin saw the elimination of a group of people as an "obscure problem."[35]

But, while Darwin believed that natural selection was the cause of these extinctions, he recognized that there were many other causes as well. Darwin never foresaw that his theory would be actively used to promote genocide because he explicitly stated that natural selection was an unplanned occurrence. To actively plan and execute a natural selection process (genocide) is directly contrary to Darwin's theory. However, the work of Hitler and the German state during World War II clearly highlights how the use of biology and eugenics can turn genocidal.

From 1933 to 1945, the Nazis utilized the biological theories of crime to justify their extermination of millions of people. Nicole Rafter has termed this period of history, "criminology's darkest hour."[36] Germany developed a criminal-biology science to identify, isolate, and ultimately eliminate people who they believed were hereditary criminals. In application, the head of Germany's Ministry of Health stated that the Roma (derisively called "gypsies") were "the products of matings with the German criminal asocial subproletariat" and not capable of assimilating due to their mental deficiencies.[37]

These studies were used to promote the idea of racial purity in Germany, which could only be achieved if "inferior" races were prohibited from reproducing. Groups that were deemed to be racially inferior included the Roma, the Jews, and the mentally and physically handicapped. In the ultimate prohibition of their ability to reproduce, millions of people from these groups were murdered during the Holocaust.

From these warped ideas emerged an Aryan criminology inside Germany that was used to justify the killing of "inferior" people. The central core of Aryan criminology held that biology determined criminal behavior and these traits would be passed on to future generations. While the Holocaust cannot be reduced to simply an exercise of criminal-biological science, the support that this theory gained lent it an air of legitimacy. Hitler and his political regime fully supported the findings behind this Aryan criminology, thus offering a sense of rationalization for the government and public who executed the genocide against the Jews, Roma, homosexuals, and the disabled.

Criminological Theories

There has been a growing literature on criminological theoretical approaches to genocide. John Hagan's collective action theory is one; another approach was developed by Augustine Brannigan and Kelly Hardwick. Further work has been developed by Joachim Savelsberg, Nicole Rafter, and Kjell Anderson.

Brannigan and Hardwick applied Gottfredson and Hirschi's general theory of crime (GTC) to genocide arguing that if the general theory of crime is truly general, then it should be able to explain genocide.[38] The authors believe that the GTC is more than just low self-control, but a combination of low self-control and social circumstances that either constrain or expedite behavioral outcomes. Basically, crime is the product of the actor (low self-control) and opportunity.[39]

Brannigan and Hardwick believed that génocidaires exhibited a lack of self-control, but this was different than the similar condition found in garden variety criminals. Primarily, genocide reflects the vulnerability and defenselessness of the targeted group especially when the state fails to broker peace in conflicts between competing racial or ethnic groups. These situations can be monitored and controlled, but if left unchecked then the opportunity to commit genocide arises.

Using the general theory of crime, they find it unlikely that all those involved in genocide suffer from low self-control. However, this does not mean that the trait of low self-control is irrelevant. It is less important to match the profile of low self-control to individual actors, than it is to apply it to the understanding of the mechanisms that create the opportunity for such behavior to flourish.

Robert Agnew developed strain theory to explain why people might commit crime. Generally, when a person is experiencing strain or stress in their life and they lack ways to cope with the strain they might resort to crime. Agnew has since broadened his theory in an attempt to explain terrorism. We can thus take his explanation of terrorism and apply it to genocide.

Agnew spoke of collective strains that lead to terrorism. Collective strains are strains experienced by members of an identifiable group most often a race/ethnicity, religion, or political group.[40] When collective strain is coupled with other factors such as extremist ideologies, then genocide could emerge.[41] The greater the strain the more likely that the state will resort to an illegal solution. Collective strain leading to genocide could include threats to power, war/crisis, or other perceived threats to the state.

As we have seen, in these types of situations, the state could devolve into a sense of normlessness or disruption. The state could then propose a genocidal solution to this disruption.[42] By doing so the state has responded through decisive action even if it is illegal. Genocide is more likely as a solution in those states with an out-group viewed as an existential threat to the state.[43] In this way Agnew's collective strain explanation of terrorism can be used to help explain genocide.

Another crime theory that could be used to understand genocide is control balance theory. In control balance theory, the main idea is that deviant behavior is caused by an imbalance in control. The decision to engage in crime is the result of "the gain in control to be achieved" by committing the deviant act.[44] The individual is seeking to gain control because they currently experience an imbalance.

A control imbalance refers to the amount of control they can exercise relative to the amount of control they are subject to.[45] Those who have control surpluses meaning they exercise more control than they are subject to (like dictators) are likely to engage in exploitation and plunder.[46] Plunder is exemplified through political leaders initiating pogroms to exterminate a whole group of people deemed undesirable.[47] Control balance theory is an example of adapting traditional crime theory to explain genocide. Other criminologists have developed new ways to use criminology to explain genocide.

John Hagan and Wenona Rymond-Richmond have proposed a collective action theory of genocide.[48] Their collective action theory begins at the macro-level and discusses how the micro-, meso-, and macro-levels interact to result in genocidal victimization. Briefly, their collective action theory of genocide states that: (1) land competition and supremacist ideology produced Arab versus Black identities; (2) these motivate individualized racial intent further promoted by field commanders with high levels of **"social efficacy"** and ties to (and support from) the Sudanese government; (3) this leads to frenzied collective action in which the yelling of racial epithets produces collectivized racial intent resulting in genocide.[49]

SOCIAL EFFICACY

Social efficacy refers to the idea that a community is willing to work together to achieve goals. This requires trust and willingness to find solutions as a team. ◄

According to Hagan and Rymond-Richmond, the government of Sudan fostered the racial and ethnic divisions between Arabs and Black Africans by recruiting and mobilizing Arab militias. It was not difficult to recruit these nomadic Arabs because of the need for land and water resources. Their collective action theory of genocide is designed to analyze both the individual and collective level of the racial division. They provide the link between the individual-level and the state-level action that is genocide.

The collective action theory was a jump forward in criminological theorizing about genocide. While the theory is very specific to the Darfur genocide, it can be broadened in an attempt to apply to more episodes of genocide. The focus on racial intent can be opened to include any protected group (race, religion, ethnicity, national origin). The theory's main idea is that genocide occurs from the top (state) and the bottom (individuals). In between the individual and the state is the collective action usually stoked by "othering" and other methods we've discussed.

Joachim Savelsberg would agree that the individual is only part of the explanation of genocide influenced by larger scale ideas. In his examination of the **My Lai** massacre, he found that racist terms invited othering and reduced the inhibition to kill. This behavior was very similar to the Darfur genocide and its othering process.

MY LAI

The My Lai massacre occurred in Vietnam in 1968. United States troops were expecting to encounter Vietcong combatants in the village, but when they arrived only elderly, women, and children were present. Lieutenant William Calley ordered his company to begin shooting the villagers. More than 500 villagers died before the slaughter was over. The violence ended when Hugh Thompson landed his helicopter between the troops and the villagers and threatened to open fire on the military members if they continued. William Calley was convicted of murder and sentenced to life imprisonment. However, his sentence was reduced to ten years and he was paroled in 1974. ◄

Savelsberg also finds culture to be an important cause of genocide. He describes a "culture of cruelty" that is often created to allow for genocide to flourish.[50] This use of culture is similar to the criminological use of culture as an adaptation to adverse conditions. This means that adverse or negative circumstances can create a culture where violence is accepted or at least tolerated. If this goes far enough, genocide may seem like a response to the negative situation.

In addition, there is a connection between the criminological theory of anomie and the genocide predecessor of war, instability, or crisis. The link lies in the breakdown of social ties. Anomie is the lack of social rules whereby an individual does not feel connected to society. Thus, committing crime is not prohibited because of the lack of social ties. Similarly, any crisis might lead to the breakdown of community and social connections.[51] If this breakdown causes loss of social connection, any crime becomes more likely, even serious crimes like genocide.

Augustine Brannigan combines anomie and the general theory of crime to explain genocide. He believes that society has evolved from a barbaric vigilante system to a more civilized society where we exchanged personal justice for protection by the state.[52] However, when state control supersedes self-control then genocide is possible.[53] The Holocaust, according to Brannigan, was a reversion to barbarity brought about by the suppression of self-control and abundance of state control (another control imbalance) which made the population vulnerable to manipulation.[54]

If this is true, then the lack of self-control may be an explanation for genocide. When lack of self-control is combined with anomie, then it may be even more likely to result in criminal behavior. Anomie is experienced as a lack of norms and even laws; this thereby creates a situation where crime is not punished but perhaps encouraged.[55] Brannigan sees self-control and anomie being related where a change in one affects the other. When anomie is high and self-control is low, state control could influence genocidal behavior.

The following table explains the relationship between anomie and self-control (Table 3.1).

As Brannigan predicts participation in genocide is more likely in a high anomie and low self-control environment. Nicole Rafter has developed the concept of "genocide propensity" to explain when a state might fall into this environment and resort to genocide.[56] Genocidal propensity is a concept combining several macro-

Table 3.1 Relationship between anomie and self-control

Anomie	Self-control: Low	Self-control: High
High	High Anomie and Low Self-Control A person is not connected to society and cannot control their own behavior. Participation in genocide likely.	High Anomie and High Self-Control While the individual is not connected to society, their own self-control inhibits their likelihood of committing crime.
Low	Low Anomie and Low Self-Control While feeling connected to society, their lack of self-control could influence their likelihood of committing crime.	LowAnomie and High Self-Control The person feels connected to society and also has good control over themselves. Likelihood of crime is low.

level factors that a state might experience leading to genocide. These include: colonialism, war, instability, ethnic/racial polarization, ideology, and prior genocide.[57]

Genocidal propensity is built upon the idea of criminal propensity that says that certain factors make an individual more likely to commit crime.[58] In genocidal propensity we find a collection of factors that puts groups (not the individual) at risk for committing genocide. The goal of genocidal propensity is to prevent genocide before it occurs by identifying those factors that put a country at risk. If these factors create an accurate risk assessment, then we might be on the way to preventing genocide and not just responding to it after it has happened.

Combining the micro-level analysis of Brannigan and the macro-level analysis of Rafter, Kjell Anderson seeks to fill the gap connecting micro- to macro-analysis. Anderson argues that too many theories ignore the process through which macro factors influence individual (micro) behavior.[59] Anderson sees génocidaires as responding to their situation in life in a way to find reason.[60]

He takes from situational action theory that posits that crime is a function of propensity and opportunity.[61] He then adds techniques of neutralization to explain how individuals can accept behavior that previously would have been illegal or immoral.[62] By using the techniques of neutralization the individual can evolve to accept the new "normal," even if it is genocide. The génocidaire then has accepted their genocidal behavior as the fault of others or by denying injury or victims (see Chap. 2 for discussion of techniques of neutralization).

Conclusion

As can be seen by the multitude of theories of genocide, there is no consensus on what causes genocide. In fact, genocide scholars were cautioned against adopting a theory of genocide prematurely. As editor of the *Journal of Genocide Research*, Henry Huttenbach warned researchers not to blindly accept any theory of genocide yet because it would deaden the field of theory in genocide studies.[63]

From a sociological and criminological standpoint, this fear appears unnecessary. We can draw an analogy with the study of street crime. There are a variety of theories of crime, many that contradict other theories. This has not stopped the theorizing of crime, but in some ways has encouraged it through critiques and elaborations. Likewise, the theorizing of genocide will advance by integrating some elements of the existing theories into new theories.

A truly interdisciplinary theory of genocide would take from as many fields of study as possible to develop a deep understanding of genocide. As such we should be aware of the many theories that exist as we continue our journey to comprehend what is seemingly incomprehensible.

Discussion Questions

1. Which theory do you think best explains genocide? Why?
2. Can you find any connections between the multitude of theories discussed?
3. If you were asked to explain why genocide occurs, what would you say? Relate your reasoning to the theories discussed.

Notes

1. United Nations (1999). *The fall of Srebrenica.* Accessed November 24, 2010 at www.un.org/peace/srebrenica.pdf: 80.
2. Carmichael, Cathie (2006). Violence and ethnic boundary maintenance in Bosnia in the 1990s. *Journal of Genocide Research,* 8(3), 283–293, 284.
3. Hiebert, Maureen S. (2008). Theorizing destruction: Reflections on the state of comparative genocide theory. *Genocide Studies and Prevention*, 3(3), 309–339.
4. Ibid.
5. Ibid.
6. Brown, Chris (1997). Theories of international justice. *British Journal of Political Science*, 27(2), 273–297.
7. Fein, Helen (1990). Genocide: A sociological perspective. *Current Sociology*, 38(1).
8. Palmer, Alison (1998). Colonial and modern genocide: Explanations and categories. *Ethnic and Racial Studies*, 21(1), 89–115.
9. Brannigan, Augustine (1998). Criminology and the Holocaust: Xenophobia, evolution and genocide. *Crime and Delinquency*, 44(2), 257–277.
10. Pramono, Siswo (2002). An account of the theory of genocide. Paper presented at the Jubilee conference of the Australian Political Studies Association, Australian National University, Canberra, October 2002.
11. Freeman, Michael (1991). The theory and prevention of genocide. *Holocaust and Genocide Studies*, 6(2), 185–199.
12. Scherrer, Christian P. (1999). Towards a theory of modern genocide. Comparative genocide research: definitions, criteria, typologies, cases, key elements, patterns, and voids. *Journal of Genocide Research,* 1(1), 13–23.
13. Fein, Helen (1993). Accounting for genocide after 1945: Theories and some findings. *International Journal on Group Rights*, 1, 79–106.
14. Supra note 6.
15. Moses, A. Dirk (2008). Toward a theory of critical genocide studies. Online Encyclopedia of Mass Violence.

16. Rummel, Rudolph. *Power kills*. Available at: https://www.hawaii.edu/powerkills/
17. Harff, Barbara (2003). No lessons learned from the Holocaust? Assessing risks of genocide and political mass murder since 1945. *American Political Science Review*, 97(1), 57–73, 63.
18. Krain, Matthew (1997). State-sponsored mass murder: The onset and severity of genocides and politicides. *Journal of Conflict Resolution*, 41(3), 331–360.
19. Cushman, Thomas (2003). Is genocide preventable? Some theoretical considerations. *Journal of Genocide Research*, 5(4), 523–542.
20. Morrison, Wayne (2004). Criminology, genocide, and modernity: Remarks on the companion that criminology ignored. In Colin Sumner (Ed.), *The Blackwell Companion to Criminology* (pp. 68–88). Malden, MA: Blackwell Publishing.
21. Durkheim, Emile ([1895] 1982). *The rules of the sociological method*. Steven Lukes, (Ed.). (W.D. Halls, Trans.). New York: Free Press.
22. Supra note 11.
23. Supra note 16.
24. Supra note 10.
25. Verdeja, Ernesto (2002). On genocide: Five contributing factors. *Contemporary Politics*, 8(1), 37–54.
26. Supra note 6.
27. Rafter, Nicole (2016). *The crime of all crimes: Toward a criminology of genocide*. New York: New York University Press.
28. Pruitt, William R. (2011). Toward a modified collective action theory of genocide: A qualitative comparative analysis. [Unpublished doctoral dissertation]. Northeastern University.
29. Ibid.
30. Koenigsberg, Richard A. (2009). *Nations have the right to kill: Hitler, the Holocaust, and war*. New York: Library of Social Science.
31. Ibid., at 3.
32. Korematsu v. United States (1944). 323 U.S. 214.
33. Rafter, Nicole (2008). *The criminal brain: Understanding biological theories of crime*. New York: New York University Press.
34. Barta, Tony (2005). Mr. Darwin's shooters: On natural selection and the naturalizing of genocide. *Patterns of Prejudice*, 39(2), 116–137.
35. Ibid., at 129.
36. Supra note 27 at 4.
37. Supra note 27 at 185.
38. Brannigan, Augustine & Hardwick, Kelly H. (2003). Genocide and general theory. In Chester L. Britt & Michael R. Gottfredson (Eds.), *Control Theories of Crime and Delinquency* (109–131). New Brunswick, New Jersey: Transaction.
39. Ibid.
40. Agnew, Robert (2010). A general strain theory of terrorism. *Theoretical Criminology*, 14(2), 131–153.
41. Anderson, Kjell (2018). *Perpetrating genocide: A criminological account*. London: Routledge.
42. Ibid.

43. Ibid.
44. Tittle, Charles R. (2004). Refining control balance theory. *Theoretical Criminology*, 8(4), 395–428.
45. Ibid.
46. Savelsberg, Joachim J. (2010). *Crime and human rights*. Los Angeles, CA: Sage.
47. Tittle, Charles R. (1995). *Control balance*. Boulder: Westview Press: 191.
48. Hagan, John and Rymond-Richmond, Wenona (2009). *Darfur and the crime of genocide*. Cambridge: Cambridge University Press.
49. Ibid.
50. Supra note 46.
51. Ibid.
52. Brannigan, Augustine (2013). *Beyond the banality of evil: Criminology and genocide*. Oxford: Oxford University Press.
53. Ibid., at 72–73.
54. Ibid., at 73.
55. Supra note 38.
56. Supra note 27.
57. Ibid.
58. Ibid.
59. Supra note 41.
60. Ibid.
61. Ibid.
62. Ibid.
63. Huttenbach, Henry R. (2004). Towards a theory of genocide? Not yet! A caveat. *Journal of Genocide Research*, 6(2), 149–150.

Criminology-Related Websites

American Society of Criminology Division of International Crime: https://international-criminology.com/

American Society of Criminology Division on Critical Criminology and Social Justice: https://divisiononcriticalcriminology.com/

4 Who Commits Genocide?

"PIO: Maybe we did not hate all the Tutsis, especially our neighbors, and maybe we did not see them as wicked enemies. But among ourselves we said we no longer wanted to live together We even said we did not want them anywhere around us anymore, and that we had to clear them from our land. It's serious, saying that—it's already sharpening the machete.

Me, I don't know why I started detesting Tutsis. I was young, and what I liked most was soccer: I played on the Kibungo team with Tutsis my own age, we passed the ball around without any hitch. I never noticed any unease in their company. Hatred just showed up at killing time; I latched on to it through imitation, to fit in."[1]

"I had killed chickens but never an animal the stoutness of a man, like a goat or a cow. The first person, I finished him off in a rush, not thinking anything of it, even though he was a neighbor, quite close to my hill…I mean, at the fatal instant I did not see in him what he had been before; I struck someone who was no longer either close or strange to me, who wasn't exactly ordinary anymore."[2]

Pio is just one example of someone who commits genocide. Before the genocide he led a relatively "normal" life. How did he become a killer? Was he predisposed to becoming a génocidaire and if so, why? While Pio represents an individual, we will also explore how states and other organizations can participate in genocide.

W. R. Pruitt, *An Introduction to the Criminology of Genocide*,
https://doi.org/10.1007/978-3-030-65211-1_4

Introduction

The question of who commits genocide is deceptive. It can appear to be an easy question: Who committed the Holocaust? Hitler. Who committed the Darfur genocide? Omar Al-Bashir. Who committed the Armenian genocide? Talat, Enver, and Cemal Pasha. But these answers are covering for the full response. In reality, none of the above-mentioned génocidaires took a weapon and physically killed the target population. Though that does not mean that they do not bear responsibility for the action.

When determining who commits genocide, we should consider the requirements of how we determine who commits crime in general. For a person to be convicted of a crime, there are two elements that must be proven beyond a reasonable doubt. The first is intent (mens rea) and the second is the act (actus reus). As mentioned in Chap. 1, genocide is a specific intent crime. This means that in order to convict someone of genocide they must have the intent to destroy a group in whole or in part.

Intent can be proven in many ways including one's words, written documents, and even other actions taken to support genocide. An example of using one's words as intent comes from the genocide of the Herero in South West Africa (today Namibia). During the genocide, German General Luthar von Trotha said, "the entire Herero people must be exterminated."[3] The Germans kept many records during the Holocaust documenting where people were deported to and their final treatment. In Sudan, the government provided air support to militias when attacking villages. All of these can go toward proving intent to commit genocide.

Aside from spoken words, these actions can be attributed to many different people. This is how we go about determining who has committed genocide. Who had the intent to eliminate the target group? This may go from the individual who physically kills a person to the head of state who knowingly allows these actions to continue.

The second element of a crime is the actus reus. This means that the person has taken some action to accomplish the criminal behavior. These acts can vary from physically attacking someone to providing support and material to accomplish the genocide. When the president of Sudan, Omar Al-Bashir, provides weapons and military aircraft to help eliminate villages in Darfur, he has taken action to support genocide. This is why the International Criminal Court has indicted Al-Bashir for genocide.

So, who commits genocide? There is no easy answer. In fact, no genocide is accomplished by just a few people. There is almost always a complex system of people behind the crime. As we try to determine the answer to this question, the field of criminology again offers some possible responses. In criminology, there is the concept of state crime and organizational crime. In both cases, it is not an individual who commits crime, but a group of people representing the state or other organization. The concept of collective violence can also be useful to understand genocide perpetrators. In collective violence, it is not the single person who we look for but instead a collective—a group of people. Groupthink was discussed in Chap. 2; collective violence can be the result of groupthink.

When we consider who commits genocide we must expand beyond the traditional thought that an individual must be responsible. For genocide, liability can lie with the state, with organizations, or with collectives of people. In all cases, there can ultimately be a defendant in the courtroom to accuse, but as criminologists we must expand our understanding to include entities composed of individuals but who act as groups.

State Crime

Can a state commit crime? Many people would say no automatically because they think of a criminal as an individual. But in criminology there is an area known as state crime. We first must accept the fact that a state can commit crime. How can a state do so? That is what the field of state crime is trying to determine. So for now, just accept that a state, which is a collection of individuals, is capable of committing crime. As we go through the research, continue to question the presumption that only an individual can commit crime.

State crime can be defined as "acts defined by law as criminal and committed by state officials in the pursuit of their job as representatives of the state."[4] Here state officials commit the crime in their official capacity. But state crime can also be "socially injurious acts designed to alter, expand, or reproduce key elements of the political order."[5] In this case, the crime is committed in order to have a political response. This response is often the retention of political power in the hand of a select few.

State crime has not been studied as much by criminologists as traditional street crime. Most state crime scholars agree that the state should be treated as a criminal actor because some crimes are just unthinkable outside of the state context and some crimes are the result of explicit state policy.[6] When individuals in the state government make decisions to kill/eliminate a group of people using the state tools and materials to accomplish their goal, the state is involved in committing the crime.

Further, international law creates a foundation for defining state crime in terms of human rights, social harm, or economic harm.[7] International law permits the treatment of a state as a criminal actor because no single state is responsible for defining crime in the international community. International law is not defined by one nation but instead by a collection of states agreeing that certain acts are universally wrong.

In international law, this concept is known as **jus cogens**. Jus cogens refers to crimes so abhorrent that a majority of nations agree that they violate principles of law. This agreement means that even if a country does not have a law banning the behavior, the state can still be held liable because the majority of nations agree that the act is illegal. In this way, no state can exclude itself from criminal liability by changing its definition of crime.

JUS COGENS

From the Latin meaning "compelling law." These represent norms that every country must abide by. No country can escape responsibility by passing laws to make these crimes legal because the majority of nations agree the behavior is universally prohibited. ◄

This has not stopped states from trying to avoid liability relying on the idea of sovereign immunity. In general, sovereign immunity means that each nation has the right to control what happens inside their borders without interference from other countries. **Sheldon Glueck,** a well-known criminologist, attacked the doctrine of sovereign immunity and quickly dismissed it. Sovereign immunity is based on the idea of national comity and courtesy with the expectation that the sovereign will act in a law-abiding and trustworthy manner.[8] If a sovereign nation violates these expectations it has abrogated its immunity.

SHELDON GLUECK

While Sheldon Glueck produced important criminological knowledge during and after World War II on the issue of genocide, he is best known for his work with his wife on juvenile delinquency. Much of Glueck's work on genocide was forgotten for several years until recovered by recent interest in the area of state crime. ◄

When a sovereign willfully orders his people to commit flagrant violations of law, he has clearly voided his immunity and made himself liable.[9] Sheldon Glueck may have been the first criminologist studying state crime. His work was crucial to the Nuremberg prosecutions. Glueck called the idea that the Nuremberg trial was ex post facto baseless.[10] Glueck expressed his feelings thusly:

> The accused knew that they could be executed for their deeds without being granted the privilege of any trial at all. Can they now be heard to complain that they had no notice that they would have to stand trial under an interpretation of international law which they do not like because they deem it to involve retroactivity?[11]

Glueck also rejected the defense of superior orders. He stated that acting on an illegal order is not justifiable when the defendant had reason to know the order was illegal.[12] Glueck also was supportive of the idea of an international criminal court to deal with the most serious international crimes. Most of Glueck's work on genocide was forgotten for decades, but his work shows how there was always a place for criminology in examining genocide. We may have abandoned this field for years, but we are now fixing that mistake.

Recent state crime criminologists have found that many criminological theories are individual decision-based theories at a micro-level of analysis. These types of theories are not very useful when analyzing state crime because state crime is usually a macro-level event resulting from several different causes and not one single cause.[13] State crime calls for a macro-level theory.

The criminologist Dawn Rothe has proposed a theory of state crime that includes three conditions which may produce state crime: (1) a state motivated by economic pressure, political goals, and anomie; (2) an opportunity where the state controls information, propaganda, and the military; and (3) constraints such as the media, public opinion, and political pressure are ineffective.[14] These conditions can be seen in many episodes of genocide. A state may decide to commit genocide to maintain its political power and usually controls the military and often the media outlets.

The Rwandan genocide fits almost all of Rothe's conditions. The ruling political party was afraid of having to share power with the minority Tutsi population. By eliminating the Tutsi, the Hutu would retain its hold on power. The Rwandan government controlled and issued propaganda denigrating the Tutsi and encouraging Hutu to kill them. There was weak political pressure from the United Nations to stop the genocide which allowed the atrocities to last for 100 days.

Similarly, others have proposed that state crime is likely when pressure for goal attainment intersects with the availability of illegitimate means in the absence of effective social control.[15] Within this framework the state structure can then create criminogenic pressure based on its political, economic, and cultural beliefs.[16] When the state frames their political or economic enemy as a certain minority group, pressure may build until it releases in an act of genocide. If crime is a rational decision, then using genocide to eliminate an enemy may seem the best response.

The field of state crime is a growing area of research that has contributed greatly to the understanding of large-scale criminal acts committed by states around the world. Theorizing and research on state crime draws heavily from the insights derived from the broader field of study of organizational crime.

Organizational Crime

Interest in organizational crime evolved from Edwin Sutherland's critique of criminology for not studying crimes of the powerful.[17] Similar to genocide, state crime, and critical criminology, the study of organizational crime has been relatively isolated within criminology though not ignored.[18]

Organizational crime is crime perpetrated by organizations or by individuals acting on behalf of organizations.[19] A more nuanced definition of organizational crime states: "Organizational crimes are illegal acts of omission or commission of an individual or a group of individuals in a legitimate formal organization in accordance with the operative goals of the organization, which have a serious physical or economic impact on employees, consumers or the general public."[20]

This definition can be broken down into its component parts. First, organizational crime involves illegal acts either through omission (failing to do something) or commission (taking an overt act) (the actus reus of crime). Second, organizational crime is committed by an individual or a group of individuals working for the organization in order to benefit the organization (the mens rea). Thirdly, organizational crime requires the presence of a legitimate formal organization, such as the state. Fourth, organizational crime must have a serious physical or economic impact and the adverse physical or economic impact must be on employees, consumers, or the general public.

In organizational crime, courts have been willing to punish both the individual who committed the criminal act and the organization that condoned the behavior.[21] When courts treat both individuals and organizations as criminally responsible, they have recognized that an organization can exist as a free-standing entity. A similar conclusion regarding the state would solidify the argument that the state is similar to an organization in behavior.

There are several reasons why organizations might be considered criminally liable by the courts. First, organizations are a collection of power positions that influence the thoughts and actions of the people in those positions.[22] Further, the people who occupy the aforementioned positions of power are replaceable.[23] The organization does not cease to function when some employees leave their position; the organization remains intact and functional.

Thus, the structure of an organization might influence deviance by limiting information to members of the organization as Rothe mentioned in the state's control of the media.[24] By limiting information availability the organization can isolate those with knowledge of the deviance away from the elites who lack knowledge. These elites can then later, truthfully, say that they were unaware of the deviance being committed and make a scapegoat out of a small number of employees.

Organizations can also support deviant behavior through establishing norms, rewards, or punishments that encourage such behavior.[25] For example, if a company gives bonuses to employees who make the most sales, the employee may resort to any behavior in order to gain the reward. Finally, an organization can directly initiate deviance through their position of power.[26] Having power over individuals means the organization can order them to commit deviant acts; it remains the individual's choice whether or not to participate.

Criminologist John Braithwaite offered a theory of organizational crime based upon Sutherland's differential association.[27] Braithwaite believes that organizational crime is more likely to occur when there are blockages of legitimate opportunities to achieve organizational goals and illegitimate opportunities are available.[28] When winning elections to retain political power is not possible, then genocide to eliminate opposition might seem like the best option.

Further, blockages of opportunities may create subcultures and organizational crime is more likely to occur when these subcultures have great resistance to law.[29] Within the state there may be subcultures that create their own set of rules. The German Gestapo, while created by the state, became a subculture open to only select individuals who acted upon their own set of norms and rules.

Braithwaite called for a "theory of tipping points" which would explain when the balance between conformity and non-conformity favors one side over the other. Determining this tipping point might act as a tool to prevent genocide. If it could be determined when the tipping point was near, intervention might be able to stop genocide before it starts.

The State as an Organization

The state may be viewed as a particular type of organization. The state is "a centralized set of institutions and personnel wielding authoritative power over a nation."[30] The government, which represents the state, has the obligation of ruling and addressing the nation's problems.[31] As stated above, organizational crime involves illegal acts of an individual or group of individuals in a legitimate formal organization acting in compliance with the organization's goals.[32]

The government of a state is a legitimate goal-oriented organization. A government obtains legitimacy in many different ways including admission to the United Nations or other international body, support in elections from the people of the state, or through exertion of a dominance of power. In addition, the government has its goals that it seeks to attain through the legislative and executive branches: to provide support and maintenance for its population. The nation's goals will include ways to achieve prosperity for the state. There may also be several other goals that the state seeks to achieve based on the government regime and the economics of the state.

Represented by its government, the state cannot act on its own accord; it must have people who act on its behalf—those in the government. It is true that no organization can run without people, but people alone are not enough to make an organization.[33] Both a government and an organization exist independently of the people who work in the system. Those in the system are replaceable; politicians can be voted out or thrown out during a coup. If the people are replaced, the state does not collapse or fail to exist; the state is still a recognized entity regardless of turnover in officeholders.

Due to what we have discussed above most state crimes take the form of organizational crimes rather than individual crime.[34] Therefore, the structure and organizational culture of the state may make the execution of crime easier. It has been claimed that "the structure and ideology of totalitarian governments, for instance, are prone to create institutions of social control and political policing in which terrorizing, physically abusing, or even killing perceived political enemies becomes a taken-for-granted part of everyday life."[35] Thereby, government agents come to accept the organizational culture created by those in power in which objectively evil acts become necessary and legitimate means to reach organizational goals.

When the state is considered to be an organization, this provides another way to examine how a state can commit crime. While the individuals in the state are the ones who ultimately take the physical acts to commit crime, they do so to benefit the state and sometimes at the request of state rulers. This should indicate that states can commit genocide, they can be criminal actors.

Collective Violence

Genocide may be viewed as an act of collective violence, thus theorizing on collective violence is relevant in our discussion. Collective violence is defined by the World Health Organization as "The instrumental use of violence by people who identify themselves as members of a group—whether this group is transitory or has a more permanent identity—against another group or set of individuals, in order to achieve political, economic, or social objectives."[36]

This type of violence though can take many different forms; there is no single manner in which to execute collective violence. What is shared by all incidents of collective violence is the fact that the events are committed collectively rather than individually.[37] Also, the goal of collective violence is to influence—by achieving or impeding—social, political, or economic change.[38] The influence that proponents of collective violence desire to achieve can be used to cause inequality as much as it is possible to achieve equality.

Due to the fact that collective violence is executed with a final result in mind, it may be seen as a rational act. Human beings turn to collective violence as a response to a perceived threat, where benefits outweigh risks, making collective violence a rational act.[39] If collective violence is rational, then we cannot blame it on random behavior or simplify it to conflict between groups.

Rational behavior implies a decision-making process that can be analyzed in hopes of preventing future acts of collective violence. Rational choice theory states that people decide to commit crime when the benefits outweigh the costs. In terms of genocide, if the goal is to achieve political power, that benefit must outweigh the cost of eliminating the minority group. Since the target group likely has limited influence their destruction may not bring heavy costs.

As a phenomenon, collective violence has occurred from early history in the form of genocide, mob violence, and gangs. The ideology behind collective violence rests upon the subordination of the individual to the group.[40] Then the group becomes independent of the individual members that make up the collectivity[41] but the elite maintain a power position. The individuals have subordinated their interests to that of the group and the group is led by a power elite.[42]

This power elite can shape the focus and intention of the collectivity, thus controlling the group both ideologically and behaviorally.[43] From this standpoint, the group may be placed in conflict with another group who has a different ideology or goal. When the other group becomes identifiable, the competition becomes personalized and individualized.[44] This individualized competition in the group structure most often takes the form of violent conflict.[45]

Between these two groups, a structure of subordination arises where one group will rise in prominence and power while the other takes the role of subordinate power. When these relationships are based on social categories (race, ethnicity, religion), collective violence will occur if there is a real or perceived assault on the structure.[46] Once this subordinate standard is no longer accepted or functional, the likelihood of collective violence increases dramatically.

What appears to be a well settled element of collective violence is the fact that collective violence involves identifying "the other." Framing involves shaping the meaning and understanding of the group's goals and antagonists.[47] This framing will offer an identity that the group can adhere to and a reason for their actions.[48] This identity promotes partisanship and solidarity among the group members.

Partisanship has been hypothesized to be a precondition to collective violence.[49] The more partisan the group members are, the more likely that collective violence will occur because of the strong connections and **homogeneity** of the group itself.[50] The partisan relations and identities may then create equivalence relations, which include value judgments of the other.[51] These judgments often take negative formats such as "Arabs = terrorists." Once established, these value judgments are difficult to change and may actually strengthen if they are disputed by others.[52]

HOMOGENEITY

Homogeneity refers to a group that shares many, if not all, thing in common. This group is uniform in its beliefs and actions. ◄

Our knowledge of collective violence has much to contribute to the study of genocide. Most research on genocide cannot occur until after the incident has ended and the lives of hundreds, thousands, and possibly millions of people are gone. This creates a unique problem for genocide scholars to address—the issue of reasoning back from the conflict to the factors believed to have influenced the conflict. In that way, the transition to group action is often overlooked.[53]

In some cases, the factors leading to the genocide are used to explain the violence without explaining why most confrontations do not result in violent behavior.[54] As seen, collective violence helps explain why groups engage in violent action in certain circumstances and not others. The final point is that group solidarity is imperfect and while people may share certain traits or characteristics based on ethnicity or lineage, each individual has their own interests that might be at odds with their fellow group members.[55] This imperfect solidarity begins to explore why some members of a dominant group (Nazis, Hutus, Turks) do not participate in genocide, but instead offer aid to victims.

Individual Génocidaires

As we saw above, Sheldon Glueck was one of the first criminologists to study the issue of state crime. He attempted to answer the questions of "who are the war criminals?" following the devastation of World War II. In his attempt, Glueck recognized that there were both individuals and organizations involved in committing the crime.

Starting with individuals, Glueck set out three broad categories of people who were responsible for war crimes. First, he focused on any person, regardless of political or military rank, who acted in their official capacity.[56] By specifically saying that political and military rank did not matter, Glueck was open to prosecuting heads of state and other high-ranking leaders who often escaped punishment.

He went further explaining that these individuals were liable for their behavior in multiple ways. If they violated the laws of war they should be punished. If they violated the generally recognized principles of criminal law (i.e., jus cogens) they were liable to be punished. Finally, if these individuals ordered, consented to, or conspired in the commission of any of these acts, they were responsible.[57]

By including multiple acts Glueck broadened who could be held accountable. A person who ordered war crimes, including genocide, can be held liable even if they do not personally kill anyone. Individuals who consented or conspired in the acts can also be held liable. These people also may not have personally committed the act but agreed to it.

Glueck's second group of responsible individuals includes those who had the power and authority to prevent the atrocities, but failed to stop them.[58] Again this group included those who may not have participated but failed to act. There is a rule in the criminal law that allows people to be prosecuted for failure to act. In general, that rule states that when there is a duty to act, failure to act can be criminal. In this case, military and political leaders have a duty to act when engaged in making decisions about war or other criminal acts.

A military leader or president who allows his subordinates to participate in genocide have made themselves liable because they have the power to stop it. At the time, this proposal from Glueck was new and controversial. But as a criminologist Glueck was convinced that these people bore as much responsibility as those executing their orders.

Outside of the military and political leaders, Glueck also felt that businessmen and industrialists of power were liable if they indirectly participated or conspired to commit crimes.[59] This idea was designed to deter business leaders from taking advantage of circumstances to enrich themselves. The goal was to have non-military or political leaders take responsibility for their behavior.

Glueck foresaw objections that might be made against his broad definition of war criminal. For example, during the Nuremberg trials, many defendants claimed that they were simply following orders. This defense was designed to push responsibility onto the leaders and off of those who executed the orders.

Glueck did not find this to be a valid defense. He stated that anyone told to gas civilians or prisoners of war knew that he was committing a crime. Glueck proposed that "the act of a soldier in obedience to a military order of his superior is not justifiable if, when he committed it, he either actually knew or, under the circumstances, had reasonable grounds for knowing that the act ordered is illegal."[60] Glueck's proposal became known as the "Nuremberg principle" and is still in use today.

Further, Glueck was open to prosecuting heads of state, an inconceivable notion at the time. Heads of state are commonly granted sovereign immunity protecting them from prosecution. Glueck though argued that immunity is based on international courtesy. This courtesy depends on whether the sovereign conducts himself as a law-abiding chief of state.[61] In the case of war crimes and genocide, the head of state has not been acting as a law-abiding and trustworthy leader and thus there should be no barrier to prosecution.

Most of Glueck's proposals on war criminals, including génocidaires, are still followed today. He set out the categories of people who are liable for their behavior and limits their defenses and immunity protection. This does not explain why these individuals participated in genocide, but it does clarify which individuals can and should be held criminally liable.

The Browning-Goldhagen Debate

In 1961 Hannah Arendt attended Adolf Eichmann's trial in Israel. She wrote several pieces about the trial for newspapers. Later she compiled these into a book about her perception of Eichmann and what was the trial of the century at the time.[62] In her report Arendt coined the phrase **"the banality of evil"** to describe Eichmann.[63]

THE BANALITY OF EVIL

Banal refers to anything that is unoriginal. This phrase is used to mean that evil acts are not always committed by evil people. In this case, evil is not original but an act perpetrated by bureaucrats without much independent thought. ◄

Arendt saw Eichmann not as a vicious and soulless killer, but as a bureaucrat. The banality of evil was her way of describing what she saw as a man who had followed orders as part of a bureaucratic system and not necessarily acting on his own free choice.

Arendt found that evil acts do not require evil people. An ordinary person could commit unthinkable acts as part of an organization even if they do not believe in what they are doing.[64] This may not mean that the perpetrator does not act upon ideology, only that it is secondary to his bureaucratic mentality.[65] Arendt's analysis became popular with the public because it explained one of the worst crimes in humanity by laying responsibility on the state and less on trying to determine individual motives.

However, over the years many began to question whether Arendt was too forgiving of Eichmann and génocidaires like him. Three decades after Eichmann's trial the question of why individuals commit genocide was still unanswered. But within a few years two competing explanations evolved to explain individual motivation. These explanations were at opposite ends of the spectrum and led to an intriguing academic debate on the motivation of génocidaires in Germany during the Holocaust.

The first idea of how Germans participated in the Holocaust came from Christopher Browning and his book *Ordinary Men: Reserve police battalion 101 and the Final Solution in Poland*. As the name suggests, Browning believed that the low-level Germans who executed the Holocaust were ordinary men in extraordinary circumstances. Browning's thesis was that any person could become a génocidaire in the right circumstances.[66] Not all Germans were evil, hate-filled monsters killing Jews for pleasure—similar to Arendt's banality of evil. Though Eichmann's elevated position in the German government meant he was less "ordinary" than other Germans.

Browning suggests that the extraordinary circumstances in place as the time combined with other factors led many Germans to participate in the Holocaust even if they did not carry anti-Semitic views. The other factors included peer pressure from those around them, the urge to conform, and the dehumanization of the Jews.[67] As we have already seen, conformity and dehumanization were essential to creating the circumstance need to engage in genocide.

In Browning's analysis, many of the Germans who participated in genocide were just like you and me. This meant that anyone could become a génocidaire; this was a difficult idea to accept for some. Many people prefer to think of génocidaires as inhuman and not anything like the rest of us. Browning challenged that thinking and showed how "ordinary men" could commit extraordinary crimes.

Browning also pointed to the German belief in bureaucratic obedience as part of the reason for German participation. Once the government power was seized by a select few elites their goals were implemented with great efficiency.[68] Those involved in the process did not have to hold extreme anti-Semitic views to fall in line with the orders of their government.[69] These ideas forced people to recognize that we all are subject to committing acts we would normally never do (see the Milgram experiments in Chap. 2).

Only a few years after Browning's analysis, Daniel Goldhagen released his analysis of German participation in the Holocaust. Goldhagen's position was not that the German's were ordinary but that the vast majority of Germans during the Nazi period were prepared to kill Jews.[70] According to Goldhagen, eliminationist anti-Semitism became the official policy of Nazi Germany which inflamed the existing anti-Jewish beliefs among ordinary Germans.[71]

The ordinary German was not coerced to kill, he desired to do so because of his anti-Semitism.[72] Unlike Arendt and Browning, Goldhagen does not see obedience to authority, peer pressure, career advancement, or bureaucratic obedience as the explanation for German participation in the Holocaust. He sees German participation as the result of rabid anti-Semitism; "killing the Jews was for many a deed done not for Nazism, but for Germany."[73]

Goldhagen's theory that ordinary Germans participated due to their own anti-Semitism was contrary to Browning's circumstance specific analysis. If Goldhagen was right, then ordinary people could not commit genocide unless they were possessed of a certain belief system. This meant that ordinary people were not vicious killers. It is a popular idea because it does not require us to question ourselves about how we would act in a similar situation.

Browning challenged Goldhagen's proposition saying that anti-Semitism was not a sufficient explanation.[74] Browning does not doubt that anti-Semitism was an important factor but alone it cannot explain the Holocaust. He further claims that Goldhagen's view of Germans is that they are all the same with no nuance.[75] Browning's own findings counter that argument since some of the Germans were not willing to execute Jewish people.[76]

One question in both Browning and Goldhagen is that of agency. Did the génocidaires have agency over themselves to make decisions? Arendt suggested Eichmann lacked some agency because of his acting in accordance with the bureaucratic rules. Browning suggests his ordinary Germans did have agency as some chose not to participate. But Goldhagen's thesis suggests the Germans lacked some agency due to the fact that they were blinded by their hatred of the Jews.

As an example, Browning points to several officers in the police battalion who walked away instead of killing. Browning says this proves that not all Germans were prepared to kill and it was the circumstances, not hatred, that led to their decision to act. Goldhagen recognizes that there were some Germans who refused to kill and even some who may have saved Jews, but he points out that no German was ever punished for not killing. Therefore, all Germans were free to choose not to participate, so those that did participate must have done so freely out of their own racial hatred.

The Browning-Goldhagen debate continues today. Is it possible that some Germans participated in the Holocaust because of the circumstances while others did so because of their anti-Semitism? Yes, both are plausible explanations. As we have seen with the varying theories of genocide neither of these theses is likely completely true.

If we have agency to decide whether to participate in genocide or not, then we can ascribe that decision to each individual. But if we lack agency, who made the decision to act? Were the Germans simply responding to their government dictates or did they take action of their own choice? It is questions like these that still remain to be answered when looking at the individual génocidaires that are prosecuted for their behavior.

> **Critical Think Exercise** Can you apply the Browning-Goldhagen analyses to other cases of genocide? When looking at other episodes of genocide, ask why individuals may have participated. Can you see a way to apply Browning and/or Goldhagen?

Organizational Génocidaires

In addition to individuals committing genocide, there are also groups or organizations that join together to commit these crimes. Committing crime in groups has some perceived advantages. It is often assumed that a group will provide extra protection—it may be difficult to identify every person committing an illegal act in a large group. Committing crime in a group sometimes allows for greater violence—the violence is performative; the members are showing off how violent they can be to others.

Similar to individual génocidaires there is no single motivation for those involved in organizational genocide. The organization will shape and limit the behavior of the people in the group.[77] Where organizations can really assist in the execution of genocide is taking the abstract and turning it into the concrete. The idea of genocide remains solely an idea until it is put into action. Putting genocide in action is where organizations often step in to fill the gap between idea and action.[78]

The most common organization involved in genocide is the military. As we will see in Chap. 5 the military is often the main perpetrators of genocide. There are many reasons for this but the main reason is that the military is controlled by the state and the state is usually the one implementing genocide. Most states have already established militaries by the time genocide occurs. This means that the military is structured and capable of executing genocide.

The military is structured so that there is little to no objection to following orders.[79] This pressure to conform is sometimes necessary in order to complete one's mission successfully. But when highjacked by the state for genocidal purposes this compliance to following orders can make the military the most efficient way of killing "the other." Soldiers are trained to kill without questioning orders; when combined with the structural nature of the military which allows for compartmentalizing information, some soldiers may be committing genocide without even knowing it.[80]

In addition, the military is already armed with the tools of genocide. Guns and other arms are readily available for soldiers to use both legally and illegally. While this may seem to give the military a free pass to commit genocide, there are expectations that when ordered to kill citizens who are not posing a danger to the state, the military will push back against such orders. As Glueck pointed out, a defense of "following orders" is no defense at all.

In many cases of genocide there are paramilitary groups involved. These groups are not always organized or controlled by the state. Paramilitaries are often trained in violence, but without the formal code of conduct that applies to the military.[81] This creates a killing force with no rules. There may be a leader of the group but they are usually much more loosely organized than the military.[82]

This looser structure makes it more difficult to identify those involved in the paramilitary and how they respond to orders. Are they acting individually or is there a leader telling them what to do? If acting individually then it is much harder to locate, prevent, or punish them. With this inherent deniability, the state may use a paramilitary group to execute genocide on its behalf because the state can deny involvement and claim that the paramilitary is acting on its own.

Paramilitary groups were used by Serbia during its war with Bosnia. Known as Arkan's Tigers, the group was built from football clubs in Serbia that had a history of violence.[83] Then-president Slobodan Milošević saw the usefulness of this militia group as Yugoslavia began to break up. He used the Arkan's Tigers to take action for which he wanted to later deny responsibility. Croatia declared independence on June 2, 1991 and the Tigers were involved in pillaging and looting.[84]

Then when Bosnia declared independence, Arkan's Tigers entered the country and was involved in one of the first "ethnic cleansing" operations.[85] As we saw in Chap. 1 on defining genocide, ethnic cleansing implies targeted killing based on ethnicity. This euphemism for genocide should not deter from the fact that the Tigers were committing genocide based on ethnicity. Stories of the Tigers in Bosnia included them entering homes of prominent Muslims, dragging them into the street, and killing them openly.[86]

Only a few years later in Rwanda, the Interahamwe became an essential part of the Rwandan genocide. The Interahamwe was formed by then-president Habyarimana from young boys in his political party. At the time there were few other options for these young men; there were few, if any, jobs and a poor national economy.[87] The young men were trained in violence—how to commit it and who to target.

In preparation for the genocide the Interahamwe purchased 85 tons of weapons and 581,000 machetes. They piled these weapons with the intent to kill Tutsis. When the genocide began Interahamwe members set up road blocks and slaughtered thousands of Tutsis.[88] The Interahamwe were crucial to the extent and brutality of the genocide.

Arkan's Tigers and the Interahamwe are just two examples of paramilitary groups used to execute genocide. Use of paramilitaries is primarily for deniability. Connecting the paramilitary and the state can be difficult. The state often claims that the paramilitary is acting on its own.[89] Even though evidence suggested that Milošević was involved with the Arkan Tigers, he adamantly denied it and claimed that militias were banned in Serbia so they could not be acting for the state.

It is this ability to cover one's tracks that make paramilitaries so attractive to génocidaires. In addition to deniability, using paramilitaries acts as a force multiplier. Militias are an easy way to add numbers to the regular military.[90] By using militias to carry out genocide the state frees up its own military to execute other duties including genocidal acts. Together the state military and the paramilitaries can execute genocide most efficiently.

A final benefit of militias is the use of violence without limits. State militaries are bound by rules of conduct and the laws of war. This means that they cannot attack civilians and non-combatants. Militias however are not bound by these rules and laws of conduct. Therefore, they can, and do, use violence that would be illegal if committed by the state.

Genocide is already a crime so it may seem unnecessary to examine the use of paramilitaries as an extension of illegal activity. But the use of paramilitaries permits the state to hide its genocidal behavior in many cases. It also allows for the state to distance itself from the genocide. And militias can execute a genocide quickly and indiscriminately regardless of the state's involvement.

Above we discussed how the state could act like an organization. From this we can see how the state's organizational characteristics facilitate involvement in genocide. First, the state is a bureaucracy. In a bureaucracy, rules are set to govern behavior and individuals are expected to set aside their personal beliefs and follow the rules.[91] In the military soldiers are expected to follow orders and not question them (unless the order is clearly illegal).

In addition, bureaucracies are amoral. An organization or a state cannot have morality which is an individual trait. So, amorality allows for behavior that would otherwise be questioned by one's personal belief system. Finally, a bureaucracy can be so complex that one individual may not be able to see the whole picture. They may play a small part that they are somewhat ignorant of the final outcome. However, this idea is questionable. Small players take part in large-scale events often. But this might permit offenders an attempt to downplay their role in the genocide.

Organizations also strive for conformity. Again, military training is part of indoctrinating soldiers into conforming their behavior to the rules of the organization. When someone does not conform they are isolated and often harassed.[92] This shaming will often force people to conform even if they would otherwise object or refuse to be involved. For many people when the state tells you to do something, you do it. This is how genocide can be executed by "ordinary" people.

Routinization is also a key aspect of organizations that can assist in committing genocide. Most organizations have a set routine—office hours, job expectations, lunch breaks, etc. When one works in this type of setting, the job becomes a routine. You probably have your own routine that you are used to—wake up, shower, have breakfast, go to class, study, party, go to bed; and do it all over again the next day.

It may seem odd that committing genocide could become a routine, but it is possible. Génocidaires in Rwanda reported that they treated their genocidal actions as a job. They would get up in the morning, go out to participate in the genocide, return home at the end of the day and do it again the next day. Being caught up in the routine of genocide can blur the bigger picture of what is happening.

This can create **"willful ignorance"** of what is actually occurring.[93] Willful ignorance occurs when someone avoids becoming informed about something in order to avoid the truth. Avoiding the truth of what is happening means that the individual does not have to make difficult choices. If you were aware that your actions were leading to genocide, would you continue to do the work?

WILLFUL IGNORANCE
Willful ignorance is not a legal defense. The law considers willful ignorance to satisfy the intent element of a crime since choosing to ignore information that might be negative should not protect you from liability. ◄

The final aspect of an organization that helps contribute to genocide is the inherent complexity. Many organizations, including states, have diffusion of responsibility and authority.[94] This means that there are many layers of people responsible for different things at different times. Think of your home country, who is in charge? Is there a president or prime minister? Can they make unilateral decisions? Probably not. So who then is in charge? Likely there are many people in charge of varying aspects at varying places.

This complexity can make it difficult to pinpoint who is actually making the decisions. When genocide becomes the answer to a state's problems, who is to blame? We will come back to this later when we discuss the legal responses to genocide. But for now it is important to recognize that an individual can lose their own sense of self in this complex nature.[95] When this happens, the individual is subsumed into the organization and what the organization wants, they will usually get.

The state thus has characteristics of organizations that can facilitate the enacting of genocide: bureaucracy, conformity, routinization, and complexity. When we view the state as an organization we can see aspects that can contribute to the commission of genocide.

► **Critical Thinking Exercise** During the Holocaust trains were used to transport the Jewish population to labor and extermination camps. Think of the person whose job it was to organize the train schedule. This person could easily separate himself from the genocide by thinking that his job is simply to schedule trains and that does not kill anyone. However, the trains were certainly leading to death for many. What should we do to the train scheduler? Is he liable to the same extent as others? Why or why not?

Conclusion

As with many questions that we have analyzed, there is no easy answer to who commits genocide? The often-simple answer is that the state commits genocide and that is usually at least a partially correct answer. Once we accept that a state is capable of committing crime, we can place some responsibility on the state as an organization. In later chapters we will discuss who in the state can be prosecuted and held legally liable for genocide.

While there is not one answer to the question of who commits genocide, the truth is that anyone could commit genocide. It's likely that you just said that you would never commit genocide, but how do we know that is true? Like crime in general, anyone might commit it when the circumstances are right. Most people think that they would never commit crime, until they lost their job, can't pay rent, or buy food for their family.

Combining what we know about who commits genocide with why they commit genocide can help us in terms of prediction. If we see a country experiencing warning signs and if there is any evidence of who might be preparing to commit genocide maybe we can intervene. Prediction and intervention have been goals of the United Nations Convention on Genocide from the start but it has almost never happened. There are many reasons why this is true, but as we will see in the next chapter, prediction is not always easy.

When you review the case studies of genocide in the next chapter, you should try to examine each case for warning signs and who might be involved. Can you identify potential génocidaires? If yes, then you should consider what supports that assumption. If you cannot identify perpetrators, start thinking outside of the box—maybe it is the president, the priest, the teacher, or someone you know.

Recognizing that each one of us is capable of committing genocide is not easy or enjoyable. But if we stop thinking that génocidaires must be crazy, or mentally ill, or vengeful, we can better understand how people become drawn into genocide. Also, recognizing our own vulnerability will hopefully help us lose the biases of who commits genocide. If anyone can do it, so can you. This should create a heightened awareness of our own susceptibility and we can confront that within ourselves. Then later we can confront the vulnerabilities of others.

Discussion Questions

1. How can an individual justify their involvement in genocide?
2. Can you think of any organizations that share characteristics with the state that might also perpetrate genocide? What would these organizations gain from doing so?

Notes

1. Hatzfeld, Jean (2003). *Machete season: The killers in Rwanda speak.* New York: Picador, 218.
2. Ibid. at 23–24.
3. Bridgman, Jon and Worley, William S. (2004). Genocide of the Hereros. In Samuel Totten, William s. Parsons, and Israel Charney (Eds.) *Century of Genocide (2nd Ed.): Critical essays and eyewitnesses accounts* (pp. 15–51). New York: Routledge: 44.
4. Chambliss, William J. (1989). State-organized crime: The American Society of Criminology, 1988 Presidential Address. *Criminology,* 27(2), 183–208: 184.
5. Lynch, Michael J. and Michalowski, Raymond J. (2006). *Primer in radical criminology: Critical perspectives on crime, power and identity.* Monsey, NY: Criminal Justice Press, 186.
6. Brants, Chrisje (2006). Gold-collar crime: The peculiar complexities and ambiguities of war crimes, crimes against humanity, and genocide. In Henry N. Pontell and Gilbert Geis (eds.), *International handbook of white-collar and corporate crime* (New York, NY: Springer, 2006) pp. 309–326: 319–320.
7. Rothe, Dawn L. (2009). *State criminality: The crime of all crimes.* Lanham, MD: Lexington Books, 6.
8. Glueck, Sheldon (1944). *War criminals: Their prosecution and punishment.* New York: Knopf.
9. Glueck, Sheldon (1946). *The Nuremberg trial and aggressive war.* New York: Knopf.
10. Ibid.
11. Glueck, Sheldon (1946). The Nuernberg [sic] trial and aggressive war. *Harvard Law Review*, 59, 443.
12. Ibid.
13. Supra note 7 at 10.
14. Ibid., 91–113.
15. Kramer, Ronald C. and Michalowski, Raymond J. (2005). War, aggression and state crime. *British Journal of Criminology*, 45(4), 446–469: 453–454.
16. Ibid., 453.
17. Braithwaite, John (1989). Criminological theory and organizational crime. *Justice Quarterly,* 6(3), 333–358: 333.
18. Friedrichs, David O. (1996). Governmental crime, Hitler and white collar crime: A problematic relationship. *Caribbean Journal of Criminology and Social Psychology,* 1(2), 44–63.
19. Supra note 15 at 334.
20. Schrager, Laura S. and Short, Jr., James F. (1997). Toward a sociology of organizational crime. *Social Problems,* 25, 407–419: 411–412.
21. Gross, Edward (1980). Organizational structure and organizational crime. In Gilbert Geis and Ezra Stotland (eds.), *White collar crime: Theory and research* (Beverley Hills: Sage), 52–76.

22. Ermann, M. David and Lundman, Richard J. (2002). Corporate and governmental deviance. In M. David Ermann and Richard J. Lundman (eds.), *Corporate and Governmental Deviance: Problems of Organizational Behavior in Contemporary Society* (New York: Oxford University Press) 3–49.
23. Ibid., 6–7.
24. Ibid., 8–9.
25. Ibid., 24–25.
26. Ibid., 19–20.
27. Supra note 17 at 338.
28. Ibid.
29. Ibid.
30. Rose, Nikolas and Miller, Peter (1992). Political power beyond the state: problematics of government. *British Journal of Sociology*, 43(2), 173–205: 176.
31. Ibid.
32. Supra note 20 at 411–412.
33. Supra note 21 at 59.
34. Supra note 5.
35. Ibid.
36. Mattaini, Mark A. and Strickland, Joseph (2006). Challenging collective violence: A scientific strategy. *International Journal of Psychology*, 41(6), 500–513: 501.
37. Barkan, Steven E. and Snowden, Lynne L. (2001). *Collective violence*. Boston: Allyn and Bacon.
38. Ibid.
39. Supra note 36.
40. Gould, Roger V. (1999). Collective violence and group solidarity: Evidence from a feuding society. *American Sociological Review*, 64, 356–380.
41. Ibid.
42. Klein, Josh (2007). Where should we stand to get the best perspective on collective violence? *Critical Sociology*, 33(5–6), 957–980.
43. Ibid.
44. Grimshaw, Allen D. (1970). Interpreting collective violence: An argument for the importance of social structure. *Annals of the American Academy of Political and Social Sciences*, 391(1), 9–20.
45. Ibid.
46. Ibid.
47. Supra note 36.
48. Ibid.
49. De la Roche, Roberta S. (2001). Why is collective violence collective? *Sociological Theory*, 19(2), 126–141.
50. Ibid.
51. Supra note 36.
52. Ibid.
53. Supra note 40.

54. Ibid.
55. Ibid.
56. Glueck, Sheldon. (1944). What shall be done with the war criminals? Pamphlet prepared for the American Historical Association's G.I. Roundtable Series. Available at: https://www.historians.org/about-aha-and-membership/aha-history-and-archives/gi-roundtable-series/pamphlets/em-11-what-shall-be-done-with-the-war-criminals-(1944)
57. Ibid.
58. Ibid.
59. Ibid.
60. Ibid.
61. Ibid.
62. Arendt, Hannah (1963). *Eichmann in Jerusalem: A report on the banality of evil.* New York: Penguin Books.
63. Ibid.
64. Moses, A. D. (1998). Structure and agency in the Holocaust: Danial J. Goldhagen and his critics. *History & Theory*, 37(2), 194–219.
65. Ibid.
66. Browning, Christopher (1992). *Ordinary men: Reserve police battalion 101 and the Final Solution in Poland.* New York: Harper Perennial.
67. Supra note 64.
68. Ibid.
69. Ibid.
70. Goldhagen, Daniel J. (1996). *Hitler's willing executioners: Ordinary Germans and the Holocaust.* New York: Vintage.
71. Goldhagen, Daniel J., Browning, Christopher R. (1996). Symposium: The "Willing Executioners"/"Ordinary Men" Debate. United States Holocaust Memorial Museum. Available at: https://www.ushmm.org/m/pdfs/Publication_OP_1996-01.pdf
72. Ibid.
73. Ibid. at 9.
74. Supra note 71.
75. Ibid.
76. See supra note 66.
77. Alvarez, Alex (2010). *Genocidal crimes.* New York: Routledge.
78. Ibid.
79. Ibid.
80. Spencer, Philip (2012). *Genocide since 1945.* New York: Routledge.
81. Ibid. See also supra note 77.
82. Ibid.
83. Supra note 77.
84. Ibid.
85. Ibid.
86. Ibid.
87. Ibid.

88. Ibid.
89. Ibid.
90. Ibid. See also supra note 80.
91. Supra note 77.
92. Ibid.
93. Ibid.
94. Ibid.
95. Ibid.

Further Reading

"On what conditions can a state be held responsible for genocide?" Available at https://academic.oup.com/ejil/article/18/4/631/453775

"Why did Ratko Mladic commit genocide against Bosnia's Muslims?" Available at https://www.newyorker.com/news/news-desk/why-did-ratko-mladic-commit-genocide-against-bosnias-muslims

Useful Websites

You can explore genocide's past and present while also seeing how to quantify in data what genocide can do: https://ourworldindata.org/genocides

The Yale University Genocide Studies Program provides case studies of several genocides including exploring those responsible for the violence: https://gsp.yale.edu/case-studies

When and Where Does Genocide Occur? 5

"Genocide has been practiced in all regions of the world and during all periods of history."[1]

This statement is so important to the study of genocide that it appears in the preface of the book The History and Sociology of Genocide before getting into the material. Unfortunately, by hiding in the preface many people still believe that genocide is a problem of poor countries, or autocratic countries, or "other" countries.

It becomes crucial to understand that genocide can occur anywhere at any time. In this way we do not let our guard down and are continuously on watch for warning signs. The case studies in this chapter show how genocide developed in several places and times.

We will crisscross the globe from Africa to Asia to the Middle East to Europe to Oceana. We will time travel from before genocide was a word to the present day. When reading these case studies try to see if you can spot the warning signs that led to genocide. Do not let location or time blind you to any relevant fact.

Introduction

Genocide is a universal phenomenon. The act has occurred in every continent (excluding Antarctica) and across centuries. As we learned in Chap. 1 the word genocide did not exist until 1944. But that does not mean that the action did not exist, it

W. R. Pruitt, *An Introduction to the Criminology of Genocide*,
https://doi.org/10.1007/978-3-030-65211-1_5

merely remained unnamed. Once named and acknowledged a question arose as to whether any action prior to 1948 when the crime of genocide was criminalized internationally can be called genocide.

In examining the when and where of genocide it is important to consider every nation capable of committing genocide. There is no magic protection against the crime of genocide. In this way, you should consider time and location in concert. The time period will influence the capability of prevention and even whether other countries are aware of what is happening. The location of genocide can be important, especially when the perpetrators are executing their crime on foreign land.

Like other crimes, genocide is more prone to occur in certain circumstances. For example, when there is an ongoing war, the violence provides a shield to commit other crimes including genocide. In both World War I and II, the war provided some coverage for the genocide of the Armenians and Jewish population respectively. War can be criminogenic, meaning that it is likely to cause criminal behavior.

The link between war and genocide can be seen in the way in which war creates insecurity, which increases the likelihood that violence will be used to counter any threat.[2] War also increases the probability that any perceived opponent will be classified as an enemy in need of destroying.[3] This was the excuse used by the Ottoman Empire in its destruction of the Armenians; the government claimed that Armenians were joining the Russian military in an attempt to defeat the Ottoman Empire and therefore they were enemy combatants who needed to be eliminated.

However, just because there is a link between war and genocide does not mean that war is necessary before genocide occurs. This is why exploring time and place is important to better understand the factors that lead to genocide. War may be one factor but other elements are often found preceding genocide. Better understanding these preceding factors can also assist in prevention. When these factors are noticed, greater attention should be paid to that country in hopes of avoiding the consequences of genocide.

Genocide Prior to 1948

Before the word genocide was created there were several examples of similar behavior that went by many names—atrocity, mass violence, colonization. By any name, the goal was the same—to eliminate a target group. When examining where and when genocide occurs, those events prior to 1948 should not be ignored. These cases of genocide can provide insight to better understand the development of genocide.

The treatment of native populations in the United States, Canada, and Australia have been referred to as genocide. These events occurred nearly two centuries before the crime of genocide evolved. Many of these genocides were part of the colonization process by which native populations were forcibly removed and killed in order for a new population to take advantage of the land.

But colonization genocide is not limited to the 1700s. In the early 1900s the Herero population in South West Africa (today Namibia) was targeted for elimination by German colonizers. Exploring this genocide can reveal the roots of colonial genocide.

1904–1908 Herero Genocide

The Herero were a pastoral people relying on farming and cattle for their way of life. The Herero had their own complex social and political organization. Hereros considered all of the land to be common property with no one person owning any particular section. Cattle were very important throughout the Herero culture. Owning cattle bestowed wealth, prestige, and political power upon the Herero. In religion, cattle played a prominent role and soured cow's milk was a staple of the Herero traditional diet.

- The Herero language contained over one thousand words for the colors and marking of cattle.

This traditional way of life did not match with the German settlers who saw themselves as the natural superior to the Herero. South West Africa (as the area was then known) was seen as ripe land for colonization purposes by the Germans. One German newspaper said: "the land, of course must be transferred from the hands of the natives to those of the whites, [this] is the object of colonization in the territory. The land shall be settled by whites. So the natives must give way and either become servants of the whites or withdraw."[4]

At the time of the genocide, Germany owned more than 25% of the Herero land and nearly half of their cattle. The Germans had promised to take care of the Hereros, but instead took their land and their cattle. Left without recourse, the Herero felt like slaves in their own country. While the government in Berlin was not present in Hereroland, they had sent Governor Leutwein to maintain order and control over the territory.

With such obvious divisions between the Germans and the Herero, it is not surprising that value judgments soon followed. First and foremost, the Herero represented an obstacle for the Germans. They were an obstacle not just to occupying the land, but also to the limited resources in the arid environment. Obstacles create frustration and strain that can lead to criminal coping. Ridding the area of the Herero would eliminate the obstacle to colonial expansion and ease the strain.

In addition, the Germans did not see the Herero as equal human beings, but as primitive natives not worthy of the land that they occupied. One missionary in the area at the time said, "The average German looks down upon the natives as being about on the same level as the higher primates (baboon being their favorite term for the natives)."[5] Viewing the Herero as baboons meant that they were not human and did not have the same feelings or emotions to consider.

The death knell for the Herero people came on January 12, 1904. On this date, the Hereros rose up against the German settlers killing more than 100 settlers and soldiers. After this attack, the German government sent in General von Trotha with military support to squash the rebellion. In order to accomplish this goal, von Trotha ordered the elimination of the Herero people regardless of age or sex. His simple cry was that "the entire Herero people must be exterminated."[6]

After the war with the Herero began and the genocide was underway, von Trotha issued his "Extermination Order," which detailed that the Herero people must leave the territory or face death. There was not to be any compassion for women or children, and if they approached German officers, the officers were to shoot above their heads to encourage them to retreat.

After cornering the Hereros, von Trotha set up an easy escape route that led straight to the Omaheke Desert. As the Herero fled into the desert, if any groups tried to escape in a different direction, German troops forced them back into the main group toward the desert.

> After the battle all men, women, and children who fell into German hands, wounded or otherwise, were mercilessly put to death. . . all those found by the wayside and in the sandveld were shot down or bayoneted to death. . . They were just trying to get away with their cattle.
>
> –Herero survivor

After the Herero made their way into the Omaheke Desert, von Trotha cordoned off the area with a 250-kilometer fence making it nearly impossible to escape the desert. One German study of the offensive noted that "the arid Omaheke was to complete what the German Army had begun: the extermination of the Herero nation."[7]

Pursuing German soldiers indiscriminately killed Herero who had fallen behind or could not make it into the desert. Once in the desert, German troops patrolled any water holes they found and drove away or killed any Herero who attempted to approach. At some point, the Germans poisoned the water holes to keep the Herero from obtaining any water. Many Herero had to decide between dying of thirst or of poisoned water.

Those who survived the initial genocide were sent to concentration camps where a further 45% perished. By the end of the German assault on the Hereros, only roughly 16,000 Herero survived out of an initial population of 80,000; 80% of the Herero population was annihilated.

***

During World War I Raphael Lemkin saw the destruction of the Armenian population in the Ottoman Empire (today Turkey). It was this action that led him to develop the word genocide to explain the crime without a name. The Armenian case is a prototypical genocide. Much of what happened here was repeated in the Holocaust and other genocides.

Exploring the Armenian case highlights how war can act as a fog for other crimes. Also this case is often argued over whether intent existed to eliminate the Armenians in whole or in part. Since intent can be proven in many ways the behavior of the Ottoman Empire should be analyzed to see how one might prove intent for the crime of genocide.

1915 Armenian Genocide

The Armenian genocide of 1915 did not erupt from nowhere. There was a history of maltreatment against the Armenians and other massacres predating the genocide. The Armenians were a Christian minority group living in the predominantly Muslim Ottoman Empire. They not only were given limited autonomy to govern themselves, but also had to accept an inferior position in many ways. Armenians were subject to taxes and rules that the Muslim population was not.

In 1894, the Armenian population began to protest this disparate treatment. As a result, Sultan Hamid II sent in the military and 3000 Armenians were killed. In August 1894, Ottoman troops executed a 23-day massacre against Armenians protesting high taxes. A year later, in October 1895, a 10-day attack followed when Armenians presented a petition to the Sultan for fair taxes and autonomy.

These attacks and massacres acted as a precursor to the genocide in 1915. The decision to execute genocide may have been partially based on the rational choice model. Prior massacres against Armenians seemed to accomplish the goal of keeping them subordinate. When faced with the perceived threat of Armenians during World War I, the Ottoman Empire may have believed that their previous actions would work again.

Political unrest began in the early 1900s. By 1908, the Committee of Union and Progress (CUP) had overthrown the government and taken power. In 1913, an internal CUP coup resulted in an ultra-nationalistic faction taking power. The government then promoted nationalism, including the idea of "Turkey for the Turks." Any non-Turks were considered disloyal; the Armenians became a prime target.

At the same time, the Ottoman Empire was facing internal wars that ultimately reduced the Empire in size and influence. When Bulgaria, Serbia, and Greece won independence from the Empire, the Ottoman's had lost 424,000 square miles of land and 5 million in population. These losses certainly created a strain and pressure on the Ottoman Empire to resist any further internal disputes whether real or perceived.

Facing loss of land and influence, the Ottoman Empire shortly entered World War I and faced heavy losses early. The Ottomans were quick to blame the Armenians for the losses. This scapegoating allowed the Ottomans to place blame on a minority group and see them as an obstacle to maintaining power. Once the dictatorial government had enabled xenophobia to rage throughout Turkey, it became easier to mobilize the populace to see the need for eradicating the Armenians.

On April 24, 1915, Allied troops landed at Gallipoli, Turkey. On the same day, the government ordered the killing of 250 Armenian intellectuals. Deportation orders soon followed ordering Armenians to be forcibly removed to the Syrian Desert (similar to the Herero deportation to the Omaheke Desert). During the deportations, men were separated and killed. Many deaths were the result of exhaustion and dehydration on the way to the desert.

> The men, numbering about 800, had been tied together in groups of 14 and marched out of town before daybreak so as not to be seen by the inhabitants; under heavy guard they were taken to a ravine several hours' marching time from Harput and then shot by the gendarmes; those not killed in that way were dispatched with knives.

Within a couple of months, the government legalized their behavior by passing the Temporary Law of Deportation. By legalizing its behavior, the government made acquiescence even easier—you were only following the law.

In its final version, the deportation orders, which led to genocide, started at the national government level and were passed down to the Minister of Interior and on to the military and local government offices. By the end, the entire nation of Turkey was involved in the deportations and genocide of the Armenians.

To encourage compliance, the government issued the following instructions: "The Armenians must be exterminated. If any Moslem protect a Christian, first, his house shall be burned, then the Christian killed before his eyes, and then his family and himself." The movement of thousands of people over hundreds of miles without proper food or water was bound to cause the deaths of many people, especially children and the elderly. Dead bodies were left to rot in the hot sun; children with bloated bellies were lying in the open heat waiting to die.

Armenians were forced to march thousands of miles to executions sites. Courtesy of: United States Holocaust Memorial Museum, https://encyclopedia.ushmm.org/content/en/article/the-armenian-genocide-1915-16-in-depth

Only a quarter of those deported survived long enough to reach the Syrian Desert. Once there, they were forced to survive with no food or supplies. The killing did not stop though once they reached the desert. Killing units would come through the make-shift villages and kill the survivors; "children were smashed against rocks, women were torn apart with swords, men were mutilated, others thrown into flames alive."[8]

The Tigris and Euphrates rivers were reported to be clogged with dead bodies. This diseased the water making it unsanitary to drink. Dysentery and other diseases killed many once they arrived at the Syrian Desert. When the killing was over, somewhere between one million and one-and-a-half million Armenians were dead. All Armenian villages in Turkey were completely destroyed and their homes emptied.

***

Genocide After 1948

When the United Nations passed the Convention on Genocide, the popular statement of "Never again" emerged as a cry against genocide. Ideally the Convention would prevent future genocides and save lives. However, this lofty goal never really materialized. Often political issues would overshadow the occurrence of genocide and limit intervention and prevention.

Little attention was paid to the agreements made in the Convention when faced with genocide. The world was mired in the Cold War and communism had become the predominant threat to the world. The interest in genocide generated by World War II and the Holocaust quickly faded.

During this period there were episodes of crimes against humanity that might have risen to the level of genocide. However, no signatory nation to the Genocide Convention raised any concern over these instances. There were also episodes of genocide that would clearly fit the UN definition. Again, these genocides were usually allowed to continue without intervention regardless of the obligations created by the Convention.

1971 Bangladesh Genocide

To understand the genocide in Bangladesh we must go back to the days of colonization by Great Britain. Great Britain decided to partition its colony India based on religion. The new state of Pakistan was established to be majority Muslim. The Bengali Muslim population decided to become part of Pakistan at this time. This created two separate nations—East Pakistan (today Bangladesh) and West Pakistan (today Pakistan).

These two sections of Pakistan were separated by more than 1000 miles with differences in population, culture, and language. Bengalis were the majority of the population but their language and culture were threatened by West Pakistan.

When a military dictatorship took control of West Pakistan, the Bengalis became a repressed minority. Bengalis did not receive fair representation in the government. Their language was denied official recognition for several years. The Bengalis were also being economically exploited in that they produced the majority of the product that brought in income to the state but received little benefit from the crop themselves.

> I will reduce this majority into a minority
>
> –General Tikka Khan, Military Governor of East Bengal

In addition, Bengalis had to fight to protect their literature, music, dance, and art from being destroyed. Bengali culture was labeled as "Hindu leaning" which alienated them from the Muslim government. Amid these feelings emerged a cry for autonomy and democracy among the Bengali nation.

In the elections of 1970, the Bengali delegation received a majority of the votes. In order to prevent the Bengalis from taking control of the government, President Yahya suspended the congress indefinitely. As a result, the government of West Pakistan felt that they had to teach the Bengalis a lesson not to contest West Pakistani rule and to rebuff their attempt at autonomy and democracy. West Pakistan sought a military conclusion to the perceived threat posed by the Bengalis. As we have seen in many episodes of genocide, the target group is defined as an obstacle to overcome.

Ridding East Pakistan of its Hindu influence was seen as a possible way of controlling the remaining Muslim population. In addition to the anti-Hindu beliefs of West Pakistan, there was a general feeling that Bengalis were a culturally and racially inferior group. Bengalis were seen as being insufficiently martial and insufficiently Islamic. "The ideology to destroy the Bengali nation was that they were descendants of aboriginal Indian tribes. They do not deserve to rule but only to be ruled. Therefore, they were to be crushed in such a way that they could never again demand the fruits of election victory."[9]

Similar to the Herero genocide, the Bangladesh genocide was committed mostly by the military in military operations. While the "Final Solution" to the Bengali problem was violent and many civilians were killed, it was mainly accomplished through military fiat. President Yahya Khan told his generals prior to the genocide, "Kill three million of them, and the rest will eat out of our hands."[10] Upon General Tikka Khan's arrival in Bangladesh, he reportedly announced his final solution to the Bengali problem claiming he would kill 4 million people in 48 hours.

General Khan saw his mission as a jihad, or holy war, against the Hindus and Bengali Muslims. One military official said, "We are determined to cleanse East Pakistan once and for all of the threat of secession, even if it means killing off two million people and ruling the province as a colony for 30 years."[11] The motive was to crush the threat of secession while at the same time cleansing the area of Hindu influence.

The genocide of Bengali Muslims and Hindus began on March 25, 1971. That night, Operation Searchlight was launched killing 17 professors and 200 students at Dhaka University. Operation Searchlight was designed to be a massive armed strike against the capital city Dhaka. The following day, March 26, 1971, Bangladesh declared independence from Pakistan; two days later on March 28, 1971, Pakistan declared war on Bangladesh.

As we saw with the Armenians and the Holocaust, a genocide occurring during war can often be hidden. In Bangladesh, the genocide was not as secret as Pakistan may have hoped. Several countries knew of the genocide and ultimately India intervened to help the Bengalis. However, India's intervention did not rely on the Genocide Convention. Instead India was helping a nation in its independence struggle.

As the war began, Bengalis resorted to guerilla tactics of warfare. In response the Pakistan military began a strategy of search and destroy. These search-and-destroy missions involved massive killing, looting, burning, and raping of areas where guerilla actions had been reported. The army would first clear the area of Bengalis and then kill the Hindus of the region, especially those in the military, journalists, teachers, and students. The common pattern was to enter the village, ask where the Hindus lived, and then kill all of the male Hindus. The soldiers would then indiscriminately burn the villages and slaughter any remaining inhabitants.

In the first phase of the genocide, young able-bodied men were targeted for death. During the second phase, girls and women became the targets for genocidal rape. After nine months of fighting, Bangladesh won its independence. The price in terms of life is incalculable. There are no solid estimates of the death toll in the Bangladesh genocide; anywhere between 1 million and 3 million people are said to have been murdered.

***

1975 East Timor Genocide

Much like the genocide in Bangladesh the genocide in East Timor was the result of an independence movement gone awry.[12] The island of Timor sits in the Indonesian archipelago and is divided into West Timor and East Timor. The island was divided by its colonial masters in the Netherlands and Portugal with East Timor under Portuguese control.

For much of its colonial existence East Timor was relatively neglected by Portugal and most East Timorese lived traditional village lives. This existed for several decades until 1974 when the government in Portugal was overthrown and replaced with an anti-colonial power. Under the new regime, East Timor was going to become an independent nation after a period of decolonization assisted by Portugal.

In the unsettled time that was decolonization, Indonesia expressed a desire to take control of East Timor and annex the land into greater Indonesia. Many East Timorese did not approve of this offer and they formed their own government under the Fretilin party. Fretilin had widespread support throughout East Timor and was working with Portugal to establish a functioning and efficient government for an independent state.

The Suharto regime in Indonesia was giving statements saying that they supported East Timor in its desire to become an independent nation. However, the regime was secretly planning its own invasion of the island in order to secure annexation with Indonesia. While the Suharto regime was notoriously undemocratic, they were also anti-Communist, which made it an ally of most major powers at the time.

Part of the reason why East Timor did not want to be annexed by Indonesia was due to their different cultures. While the geographic distance between Indonesia and East Timor is slight, the cultural differences are great. Even though East Timor is part of the archipelago of Indonesia, the East Timorese view themselves as a separate and distinct nationality.

While Indonesia is predominantly Muslim, East Timor practices Catholicism and animist religions. The ethnic and culture of East Timor is also much more complex than that of Indonesia. Political traditions are different between the two peoples as are the multiple languages that are spoken on East Timor. The ethnically diverse population of East Timor cannot be subsumed or incorporated into that of Indonesia easily. Diverse religious beliefs and different languages make the East Timorese a unique and socially diverse people. These differences were overlooked by the Indonesian regime when they decided to annex the island nation.

Much of the fighting and terror of the East Timor genocide was accomplished by the Indonesian army. After one massacre, two senior military generals were heard to say that the killing was "necessary and that no regret was warranted."[13] Army commanders threatened to "liquidate…all the pro-independence people, parents, sons, daughters, and grandchildren."[14]

On December 7, 1975, Indonesian forces invaded East Timor from the land and the sea. From the beginning, the Indonesian forces went on a rampage against the East Timorese people. The Indonesian troops continued on their rampage through East Timor killing, torturing, and raping the civilian population. Search-and-destroy missions using aerial bombardments killed the civilian population and their crops.

> The soldiers who landed started killing everyone they could find. There were many dead bodies in the streets—all we could see were the soldiers killing, killing, killing.
>
> –Catholic Bishop of Dili, East Timor

There is no accurate death count of the East Timor genocide. Of the island's initial 650,000 population, 150,000 people had been killed or disappeared in the first four years of fighting. By the end of fighting nearly 24 years later, it is estimated that 200,000 people had died. But while the genocide raged it was feared that half of the population may face extinction, so it may never be known how many East Timorese were annihilated by Indonesia.

The Indonesian occupation of East Timor lasted until 1999. In 1999, President Suharto resigned and the United Nations formed a temporary government to rule East Timor. The temporary government remained until East Timor's first election in 2001. After the election quickly followed passage of a new constitution. On September 27, 2002, the country was renamed Timor-Leste using the Portuguese naming and admitted to the UN as a full member state.

***

1988 Kurdish Genocide in Iraq

The Kurdish genocide in Iraq is often overshadowed by the war between Iran and Iraq. The war acted as a shield to hide the attempted extermination of the Kurdish population. As discussed in Chap. 3 war can be criminogenic leading to other crimes including genocide.

In September 1980, disputes between Iran and Iraq over border lines erupted into war when Iran bombed several Iraqi border towns. Using the war as cover, the regime of Saddam Hussein created a designated campaign to eliminate the Kurdish population.[15] Part of the ideology of Hussein's Ba'ath Party in Iraq was the creation of an Arab nationalist character. This ideology soon spread to cover areas of the country that were not traditionally Arab in nature. The Kurds of Iraq represented a block to full Arabization of Iraq.

Living in oil rich portions of Iraq also led to the desire to either Arabize the locale or rid it of the Kurdish population. The genocide of the Kurds evolved under the strict control that Saddam Hussein wielded in his country. With an Arab ideology in place, the Kurdish population was easy to identify and criticize.

The Kurds live in an area of approximately 74,000 square miles stretching across Turkey, Iran, Iraq, and Syria. Most of the area is densely mountainous and heavily forested; the majority of Kurds lived as farmers and mountain dwellers. The Kurds consider themselves indigenous to the area even though they have never had a recognized nation of their own.

The mountains of Kurdistan made it geographically isolated from much of the rest of Iraq. In addition to geographic separateness, the Kurds represent a distinct ethnic group. Kurdish language, customs, and traditions are all unique to the Kurdish populace. While the Kurds are spread across several different nations, they have maintained their own cultural and ethnic identity. At the time of the genocide, the Kurds comprised about 20 to 25% of the Iraqi population—the largest ethnic minority in the country.

The unique cultural and ethnic identity of the Kurds made them identifiable to the Iraqis quite easily. But to further the individualization process and identifying the "other," the government of Iraq required a census to be taken throughout the country. At the census, all Iraqi citizens had to declare their ethnicity; the only option was Arab or Kurd.

Anyone who failed to participate in the census was subject to loss of Iraqi citizenship and was to be considered as army deserters. Many Kurds claimed that they were never informed of the census, which may be true due to the isolated location of most of the Kurds. Anyone willing to declare themselves Kurd faced the destruction of their home and deportation to the autonomous region. By the time of the census, many Kurdish towns and villages were no longer drawn on official maps.

In addition to the census, which clearly identified the Kurds as the "other," there were value judgments against them as well. One police officer said, "Dogs have no relations to Islam," or identified all Kurds as "saboteurs, all saboteurs we attacked with chemical weapons."[16] When the elderly mullah of Balisan went to Ba'ath Party officials at Seruchawa to plead for an improvement in conditions in the complex, he was told contemptuously, "You're not human beings."[17]

Prior to the genocide in 1988, al-Majid, who was in charge of the Kurdish area, issued several decrees limiting the rights of the Kurdish people. On April 6, 1987, he took away the property right of all "saboteurs"; on April 10, he suspended all of the legal rights of villagers in prohibited areas (where most of the Kurdish population was located); on May 1, al-Majid ordered the execution of first-degree relatives of saboteurs; on May 14, he authorized the execution of wounded civilians; and on June 3, he forbid farming and the importation of goods into the area.

The genocidal attacks on the Kurds, known as Anfal, followed a regular pattern. The targeted area would be surrounded and then bombed from the air, including the use of chemical weapons. Once the population began to flee the bombing, ground troops would enter the area and mount a ground attack on those fleeing.

People who surrendered to the ground troops were never seen again. Others who were captured during the raid would be transported to camps where the men and women would be separated and the men killed en masse. It was not unusual for men to be tied together, made to stand in a line at the tip of a pit and then shot in the back and allowed to fall into the pit, which served as their grave.

Some of the grave sites contained dozens of separate pits containing thousands of victims. Most of the Anfal attacks occurred after some military interaction with Iran during the Iraq-Iran war. The army would withdraw from the front lines of war to engage in the genocide of the Kurds. There is no accurate count of the number of victims of the Anfal campaign.

Since the Kurds lived in Iran too during the war, we should explore why Iran did not engage in genocide against its Kurdish population. Iran looked very similar to Iraq during the 1980s, a theocratic regime with no room for dissent. While the Kurds were present in Iran, there does not seem to be the same level of Arabization in Iran as there was in Iraq.

While Saddam Hussein was obsessed with making Iraq an Arab nation, Iran was content to be an Islamic regime. This lack of Arabization desire may explain why the groups within Iran did not find their Kurdish neighbors to be a problem. With no ethnic division, the Kurds in Iran did not pose an obstacle to the Iranian government.

In fact, during the Anfal campaign near the border with Iran, many Kurds fled into Iran to escape death in Iraq. There is no evidence that Iran was bothered or tried to turn away Kurdish refugees at the border. There is no evidence of hatred or a desire to rid Iran of the Kurds by the state, the military, or the people of Iran.

While losses in the Iraq-Iran war seemed to trigger genocidal attacks on the Kurds in Iraq, there was no such attack on Iranian Kurds following any battles. It may be that the Iranians were more successful in their campaign against Iraq and had not residual aggression to mete out. While Iran shared Iraq's autocratic political status as well as a Kurdish population within its border, the country did not devolve into genocide. Understanding why similar circumstances resulted in different outcomes can help us understand the reason some nations commit genocide and others do not.

***

1994 Rwandan Genocide

Rwanda is a small, land-locked country in central Africa. While small in area, many people populate the country. There are two main ethnic groups—Hutu and Tutsi. Hutus comprised about 85% of the population at the time of the genocide. The Tutsis represented about 14% of the population. The native population, known as Twa, comprised about 1% of the population.

Rwanda began its existence as a Belgian colony. It was under this colonization that the Hutu and Tutsi ethnic groups became more identifiable and caste-like in nature. Originally, the word Tutsi simply referred to a person who was rich in cattle. Hutu was originally used to refer to the mass public or ordinary people who were not wealthy. It was not until the Belgian colonial rule that these terms became distinct ethnic identities that could not be changed.

There may have been some physical distinctions between the Hutu and the Tutsi originally, but intermarriage had erased most of them. Beside these physical distinctions that were faded by 1994, the Hutu and the Tutsi shared a common culture. They spoke the same language, had the same customs and clan names. They attended the same schools and churches and worked with each other in the same offices and bars.

Despite representing a minority in the country, the Belgians gave the Tutsi political power over the majority Hutu population. This upset the Hutu who did not appreciate having a minority population ruling the majority. This lasted until independence in 1962. When Rwanda gained independence, Belgium switched allegiance from the Tutsi to the Hutu and assisted the Hutu in their political revolution.

In the end, the Hutu took political power and more than 130,000 Tutsi fled Rwanda. Ten years later, General Juvenal Habyarimana took control of the government and made Rwanda a one-party state under his control. The new military regime consolidated all political power in the president's party and forbid the involvement of Tutsi in the new state government.

By the time of the genocide in 1994, the political power of the Habyarimana regime was threatened by peace talks designed to increase Tutsi representation in the government. These Arusha Accords would ultimately result in a power-sharing government between the Hutu and the Tutsi. The Arusha Accords were organized by the United Nations to bring peace to Rwanda after internal war and unrest.

The Hutu majority did not want to share power with the Tutsis. Using fear, the government and others demonized the Tutsis and made them the incarnation of evil to the Hutu masses. Much of the Hutu population believed that the Tutsi were not part of the national community. They were viewed as a threat to the security and safety of the Hutu populace.

One high-ranking official in the Rwandan government told the Hutu to "know that the person whose throat you do not cut now will be the one who will cut yours."[18] In addition to presenting the Tutsi as a threat to the Hutu, the Hutu leadership created what became known as "The Hutu Ten Commandments." Among these commandments were judgments of Tutsi women as conspirators and infiltrators of the Hutu ethnicity.

They also said that all Tutsi were dishonest in business dealings, that the military should have no Tutsi members, and that the Hutu should not have any mercy on the Tutsi. Other terms used to describe the Tutsi were ibyitso and inkotanyi. Ibyitso translates as accomplice to the enemy and inkotanyi translates as cockroaches. Tutsi were also referred to as snakes that slithered into the Hutu society and disrupted Hutu solidarity. All of these value judgments were supported, if not supplied, by the government and the government-run media outlets.

The build-up to the genocide occurred over several months. From the beginning of the peace talks there was dissent among the Hutu-run government. As it became clear that President Habyarimana had no choice but to acquiesce to the peace talks, he was targeted by his own regime.

On April 6, 1994, on a return flight to Rwanda, his plane was shot down and Habyarimana and the president of Burundi were killed. Within hours of the plane crash the government in Rwanda set into motion its plan for collectivizing the Hutu against the Tutsi in a genocidal spree. Sporadic gunfire erupted almost immediately after the plane crash. Forty-eight hours later, the genocide spread from the capital region into the countryside.

Most of the Hutu population participated in the slaughter of the Tutsi. Within hours of the assassination of President Habyarimana, the government and militias had set curfews and roadblocks throughout the capital. The government ran the genocide through its military and the militias it recruited among the youth. These militias, known as Interahamwe, manned the roadblocks and killed anyone Tutsi who attempted to cross.

> These Interahamwe brought him [my brother Theoneste] back to the house. They told us that he had to be killed in order to prove that the whole family were [sic] not agents of the FPR. … During this time messages were coming in every hour, urging our family to kill Theoneste. The whole family was threatened with death unless we killed Theoneste. … After these four days, about 20 Interahamwe,

> armed with machetes, hoes, spears, and bows and arrows, came to the house. … Theoneste got up and spoke to me. 'I fear being killed by a machete; so please go ahead and kill me but use a small hoe.' He himself brought the hoe and handed it to me. I hit him on the head. I kept hitting him on the head but he would not die. It was agonizing. Finally I took the machete he dreaded in order to finish him off quickly. The Interahamwe were there during the whole time, supervising what they called 'work.' When Theoneste was dead they left.
>
> –Lemarchand, Rene (2004), 411.

The Interahamwe used the following methods of killing: machetes, massues (clubs studded with nails), small axes, grenades, guns, fragmentation grenades, beatings to death, amputations with exsanguination, buried alive, drowned, or raped and killed later. Many victims had both their Achilles tendons cut with machetes as they ran away, to immobilize them so that they could be finished off later.[19]

From the beginning, the government-run radio and television media exhorted all Hutu to get involved and murder the enemy. It was said that it was the duty of the Hutu to participate in order to save their families. When some government officials throughout Rwanda refused to participate in the genocide, they were quickly removed and replaced with more sympathetic officials.

With such carnage throughout the country, bodies were soon being dumped in the river. So many bodies were dumped that the river became clogged and could not flow as usual. In many cases, Tutsi were lured to what was promised to be safe havens, only to be slaughtered en masse at churches, schools, and hospitals. Many times Hutu were forced to kill their own neighbors or spouses to prove loyalty to the government.

The genocide in Rwanda lasted 100 days and may be the most clear-cut case of genocide since the Holocaust.[20] In just over three months from April to July, nearly one million Tutsi were massacred. The genocide in Rwanda only ended when the Rwandan Patriotic Front defeated the sitting government and installed themselves as the new power elite.

Similar to the Kurdish genocide in Iraq, but not in Iran, when Rwanda erupted into genocide, there was fear that Burundi would follow, yet it did not. Burundi in 1994 was very similar to Rwanda at the same time including a Hutu-run government. The government in Burundi was very friendly with the Habyarimana regime in Rwanda, which is why they were sharing a plane on April 6, 1994.

The main ethnic groups in Burundi, like Rwanda, are the Hutu and the Tutsi. In 1994, while there was still some animosity between the Hutu and the Tutsi in Burundi, it was not as severe or as targeted as in Rwanda. The proportion of Hutu and Tutsi are similar in Burundi as in Rwanda.

Raising concern that Burundi could devolve into genocide in 1994 was the fact that Burundi had experienced its own genocide in 1972. Much like its neighbor to the north, Rwanda, Burundi had experienced ethnic troubles for many years. After gaining its independence in 1962, there was a monarchical system of government established with a king and several princes in line to the throne.

When looking at the state of Burundi prior to the 1972 genocide, it is clear that the Hutu majority were being excluded from the power base. Within the constitutional monarchy, the true setup of the government was a Tutsi ethnocracy. Between the years of 1966 and 1993, the government was ruled by three separate military regimes. These regimes began the rise to power in 1966 when a coup d'etat occurred and the first military regime took control of the government.

While the Tutsi represented a numerical minority in the Burundi population, they represented a majority in the government. Almost every political position of importance was occupied by a Tutsi. This unequal access to the government had repercussions on the access of the Hutus to other scarce resources. Immediately prior to the genocide, Burundi was on the "brink of anarchy."[21]

Both the Hutu and the Tutsi believed that the other group would somehow cause them harm. This mutual fear easily devolved into rumors of possible attacks. These false rumors led the Hutu to attack the Tutsi in what they believed was a preemptory strike. This uprising led directly to the genocide of the Hutu.

The genocide of the Hutu began when the Hutu majority attempted a coup on April 29, 1972. Hutu members of the coup attempt killed several thousand Tutsi including women and children. This failed coup led to a quick and brutal backlash that began on April 30, 1972. While the counter violence may have started as a repression of violence toward the Tutsi, it devolved rapidly into full-scale genocide. By the end of the genocide in July, roughly a quarter of a million Hutu men, women, and children were murdered. In addition, several thousand fled into neighboring countries seeking refuge.

So why didn't Burundi experience genocide in 1994 when their president was killed in the plane crash of April 1994? Much like Iran in 1988 it may involve the fact that at the time there were not the negative value judgments that had existed in 1972. Lacking the fear that had existed in 1972, there was no need to target any particular group.

While there was no genocide in Burundi in 1994, the country did not escape from side effects of the Rwandan genocide. Some Rwandan refugees tried to enter

Burundi by crossing the river border. In an attempt to restrict the influx of refugees, many people lined the border forcing the Tutsi to return to Rwanda.

Some conditions in Burundi were similar to Rwanda, yet they did not engage in genocide in 1994. Perhaps some of that is because there was not the same level of strain in Burundi as in Rwanda. Further, the state had not been experiencing political unrest. The circumstances that often lead to genocide were absent in Burundi in 1994. If we can understand what these conditions were, we may better be able to intervene and prevent genocide.

***

1995 Bosnian Genocide

Similar to the Ottoman Empire during World War I and the resultant genocide of the Armenians, the Bosnian genocide was preceded by lost land and population and hidden by war. The seeds of the genocide in Bosnia and Herzegovina began when the former communist state of Yugoslavia collapsed.[22] In 1991, Croatia and Slovenia declared independence from Yugoslavia. The next year Bosnia and Herzegovina followed.

Bosnia and Herzegovina was one of the most ethnically diverse portions of the former Yugoslavia. By population, Bosniacs (Bosnian Muslims) represented 44%, Serbs constituted 31%, and Croats represented 17%. This ethnic diversity made division of the land impossible as every ethnic group stood opposed to the country's division.

Formally recognized as an independent nation on April 6, 1992, Serbia instigated a war to retain Bosnia as part of the Serbian nation. Croatia and Slovenia had just recently fought and won their own wars of independence. However, the leadership in Serbia did not want to allow Bosnia and Herzegovina to separate peacefully because of the large population of Serbians within its borders.

Within days of declaring independence, the fighting between the Yugoslav National Army and the Army of the Republic of Bosnia and Herzegovina erupted. The conflict lasted for several years into 1995 when the Serbian military issued a directive as to what should happen in Bosnia: "by force of arms, impose the final outcome of the war on the enemy, forcing the world into recognizing the actual situation on the ground and ending the war."[23]

The Bosniacs had lived among the other ethnic groups for many decades under the communist rule of Yugoslavia. As the nation began to separate and divide by ethnic lines, the idea of a Muslim section of the land ignited deep-seated racist notions. Early Muslim beliefs concerning food, the celebration of holidays, and clothing were the only visible differences between the Bosniacs and their neighbors. It was once said that the only difference between the Muslim and non-Muslim population was the way that the Muslims pray and what they eat.

These small and some would say insignificant differences became exposed and enlarged during the war to justify a dislike of the Bosniac population. Serbian intellectuals referred to the Muslims as an inferior, non-European culture. They were deemed to be an Arab subculture more related to their "desert ancestors" than to Bosnia. A sense of Serbian power and supremacy soon developed at the state level. Bosniacs were said to be a malignant disease that threatened to infect Europe if not eliminated.

Serbia used the fog of civil war to send its military into Bosnia with the intent to take the land from Bosnia and incorporate it into Serbia. At the same time, Serbia wanted to allow the Serbs in Bosnia to join Serbia. The civil war gave cover to the military actions erupting in genocide. The genocide decision was made the evening of July 11 and morning of July 12 by military leaders in the Srebrenica enclave. There is evidence to show that the genocide was mainly a military operation. General Mladic issued a directive ordering the ethnic cleansing of the towns of Srebrenica, Zepa, and Gorzade.

Military leader Radovan Karadzic issued the following order: "By planned and well-thought-out combat operations, create an unbearable situation of total insecurity with no hope of further survival or life for the inhabitants of Srebrenica and Zepa."[24] At the time of the issuance of this order, Srebrenica was a safe zone protected by United Nations troops. In the town were close to 40,000 Muslim men, women, and children who had fled their homes. Standing orders were to destroy the Muslim forces in Srebrenica and other safe zones should the UN troops leave the town unprotected.

On July 11, 1995, the Serbian forces broke through the UN troops at Srebrenica ending the safe zone. Deportation of the Muslim population of Srebrenica began the next day. During these deportations, the men were separated from the women and elderly. Bosniac men and boys were shot beside pits and buried in mass graves. As some tried to flee the genocide, they were caught in the woods and slaughtered. Several of the men were taken in trucks to warehouses or factories where they were executed.

Prior to executing the men they were dehumanized; soldiers would beat them with bars and then use grenades and small arms to kill those that were still alive. On a farm near the fallen safe zone, between 1000 and 1200 men were lined up in one day and systematically killed. Following the massacres, UN personnel were able to see hair, blood, and human tissue caked to the inside walls of the warehouses and factories. It is estimated that up to 8000 Muslim men and boys were killed during the months following the fall of Srebrenica.

> I would rather not know how many people I killed.
>
> –Drazen Erdemovic, convicted of crimes against humanity and sentenced to ten years

***

2003 Darfur Genocide

Darfur is located on the border of Chad in western Sudan. The area is occupied mostly by African tribes including the Fur, Massaleet, and Zaghawa. Surrounding these settlements are nomadic Arab tribes that survive by moving from place to place and using the land to subsist on. As the Arab tribes leave one portion of the land for another, the land they live is no longer arable.

What soon occurred was isolation of all arable land into the Darfur region. This arable land is what drew the Arab tribes closer to the Fur and other African tribes. Prior to the regime of Omar al-Bashir and the need for arable land, the African and Arab tribes lived among each other in relative peace. However, when African tribes attacked the government in response to their perceived preference for the Arabs, genocide broke out.

The government of Sudan sits in the northern part of the country where there are both Arab influences from the Middle East and African influences from southern Africa. The al-Bashir government chose to affiliate itself with the Arab influences over the traditional African influences. In 2003, the Sudanese Liberation Army and the Justice and Equality Movement attacked government targets accusing the government of oppressing black Africans in favor of Arabs.

The government responded to these attacks by making their own attacks against the rebel groups. As much of the African population lived in Darfur, it became a target of government and militia attacks. The Janjaweed militia joined with government forces to attack Darfur and expel the native population. The government supported the Janjaweed by providing weapons and air attacks.

> Citing orders from the president of the Republic, "You are informed that directives have been issued...to change the demography of Darfur and empty it of African tribes" through burning, looting, and killing "of intellectuals and youths who may join the rebels in fighting" (Hagan & Rymond-Richmond, 2008: 133).

The Arab tribes would arrive in the villages of Darfur, kill the men, rape the women, and burn the village to the ground. It appears that the arable land was the primary goal of the Arab tribes and the genocide was the simplest method of obtaining that land. The military soon joined power with the Janjaweed and together they made several raids on villages throughout Darfur pushing the Black Africans who survived into refugee camps in Chad. The state clearly began the genocide as a response to the Black African tribes seeking fair representation in the government.

One government directive stated that the goal was to "change the demography of Darfur and empty it of African tribes."[25] These orders were carried out by both the military and the Janjaweed. Police were disarmed prior to the genocide so that they could not reasonably defend the villages against attack.

One way that the demography of Darfur was to change was through the use of rape. The Janjaweed would rape Darfuri women with the intent to impregnate. In Sudan, the ethnicity of a child is determined through the father. So if an Arab man impregnates a Darfuri woman, the child is considered to be Arab.

These pregnancies forced women to carry children of a different ethnicity. After giving birth, many of these women were not seen as marriage prospects for Darfuri men because they had born an Arab child. These behaviors may qualify as an attempt to prevent births of African children and forcibly transferring children to a different ethnic group—both outlawed by the UN Convention on Genocide.

While there is no accurate count of the number of people killed since the beginning of the genocide in Darfur, an accepted account puts the total near 400,000. There is currently tentative peace in the region while millions of Darfuris still live in substandard refugee camps on the border between Darfur and Chad.

***

2017 Rohingya Genocide

Myanmar is a country in Southeast Asia bordering on India, China, and Thailand. From 1962 until 2011, the country was ruled by an oppressive military regime.[26] The country along with the government is majority Buddhist. Two-thirds of the country identify as Bamar an ethnic group native to Myanmar.[27]

In addition to the Bamar, there are 135 ethnic minority groups among the population.[28] The Rohingya represent a minority group in Myanmar—a Muslim minority accounting for the largest percentage of Muslims in Myanmar. The Rohingya have their own language and culture and live predominantly in Rakhine state.[29]

The Rohingya were pushed into Rakhine state by the Bamar government. Rakhine state is on the outer part of the country where natural resources are scarce.[30] Access to education and social problems were restricted as well.[31] The ability to participate in the government did not exist.

Myanmar refuses to recognize the Rohingya as a people.[32] In 1982, Myanmar's government adopted a citizenship law that denied the Rohingya equal access to citizenship leaving them stateless.[33] The Rohingya are viewed as illegal immigrants from Bangladesh. Other discriminatory orders restricted movement, marriage, childbirth, and religious practice.[34]

In 2011 the government transitioned to civilian rule but the military maintained significant power.[35] In April 2012 the first partly free elections are held. The National League for Democracy (NLD), formerly banned by the government, won several seats in parliament. Over the next few years the move toward a democracy was slow. Small attacks against the Rohingya occurred sporadically.

In June 2012, attacks between the Rohingya and Buddhists in Rakhine state resulted in deaths on both sides. These attacks escalated into targeted violence against the Muslim population.[36] In October 2012, state forces killed numerous Rohingya and forced 100,000 to flee the country.

In the 2015 elections, the NLD won enough seats to form a government. While hope was high for a new democratic government, treatment of the Rohingya did not greatly improve. Beginning in August 2017 Rohingya militants attacked several police posts in Rakhine.[37] In response the Myanmar military attacked Rohingya villages burning them down and killing civilians. The government said the purpose of the raids were to find those who attacked the police posts. Instead, the military initiated a widespread attack on the Rohingya population.

The army, joined by police and armed civilian groups, burned entire villages.[38] At least 288 villages were either partially or totally destroyed by fire in northern Rakhine state after August 2017.[39] In addition, attackers would kill men, women, and children, rape the women and girls, and disappear many survivors.[40]

Evidence gathered from survivors showed that the attacking military and militias would open fire on villages from land and air.[41] When the killing was complete the soldiers would move the bodies into piles and set them on fire.[42] Survivors reported that in addition to the military, civilian groups would participate in the attacks alongside the state forces.

In addition to murder, rape and sexual assault were rampant. Soldiers would often separate captives by gender with the intent to rape the women.[43] Sometimes following the rape the soldiers would mutilate the women. All of these actions fall under the UN definition of genocide—causing serious bodily harm.

During the first months of the attacks (August and September 2017) at least 6700 Rohingya were killed.[44] Survivors of the attacks then fled to neighboring Bangladesh. This created a refugee crisis with Rohingya being forced into overcrowded camps on the border. The Myanmar military continued the fight against the refugees by opening fire on fleeing civilians and planting land mines near the border.[45]

With an ongoing genocide, it is difficult to determine exact numbers of those killed. Best estimates say that at least 25,000 have died since fighting began in 2017.[46] More than 34,000 Rohingya have been thrown into fires and over 114,000 have been beaten.[47] More than 730,000 Rohigya have fled Myanmar since fighting began leading to one of the worst refugee crises in modern history.[48]

Aung San Suu Kyi: From Nobel Laureate to Alleged Génocidaire In Chap. 4 we looked at who commits genocide. We explored the ideas of individuals and organizations being capable of committing atrocity crimes. We could not find a single motivating factor for the individual to commit genocide recognizing that there are probably many reasons. The story of Aung San Suu Kyi represents how individuals who personally suffered from repression and fought for freedom can still ignore the suffering of others.

- Aung San Suu Kyi rose to prominence in Myanmar as an advocate for democracy during military rule. Her father fought for independence in Myanmar and was assassinated in 1947 just six months before the country gained independence. Her mother was appointed as the Myanmar ambassador to India in 1960.
- In 1964 Suu Kyi arrived in the United Kingdom to study philosophy, politics, and economics at Oxford University. She returned to Myanmar in 1988.
- At the time of her return there were protests for democracy ongoing. She soon rose to lead the democracy movement organizing rallies and using civil disobedience to promote democracy and free elections.
- These gatherings were swiftly and brutally repressed by the military who took power in September 1988. The next year Suu Kyi was placed under house arrest because of her activism. While under

house arrest in 1991 Suu Kyi was awarded the Nobel Peace Prize for her work on campaigning for democracy. She was unable to attend the ceremony.

- She was freed in 1995 but by 2000 she was placed back into house arrest for violating travel restrictions. In 2009, she was awarded the Amnesty International Ambassador of Conscience Award, the organization's highest honor.
- Even under house arrest Suu Kyi worked with the National League of Democracy (NLD) political party who was still pushing for elections and democratic rule. Suu Kyi spent ten more years under house arrest until she was finally freed in 2010.
- In the elections of 2015 the NLD won decisively. Suu Kyi was barred from becoming president by the state's constitution which was amended to ensure she would never be able to be president. Her official title is state councilor, but many people consider her the de facto president.
- Aung San Suu Kyi acting as de facto president decided that she would downplay and ignore much of the violence against the Rohingya. She repeatedly said in public that the attacks were limited and targeted for specific goals. She denied any mass violence or refugee crisis.
- What many see as her most brazen act is her defense of these actions at the International Court of Justice. Instead of recognizing the violence and attacks on the Rohingya, Suu Kyi claimed that the situation was too complex to understand. She also defended the attacks as legitimate counterattacks on violent extremists. She refused to acknowledge the rape of women and girls.
- The Nobel committee considered revoking her Peace Prize due to her actions in regard to the Rohingya genocide. Ultimately, the committee decided that the award was given for her past activities and not her current behavior. However, Amnesty International did revoke her Ambassador of Conscience Award stating that they were "profoundly dismayed at her failure to speak out for the Rohingya minority."[i]

- Suu Kyi has seen other honors rescinded due to her actions against the Rohingya. She was granted honorary Canadian citizenship in 2007 which was rescinded—the first-time honorary citizenship had been stripped—in 2018. In 2012, the United States Holocaust Memorial Museum awarded her the Elie Wiesel human rights award. In 2018 the Museum issued a formal rescission of the award after conducting its own research and determining that the actions against the Rohingya rose to genocide.[ii]
- *Can you think of any reason that Aung San Suu Kyi might have gone from fierce advocate of democracy to covering for genocide?*
- *What does Suu Kyi gain from denying genocide?*
- *Can you connect her behavior to our discussion of individual génocidaires?*
- i BBC News (2018). Aung San Suu Kyi: Amnesty strips Myanmar leader of top prize. Retrieved at https://www.bbc.com/news/world-asia-46179292
- ii BBC News (2018). United States Holocaust Museum withdraws Aung San Suu Kyi's human rights award. Retrieved at https://www.theguardian.com/world/2018/mar/07/aung-san-suu-kyi-holocaust-museum-award

Conclusion

The answer to our opening query about when and where genocide occurs is that it occurs everywhere at any time. Genocide has occurred before there was a name for it and long after the world promised "Never Again" following the Holocaust. While there are some commonalities among genocides as we have seen, one aspect that is diverse is location and timing.

Many people assume genocide is a problem only in the under-developed world, but it is not. Genocide can, and does, occur in developed nations across the globe. Since the UN Convention passed in 1948, there have been countless episodes of genocide. While we struggle to understand and predict genocide, we must be aware that location and time should not be limited. We should never say this or that country will never have a genocide because when the circumstances are just right, we have seen what happens.

Discussion Questions

1. Do you see any similarities among these cases of genocide? Try to make a chart comparing these episodes and the factors leading to each genocide. Then see if you find common factors.
2. What major differences do you see in these episodes of genocide? Do these differences point to other causes of genocide that we have not mentioned before?

Notes

1. Chalk, Frank and Jonassohn, Kurt (1990). *The history and sociology of genocide: Analyses and case studies*. New Haven: Yale University Press, xvii.
2. Straus, Scott. (2012). "Destroy them to save us": Theories of genocide and the logics of political violence. *Terrorism and Political Violence,* 24(4), 544–560.
3. Ibid.
4. Madley, Benjamin. (2004). Patterns of frontier genocide 1803–1910: The Aboriginal Tasmanians, the Yuki of California, and the Herero of Namibia. *Journal of Genocide Research*, 6(2), 167–192: 182.
5. Ibid. at 169.
6. Bridgman, Jon and Worley, William S. (2004). Genocide of the Hereros. In Samuel Totten, William S. Parsons, and Israel W. Charny (Eds.), *Century of Genocide (2nd Ed.): Critical essays and eyewitnesses accounts* (pp. 15–51). New York: Routledge, 44.
7. Drechsler, Horst. (1990). "Let us die fighting": The struggle of the Herero and the Nama against German imperialism (1884–1915). In Frank Chalk and Kurt Jonassohn (Eds.), *The History and Sociology of Genocide: Analyses and Case Studies* (pp. 231–248). New Haven: Yale University Press: 242.
8. Adalian, Rouben P. (2004). The Armenian Genocide. In Samuel Totten, William S. Parson, and Israel W. Charny (Eds.), *Century of Genocide (2nd Ed.): Critical essays and eyewitness accounts* (pp. 53–92). New York: Routledge, 57.
9. Beachler, Donald. (2007). The politics of genocide scholarship: The case of Bangladesh. *Patterns of Prejudice*, 41(5), 467–492: 483.
10. Kiernan, Ben. (2007). *Blood and soil: A world history of genocide and extermination from Sparta to Darfur.* New Haven, CT: Yale University Press, 574.
11. Supra note 9 at 476.
12. The following information comes from Chalk & Jonassohn (1990), Kiernan (2007), Saul (2001), Sidell (1981), and Silove (2000).
13. Silove, Derrick. (2000). Conflict in East Timor: Genocide or expansionist occupation? *Human Rights Review*, 1(3), 62–79: 69.

14. Supra note 10 at 581.
15. The following information comes from Human Rights Watch (1993), Kelly (2008), Knowles (1998), Leezenberg (2004), Power (2002), and Salih (1995).
16. Human Rights Watch. (1993). *Genocide in Iraq: The Anfal campaign against the Kurds*. New York: Human Rights Watch.
17. Ibid.
18. Des Forges, Alison. (1999). *Leave none to tell the story*. New York: Human Rights Watch, 86.
19. Lemarchand, Rene. (2004). The Rwanda genocide. In Samuel Totten, William S. Parsons, and Israel W. Charny (eds.), *Century of genocide (2nd ed.): Critical essays and eyewitness accounts* (pp. 394–414). New York: Routledge, 403.
20. The following information comes from Des Forges (1999), Gourevitch (1998), Lemarchand (2004), Meredith (2005), Power (2002) and Rusesabagina (2006).
21. Lemarchand, Rene. (2004). The Burundi genocide. In Samuel Totten, William S. Parsons, and Israel W. Charny (eds.), *Century of genocide (2nd ed.): Critical essays and eyewitness accounts* (pp. 321–337). New York: Routledge, 324.
22. The following information comes from Brkic (2007), Carmichael (2006), Honig (2007), Kiernan (2007), Power (2002), and United Nations (1999).
23. Honig, Jan W. (2007). Strategy and genocide: Srebrenica as an analytical challenge. *Southeast European and Black Sea Studies*, 7(3), 399–416, 402.
24. Supra note 10 at 593–594.
25. Hagan, John and Rymond-Richmond, Wenona. (2009). *Darfur and the crime of genocide*. Cambridge: Cambridge University Press, 133.
26. World without genocide. (2017). Myanmar—Genocide of the Rohingya. Retrieved at https://worldwithoutgenocide.org/genocides-and-conflicts/myanmar
27. Ibid.
28. Ibid.
29. BBC News. (2020). Myanmar Rohingya: What you need to know about the crisis. Retrieved at https://www.bbc.com/news/world-asia-41566561
30. Supra note 26.
31. Ibid.
32. Supra note 29.
33. United States Holocaust Memorial Museum. (2017). "They tried to kill us all": Atrocity crimes against Rohingya Muslims in Rakhine state, Myanmar. Retrieved at https://www.ushmm.org/m/pdfs/201711-atrocity-crimes-rohingya-muslims.pdf
34. Ibid.
35. BBC News. (2018). Myanmar profile-Timeline. Retrieved at https://www.bbc.com/news/world-asia-pacific-12992883
36. Ibid.
37. Supra note 29.
38. Supra note 33.
39. Supra note 29.
40. Supra note 33.
41. Ibid.
42. Ibid.
43. Ibid.

44. Council on Foreign Relations. (2020). The Rohingya Crisis. Retrieved at https://www.cfr.org/backgrounder/rohingya-crisis
45. Ibid.
46. Aljazeera. (2019). Former UN chief says Bangladesh cannot continue hosting Rohingya. Retrieved at https://www.aljazeera.com/news/2019/07/chief-bangladesh-continue-hosting-rohingya-190710191318011.html
47. Ibid.
48. Ibid.

Further Reading

For comprehensive coverage of genocides throughout history see:

Blood and soil: A world history of genocide and extermination from Sparta to Darfur by Ben Kiernan.

Genocide: A comprehensive introduction by Adam Jones.

DVD Resources

Genocide (1982) narrated by Orson Welles and Elizabeth Taylor.

Hotel Rwanda. (2004). Staring Don Cheadle. After watching this film you should explore the response by those inside the hotel who challenge some of the facts used in the film. One example can be found here: https://www.theguardian.com/commentisfree/2011/nov/17/hotel-rwanda-hollywood-ending

How Do We Respond to Genocide?

6

When the genocide in Rwanda erupted, Carl Wilkens, director of the humanitarian arm of the Seventh-Day Adventist Church, decided to stay in the country. He could have fled along with his wife and children, but he decided to stay behind. By staying behind, he most likely saved the lives of his housekeeper and watchman—both Tutsis.[1]

Of his brave, and what many would call foolish, decision Wilkens writes: "Simply being there *is often the most powerful factor in making the right decision—a decision we will not regret for the rest of our lives."*[2]

Carl Wilkens had to make a choice when faced with genocide on what he would do. While hopefully none of us will ever have to make such a drastic decision, we are faced with deciding how we respond when we see genocide either first-hand or second-hand.

Our reaction may be to contact our government leaders or international bodies asking for their help. We may decide to take action ourselves by raising awareness of what is happening. We could also turn away and ignore what we see.

The international community faces the same decision as individuals, though with greater ability to act. How should the UN respond when facing genocide? So far intervention has been few and far-between. The more likely response has been to respond legally after the genocide ends. Is this response enough to confront genocide?

As we look at the different ways to respond to genocide, ask how *we should respond and not* if.

W. R. Pruitt, *An Introduction to the Criminology of Genocide*,
https://doi.org/10.1007/978-3-030-65211-1_6

Introduction

The question of how to respond to genocide encompasses many different opportunities for states or the United Nations to act. What we often see though is a reluctance to act. The concept of **sovereign immunity** kept most states from interfering with the internal disputes of another state—even when those disputes resulted in genocide.

SOVEREIGN IMMUNITY

Sovereign immunity is the idea that every state is a sovereign unto itself and should be able to do what it wants within its own borders. See Chap. 4 on how criminologist Sheldon Glueck dismissed sovereign immunity in regards to genocide. ◄

However, following WWII and the Holocaust, states decided that there were times when intervention in a fellow state was necessary. The United Nations and other countries promised "Never Again" after the Holocaust. This saying implied that action would be taken when necessary to protect vulnerable people.

Unfortunately, this great promise has not been borne out. Too many times genocide has occurred again and again. So the question about how we respond is important because for too long we have failed to respond at all. As we go through the ways genocide has been responded to in the past, think about how we should be addressing genocide going into the future.

The UN Convention on Genocide should be the starting place to explore how we respond to genocide. However, as we saw with defining genocide, the Convention has flaws. The Convention is vague when it comes to specifics on how states or the UN should respond to genocide.

The UN response to the Rwandan genocide is an example of how intervention failed and thousands died as a result. However, we will also look at NATO's response in Kosovo, which many credit as preventing a genocide. Partly because of these situations, a new doctrine called the responsibility to protect (R2P) evolved laying out responsibilities when faced with genocide. But like many previous efforts the R2P has failed to be effectively implemented.

The full title of the Genocide Convention is: United Nations Convention on the Prevention and Punishment of the Crime of Genocide. From Lemkin's early work, the Convention speaks to both prevention and punishment. Prevention has been difficult to implement, but the UN and states have been more active in the punishment of genocide.

Perhaps as a **mea culpa** for its failure to prevent genocide in Yugoslavia and Rwanda, the United Nations created an international tribunal for each nation to punish crimes including genocide. After spending millions of dollars on these courts, the final outcome is dubious at best. These courts convicted several génocidaires, but many more went unpunished.

MEA CULPA

Mea culpa is a Latin phrase meaning "through my own fault." This phrase is often used as an apology. ◄

In the footsteps of the UN international tribunals, there evolved the International Criminal Court (ICC). The ICC was established by the United Nations as an independent court to handle the most serious crimes. Again, the success of the ICC is mixed; as we will see this is partly due to the lack of involvement of several countries.

In addition to the international courts established by the UN, several states have held trials to hold génocidaires accountable. These cases often occur in states where those fearing prosecution have fled to hide from the international courts. When states prosecute génocidaires for their crimes that occurred in a different country, they are exercising **universal jurisdiction**. Usually jurisdiction lies with the nation where the crime occurred, but with international crimes like genocide, universal jurisdiction allows any state to claim jurisdiction to prosecute in order to hold perpetrators accountable.

UNIVERSAL JURISDICITON

Raphael Lemkin supported the idea of universal jurisdiction in 1948 when he was writing the UN Convention on Genocide. He believed any country should have the power to prosecute génocidaires because otherwise they could escape punishment. It took nearly 50 years before universal jurisdiction was exercised on a more regular basis. The concept is still controversial for many nations. ◄

Going forward, the ICC will be the main court to prosecute grave international crimes. Lemkin called for such a court in his original Convention but it took a half century before it became reality. We will explore how the ICC could improve its record on holding international criminals accountable for their crimes.

We will also explore more individual ways to respond to genocide. Prosecutions rely on courts and prosecutors, but every one of us can fight for a more just world by calling out genocide when it occurs. Activism is but one way to bring attention to genocide; and as U.S. Supreme Court Justice Louis Brandeis once said, "sunlight is the best disinfectant." If we bring sunlight (awareness) to genocide, then hopefully we can stop it.

United Nations Convention on the Prevention and Punishment of the Crime of Genocide

When analyzing the crime of genocide, the UN Convention should be our starting point. This treaty was written by the founding father of genocide, Raphael Lemkin, and stands as one of the first pieces of international law ever. However, no legal document is perfect and the Convention is unclear on the responsibility of states to intervene to prevent genocide. There is clearer language on the punishment of the crime.

Only two of the Convention articles deal with what could be considered prevention. Article VIII states that any state that is a member of the Convention can call upon the UN to take action "for the prevention and suppression of acts of genocide."[3] This has been interpreted to mean that any state can ask the UN Security Council to take action to prevent genocide. As we will see below this did not work in the case of Rwanda.

The only other article that could apply to prevention is Article IX which states that any dispute between member states relating to the "interpretation, application, or fulfillment of the present Convention . . . shall be submitted to the International Court of Justice."[4] This means that states can bring other states to the International Court of Justice (ICJ) which is the UN's own court. States can charge other nations with violating the Convention by committing genocide and the court could act to intervene. This process has been seldom used.

Let's look at what the United Nations has done when faced with genocide. Prior to the 1994 Rwandan genocide, the UN was involved with trying to make peace in the country. As early as October 1993 the UN Security Council passed Resolution 872 creating the United Nations Assistance Mission in Rwanda (UNAMIR).[5] UNAMIR's limited mandate was to ensure compliance with the Arusha Accords, which had established a cease fire between the government and Tutsi rebels. UNAMIR could only use force if force was used against them first. The UN had only authorized the mission to last six months.[6]

By early April 1994, UNAMIR's mandate was extended by three months.[7] On April 6, 1994 the president of Rwanda was assassinated and the genocide began. The UNAMIR soldiers were instantly immobilized by the Presidential Guard who seized control of the capital.[8] Ten Belgian soldiers working with UNAMIR were captured and killed. In response the Belgians pulled out of UNAMIR and left the country. The estimated death toll on the first day: 8000.[9]

Between April 6 and 21, the UN Security Council held discussions about UNAMIR but rarely mentioned the fate of the Rwandan people.[10] The estimated death toll by April 21: 112,000.[11] During these discussions there was no mention that UNAMIR was "morally and legally [obligated] to use all available means to halt" the ongoing genocide.[12] On April 22, less than three weeks after the genocide started, the UN reduced the UNAMIR contingent to only 150 soldiers.[13] The mandate was considered "exclusively political"[14] meaning it carried no real enforcement power and was simply a way for the UN to appear active in the face of genocide.

With only 150 soldiers, General Romeo Dallaire, the commanding officer, could not intervene to save the thousands of Rwandans dying each day. He did his best to protect as many Tutsis as he could, but laments that he could not do more. Following the Belgian withdrawal of troops, Dallaire was left with ill-prepared troops from Bangladesh and Ghana. Their inexperience also hampered any effective intervention.

Nearly two months after the genocide started, eight African nations expressed a willingness to participate in UNAMIR II if authorized by the UN.[15] The UN did not act quickly on this proposal. Weeks later, on June 15, France proposed a joint operation with other European and African nations. The Security Council debated the French initiative; China and Russia objected unless the parties in Rwanda consented.[16] The Organization for African Union refused to support the French initiative meaning that it was unlikely to recruit African troops for the plan.[17]

On June 22, the UN Security Council authorized the French intervention in Rwanda.[18] Estimated death toll by June 22: 616,000.[19] The French intervention, known as Operation Turquoise, began on June 23. By July 4, the Rwandan Patriotic Front (RPF) had captured the capital and began to restore order. Estimated final death toll: 800,000–1 million.[20]

As you can see, while the UN Security Council dawdled and debated, hundreds of thousands died. By the time of the French intervention, the genocide ended within ten days—not because of the intervention though. The genocide ended because the RPF was victorious in capturing the capital and forcing many Hutus out of the country. The Rwandan genocide ended not due to the UN but in spite of the UN.

The UN and international response to Rwanda is considered a massive failure. Though while the goal should be to learn from failure and improve, there is little evidence that that has happened. Now let's look at a more successful intervention, but one that carries its own controversies.

Kosovo is a small republic in southeast Europe bordering on Serbia, North Macedonia, Albania, and Montenegro. The Kosovo war began in February 1998. As we saw with the conflict in Bosnia, Serbia had controlled Kosovo prior to the war. The Kosovo Liberation Army (KLA) was seeking to declare independence from Serbia. The KLA was composed primarily of ethnic Kosovo Albanians.

The KLA formed in the early 1990s to fight against persecution of the Kosovo Albanians perpetrated by the Serbs.[21] By 1998, KLA attacks on Serbian authorities in Kosovo led to Serbian paramilitaries and other armed forces seeking retribution.[22] Serbian forces targeted KLA sympathizers and combatants killing up to 2000 people.[23] Many of the targeted were ethic Kosovar Albanians raising the specter of genocide if the fighting continued.

Diplomatic solutions failed to stop the violence. The North Atlantic Treaty Organization (NATO) is a military alliance between 30 North American and European nations.[24] The goal of NATO is to create a system of collective defense where member countries agree to defend other member nations when attacked.[25] NATO's role in the Kosovo war begins at the United Nations.

In September 1998, the UN passed Resolution 1199 demanding a ceasefire in the region. Negotiations with the United States Special Envoy broke down on March 23, 1999. The envoy handed the matter over to NATO. The next day NATO began a bombing campaign that lasted for 78 days.[26] The operation targeted military capabilities of the Serbs. NATO also sent humanitarian aid to Kosovar Albanian refugees.

NATO justified the bombing on humanitarian grounds. If NATO did not intervene, the argument was that the Serbs would commit genocide against the Kosovar Albanians. Since the Serbian state had already committed genocide in the mid-1990s against Bosniaks, this argument was not totally without merit. Following the 78 days of bombing the war ended. The UN passed another resolution establishing a peacekeeping force to be deployed.

The controversy came when it was argued that NATO needed the UN Security Council to approve of its bombing campaign. While some member nations argued that UN approval was necessary, others dismissed the idea.[27] The UN never officially sanctioned the NATO bombing. One argument against seeking UN Security Council approval was that China and Russia would veto the proposal and thus block humanitarian aid to the Kosovars.

Some credit the NATO bombing with preventing a genocide. If true, then this is an example of how the UN Convention on Genocide was meant to function. As it is nearly impossible to prove a negative-like genocide didn't happen, we cannot know if NATO prevented genocide. At the least though it likely saved lives by shortening the war and encouraging peace talks.

As can be seen by the fear of seeking UN approval, the UN had no role in the possible prevention of genocide in Kosovo. There was even a fear that the UN could block prevention by vetoing the bombing campaign. As such, there has been little success by the UN to prevent genocide before it happens or to even stop it once it has begun.

The Responsibility to Protect (R2P)

The international community recognized that its failures in Rwanda and the controversy over Kosovo necessitated a response. Kofi Annan, then **Secretary-General of the United Nations**, challenged the UN member nations to answer the question: "if humanitarian intervention is, indeed, an unacceptable assault on sovereignty, how should we respond to a Rwanda, to a Srebrenica, to gross and systematic violation of human rights that offend every precept of our common humanity?"[28]

SECRETARY-GENERAL

The United Nations Secretary-General is the chief administrative officer of the UN. His duties include consulting with world leaders and bringing attention to international issues. ◀

The Canadian government took the charge and set up the International Commission on Intervention and State Sovereignty (ICISS).[29] The result was a document entitled "The Responsibility to Protect." In the document, sovereignty was defined as nations having certain responsibilities for its population's welfare.[30] This meant that sovereignty could not be used as a shield to protect a country committing genocide or other serious offenses against its own people.

In addition to the state's responsibility for protecting its own citizens, a residual responsibility was placed on all countries to act when it was clear that the perpetrator state was unwilling or unable to fulfill its responsibility to protect.[31] The residual responsibility was clear that every nation had an obligation to intervene when faced with genocide and other crimes against humanity.

The R2P document was unanimously adopted by the UN in 2005.[32] Those states agreeing to the R2P have accepted the obligation to act in accordance with the doctrine including intervention where necessary. The R2P consists of three main pillars:

Pillar One: "Every state has the responsibility to protect its populations from four mass atrocity crimes: genocide, war crimes, crimes against humanity, and ethnic cleansing."

Pillar Two: "The wider international community has the responsibility to encourage and assist individual states in meeting that responsibility."

Pillar Three: "If a state is manifestly failing to protect its populations, the international community must be prepared to take appropriate collective action, in a timely and decisive manner and in accordance with the UN Charter."[33]

Since its passage, the R2P has been invoked in more than 80 UN Security Council resolutions, 50 Human Rights Council resolutions, and 13 General Assembly resolutions.[34] But the question remains whether the R2P has done anything to change the status quo. With near universal acceptance by the UN it can be said that the R2P represents a new international norm.[35] As a norm, R2P would represent the new standard response to genocide.

The goal of R2P is to ensure that when the next genocide or crime against humanity occurs, the immediate response of the world community will be to ask what action is required.[36] This would replace the current endless debates on whether action is necessary that often delay a response and allow genocide to continue unabated.

But challenges remain before R2P can be completely implemented successfully. The challenges fall into the conceptual, institutional, and political. R2P plus its limits and scope must be completely understood which can be difficult.[37] The UN and other organizations must be prepared to act meaning they have the physical capability to do so.[38] Finally, political will, glaringly absent in Rwanda and Kosovo, must exist.[39]

The R2P has been used with questionable success. In 2011, the UN Security Council authorized military intervention in Libya citing R2P. Citing violations of human rights in Libya, the Security Council adopted Resolution 1973. The resolution allowed member nations to take "all necessary measures" to protect civilians.[40] Acting on the resolution, NATO began strikes on Libyan forces. Success in Libya was questioned though as civilians may have been hit by NATO airstrikes.[41]

So while the R2P has been mentioned in many UN resolutions it is unclear if that has transformed into action and even more so prevention. Political will is often still lacking to actively intervene when necessary. The R2P has not prevented or stopped the genocide in Myanmar against the Rohingya. R2P stands as a reminder of what our responsibilities should be and how the international community often fails to meet them.

International Criminal Tribunals

Following the genocide in Srebrenica and in Rwanda, the United Nations established international criminal tribunals to prosecute those involved. In 1993, the International Criminal Tribunal for Yugoslavia (ICTY) was created and a year later the International Criminal Tribunal for Rwanda (ICTR) came into existence.

The resolutions establishing each court spoke to two main goals. This first was to bring *justice* to those responsible for atrocity crimes.[42] The second goal was to contribute to the *restoration* of peace.[43] With justice and restoration in mind, the ICTY and ICTR were officially established. The ICTY sat in the Hague, Netherlands, and the ICTR sat in Tanzania. Neither court actually sat in the countries affected.

From a criminological viewpoint, there are four reasons to punish someone for their crime. The utilitarian approach's goal is to prevent future crime. Deterrence and incapacitation are utilitarian methods. Then there is retribution which seeks to assign blame and punish proportionately but is not concerned with preventing future crime, only punishing for what has happened. Finally, there is restorative justice with the goal of restoring the victim, offender, and society to where they were before the crime.

Deterrence is the idea that if you are punishing someone for their crime, you can change behavior. Specific deterrence means that the offender will be deterred from committing more crime because of the punishment that they received. General deterrence means that the public will be deterred from committing crime because they saw the punishment of someone else. We strive to achieve both specific and general deterrence in order to have the greatest impact. For a génocidaire that means that they will not be committing genocide again and others will not do so because of seeing him punished.

The other utilitarian principle is incapacitation. Incapacitation means that the offender is put into custody, usually in prison, to protect society. They cannot harm society with crime if they are locked in prison. Their ability to commit crime has been incapacitated by being imprisoned; they are not free to harm others in society behind prison bars.

Retributive justice is offender-centered. The principle is to punish bad behavior because the offender deserves it. The punishment should be proportional to the crime meaning that it should not be too much or too little. For the crime of genocide, it is difficult to think of what might be too harsh of a punishment. The goal here is to assign blame for behavior and is focused solely on punishing the offender and not preventing future crime.

Restorative justice is more victim-centered. Restorative justice concepts include the idea that in crime both the victim and the community have been harmed. The offender's obligation is to make things right again with the victim and community. The punishment in restorative justice is not always prison as that may not restore everyone to where they were before the crime occurred. Apologies and other punishment options tend to predominate. Due to the nature of genocide, restorative justice is difficult, though not impossible as we will see.

The ICTY and ICTR trying to restore peace and find justice are combining several purposes for punishment. In the end, they may not achieve their own goals because of the attempt to do too much. No doubt the courts are seeking deterrence and incapacitation. It is likely that retribution also plays a part. While restoration of peace is one goal, restorative justice is not really part of these tribunals.

There is no death penalty at the ICTY and ICTR; life imprisonment is the harshest punishment available. When imposing sentences the court is supposed to consider factors like the gravity of offense and any individual circumstances.[44] This is similar to **mitigating and aggravating factors** that many courts consider when sentencing defendants.

MITIGATING AND AGGRAVAITNG FACOTRS

Mitigating factors are those that would reduce a sentence. A defendant suffering from mental illness or addiction might not be held to same level of culpability.

Aggravating factors are those that would increase a sentence. Particularly heinous crimes involving torture or extreme indifference to life might call for a harsher penalty. ◀

In terms of effectiveness of the ICTs we should look at the numbers of cases and defendants, but also the reception from the state where the crimes occurred. The ICTY indicted 161 defendants.[45] Of this number, 18 were acquitted while 90 were convicted and sentenced. By 2019, 59 of the sentenced defendants had finished serving their sentence.[46] The first conviction was obtained in 1996 meaning that these 59 defendants were sentenced to less than 25 years' imprisonment.

Thirteen of the indicted defendants were referred to local state courts for prosecution. Thirty-seven defendants had their indictment withdrawn or died before trial.[47] Having convicted only 90 defendants, the success rate was just 56%. Nearly half of the indicted defendants were never tried or sentenced.

Of those convicted, the average sentence was just 17 years. Only six defendants were sentenced to life imprisonment. The most common sentence was 20 years (18% of all sentences). For the severity of the crimes charged including genocide and crimes against humanity, these sentences seem short. This goes to the restoration of peace aspect of the courts. Can peace be restored if victims feel that the offenders have not been appropriately punished. A 2012 poll found that a majority of citizens in Serbia had a negative view of the court.[48] The Court then increased its outreach to Serbia in an attempt to educate them on the processes of justice at the ICTY.

By 2008, nine years before the court closed, the ICTY had spent roughly $1.2 billion.[49] By 2015, the ICTY had spent nearly $2 billion seeking justice. This represents about $12.5 million per indictment or $22.2 million for each conviction. It is not an exaggeration to say that intervention at the time of the conflict would have been cheaper.

Turning to the ICTR, we can see similar results there. The ICTR only indicted 93 individuals.[50] Of those, 62 were convicted and sentenced, a success rate of 67%. Ten cases were sent to local state courts for prosecution.[51] The ICTR was more likely than the ICTY to sentence defendants to life imprisonment. Information was available for 60 of the convicted defendants. Twenty-six of these defendants were sentenced to life (43% of all cases).[52]

The average sentence length at the ICTR was also longer than the ICTY standing at 27 years. The most common sentence was 25 years (13% of cases); sentences of 15 years and 30 years were also fairly common (12% each).[53] Only seven defendants were sentenced to less than 15 years in prison. On average the ICTR appears to be more punitive than the ICTY.

Similar to the ICTY, by the closure of the ICTR in 2015, the total cost was near $2 billion. Having indicted and convicted fewer defendants than the ICTY though makes the ICTR an overall more expensive endeavor. The ICTR spent about $21.5 million per indictment and $32.2 million per conviction. Again, it seems clear that intervention would have saved money (not to mention lives).

When the ICTR closed in 2015, Rwanda had criticized the court and had essentially stopped offering assistance. The complaints were laid out by the Rwandan justice minister who objected to the lack of reparations for the victims.[54] He also expressed displeasure that the location of the court was outside of Rwanda[55] meaning that victims and survivors could not observe justice being done. Finally, the state was bothered by allowing convicted génocidaires to speak to the media[56] thereby spreading their message of hate and denial. So it becomes questionable whether the ICTR was able to achieve its goal of restoration of peace when the victim nation did not feel properly represented.

These courts set many precedents though. The ICTR was the first court to convict a defendant for the crime of genocide. Both courts created guidelines for how sentencing of genocide and other atrocity crimes would occur. The ICTR established some aggravating factors that would justify a lengthy sentence of life. The most commonly cited factors were gravity of the offense, abuse of authority, number of victims, and superior responsibility.[57]

As genocide is a very serious crime it is not surprising that gravity of offense appeared in 68% of sentencing decisions. Abuse of authority applied most often to local leaders (like mayors) who participated or aided in the genocide; this factor was mentioned in 62% of cases. While number of victims may seem obvious this factor was used to increase sentences for those who killed large numbers in a single event; this factor appeared in 26% of cases. Superior responsibility allowed for those individuals in charge to be held liable for their action even if they did not personally murder anyone. This appeared in 18% of sentencing decisions.

As for mitigating factors justifying a reduction in sentencing, these appeared much less often. The most common factor—selective assistance to Tutsis—was mentioned in only 26% of cases. The next most common factor was prior good character appearing in 25% of decisions. Roughly 22% of defendants received some mitigation for expressing remorse. Though the same number received no mitigating factors where the court could not find any mitigation for their behavior.

Neither the ICTY nor the ICTR had its own permanent facilities for holding convicted defendants. This meant that once convicted the defendant was sent to a country that had agreed to take prisoners from the court and imprisoned in a foreign location. For the ICTY, these nations included Italy, Finland, Norway, Sweden, France, Spain, and Denmark. For the ICTR, these nations included Mali, Benin, and Swaziland.

Critical Think Exercise Why would these countries be willing to accept very dangerous criminals convicted of the worst crimes into their nation and their prisons?

The ICTY and ICTR were groundbreaking at the time. These were the first courts established by an international body to hold individuals accountable for genocide and other serious crimes against humanity. Soon after the creation of these international courts, the UN began work on what would become the first permanent international court for prosecuting serious breaches of international law.

The International Criminal Court

The International Criminal Court (ICC) was created by the Rome Statute passed on July 17, 1998.[58] The Rome Statute establishing the ICC gave the court jurisdiction over four types of international crimes: genocide, crimes against humanity, war crimes, and aggressive war. While the Rome Statute was written under the auspices of the UN, the ICC is an independent body separate from the UN. The Court is funded primarily by the member states, though it does receive contributions from international organizations, individuals, and corporations.

As of 2020, there are currently 123 states parties to the Rome Statute.[59] The majority of state member come from Africa (33 nations) followed by Latin America/Caribbean (28 states). Western Europe (25 nations), Eastern Europe (18 members), and Asia (19 nations) complete the list of members.

> **Exercise** Is your country a member of the ICC? Explore why your home country either joined the court or decided not to join the court. Are there valid concerns for not joining?

One of the controversial aspects of the ICC is how the court exercises its jurisdiction. The issue of sovereign immunity returns. Few countries want the Court to have universal jurisdiction where it could prosecute anyone from anywhere. So the ICC has jurisdiction only in certain situations: (1) the accused is a citizen of a State Party, (2) the crime took taken place in a State Party, or (3) the UN Security Council referred the situation to the Court regardless of nationality or location of the crime.

The ICC operates under the concept of complementary jurisdiction. This means that the Court can exercise jurisdiction only if a state fails to investigate or prosecute the situation or is unwilling or unable to do so. If this condition is met and one of the above three situations exist, then the ICC can exercise jurisdiction and begin an investigation.

The Office of the Prosecutor is where a case begins. The Prosecutor is responsible for both investigating and prosecuting the case.[60] The Prosecutor enjoys great control over the power to investigate. The Prosecutor has the power to decide whether to open an investigation at all. Any State Party may request the Prosecutor open an investigation. The UN Security Council can also refer cases to the Prosecutor. However, the Prosecutor retains the final say on whether to open an investigation into a situation.

Assuming an investigation is opened, the next step is to gather evidence and identify suspects. If enough evidence is gathered to justify a trial, the Court can issue an arrest warrant for a defendant.[61] If the defendant is arrested, he will be brought to the ICC for the pre-trial stage. The pre-trial stage includes an initial appearance where the defendant's identity is confirmed.[62] Then follows a confirmation of charges hearing where the Prosecutor, Defense, a legal representative for the victims, and judges decide if there is enough evidence for the case to go to trial.[63]

If there is not enough evidence to go to trial, the defendant is released. But if the case continues on it enters the trial stage. The trial occurs before a three-judge panel and the Prosecutor must prove guilt beyond a reasonable doubt.[64] Verdicts can be appealed by the Defense or the Prosecutor.[65] If a decision is appealed it goes to the Appeals Chamber. The Appeals Chamber consists of five judges who decide whether to uphold the original decision, amend it, or reverse it.[66]

Under the Rome Statute every defendant is entitled to defense attorney of their choice. The ICC has established the Office of Public Counsel for the Defense to assist accomplishing defense representation. The Defense Office is responsible for protecting the rights of the defendant during the initial stages of an investigation. The Office can also provide support to the Defense Attorney by providing legal advice or by appearing before the Court on specific issues.

There are 18 judges at the ICC who serve a 9-year non-renewable term. As of 2020, there are 6 female judges and 12 male judges. Per rules of the Court, nine of the judges must have experience in criminal law and procedure. At least five of the judges must have competence in areas of international law. The judges are elected by the States Parties to the Court; any member state can nominate a candidate. A candidate must receive two-thirds support from the member states to win election.[67]

The ICC is designed to assist victims in many ways. The Court allows a victim to apply to participate at any stage of the proceedings. The victim is then assigned a legal representative who can appear before the Court on behalf of the victim. Victims can also request reparations for the harm they have suffered. Reparations can come in three ways: (1) compensation, (2) restitution, and (3) rehabilitation.

Compensation can entail monetary payment for moral, material, and physical harm. The goal of restitution is to re-establish the situation that existed for the victim prior to the crime. This may include restoration of stolen property among other compensation. Rehabilitation is aimed to allow the victim to continue their life as normally as possible. This may include covering costs for medical, psychological, or psychiatric care.

The Rome Statute creating the ICC came into force on July 1, 2002. Since then the Court has handled only 28 cases and convicted just four individuals (one conviction was overturned on appeal). Ten indicted defendants (36% of all cases) remain at large. Similar to the ICTY and ICTR we must ask whether this Court is truly serving justice. In nearly 20 years, less than 2 dozen cases have been heard. The lengthy trials and appeals also do not ensure swift justice.

The ICC was created in response to the atrocities of Srebrenica and Rwanda, but its effectiveness remains to be seen. Part of the problem with the Court is that it must rely on cooperation from States Parties to enforce warrants and other rulings.

The ICC has no enforcement arm itself and if a member state refuses to cooperate there is little the Court can do. Omar Al-Bashir, president of Sudan, was indicted by the ICC and an arrest warrant was issued. Al-Bashir is the first sitting head of state to be indicted. However, African nations that are members of the ICC refused to enforce the arrest warrant and Al-Bashir remains at large.

Another issue with the ICC is the number of large nations that are not members. The United States, Russia, China, India, and Turkey, among other states, are not members of the ICC. As such, these states have no obligation to support the Court or its rulings. When large powerful states such as these refuse to participate a message of defiance is sent to other countries. While the Court receives much support from powerful countries, the absence of others is an issue that should be addressed.

National Courts

In addition to international courts, several countries have held genocide trials in their respective courts. These cases are often held when a defendant is found in a country that wishes to exercise universal jurisdiction for serious crimes like genocide. National prosecutions for serious international crimes are not new; they date back to at least World War II.

In 1958, ten German defendants were prosecuted for their actions of killing the Jewish population in Lithuania.[68] The defendants were members of the Einsatzgruppen killing squads formed for the purpose of killing. The defendants were charged with hundreds, and in some cases thousands, of murders.[69] They were tried in West Germany where the success rate of convicting prior German génocidaires was low.

However, the court here convicted all ten defendants. But the court did not find them guilty as principals, merely accessories.[70] This finding meant that the defendants were sentenced to relatively short prison terms. Overall the sentences ranged from 3 to 15 years. The harshest punishment of 15 years went to a defendant found guilty as accessory to 3907 murders.[71]

While this case was not necessarily a success in terms of handing out proportionate punishment, it did hold several prior génocidaires legally accountable. A few years later West German courts again tried several defendants accused of participating in the killings at **Auschwitz**. By 1965 when the court cases ended, seven defendants had been convicted of murder and sentenced to life imprisonment.[72] Ten defendants were convicted as accessories and sentenced from three to nine years in prison; three defendants were acquitted.[73]

AUSCHWITZ-BIRKENAU

Auschwitz-Birkenau was one of the Nazi German concentration and extermination camps located in occupied Poland. The camp was established in 1940 and has become a reminder of the damage wrought by genocide. To learn more, you can visit http://auschwitz.org/en/

The webpage is available in several languages. ◄

The Auschwitz case showed that German defendants could be found guilty of murder for their actions during the Holocaust. Though again many were convicted as accessories and received light sentences compared to the horrors of their crimes. But these trials proved that national courts can play a role in prosecuting génocidaires when no international court exists to do so.

Adolf Eichmann, a key organizer of the Holocaust during WWII, was captured and tried by Israel in its national courts. After the war Eichmann had fled to Argentina where he lived relatively in peace. In May 1960, Israel forces captured Eichmann in Argentina and brought him to Israel.[74] Eichmann's trial began in April 1961. In his defense, Eichmann argued that he was following orders.

As this defense had failed at the Nuremberg tribunal, it is no surprise that it has failed here too. Eichmann was convicted on December 11, 1961.[75] He was sentenced to death and hanged on May 31, 1962.[76] To date, Eichmann remains the only person put to death in Israel. While the Eichmann trial had its controversies, it proved that a state affected by genocide can still hold a legally sound prosecution.

► **Critical Thinking Exercise** The main controversy in the Eichmann trial was how he was taken from Argentina to Israel. Israeli forces entered Argentina and essentially kidnapped Eichmann without notifying Argentinian officials of their plan. Eichmann was then disguised and flown out of the country.

Do you think the way in which Israel brought Eichmann out of Argentina was wrong? Why or why not?

Other national court prosecutions include Klaus Barbie, the highest-ranking Gestapo official in Lyon, France, from 1942 to 1944. After the war, Barbie fled to Bolivia. In 1982, the Bolivian president expelled Barbie from the country for using false identification. After his expulsion he was arrested and sent to France. In France, he was charged with murder, torture, arbitrary arrests, and illegal detention.[77]

Barbie was charged with 17 counts of crimes against humanity.[78] These charges included up to 340 separate incidents. His trial began in France in 1987, more than 40 years after the end of the war. Barbie was found guilty and sentenced to life imprisonment.[79] Barbie's trial is an example of national courts holding génocidaires accountable decades after the offense. Most serious international crimes like genocide and crimes against humanity have no statute of limitation whereby defendants cannot be prosecuted after a certain amount of time has passed.

Gacaca Courts

Another example of national courts and local justice are the gacaca courts of Rwanda. Gacaca roughly translates to "justice on the grass." Historically gacaca was used as a way to settle disputes in the community without involving the formal legal system. Following the genocide, the ICTR was setup to prosecute the organizers of the genocide. But this left thousands of other defendants without a court.

In response, Rwanda adapted the gacaca system to prosecute génocidaires. The main goal of gacaca was to achieve truth, justice, and reconciliation.[80] With such goals, the court operated differently from traditional court systems. In gacaca it was expected that witness or victims would come forward to offer evidence. The defendant would have a chance to speak but no official lawyers were present.

Once the hearing was complete, defendants faced a range of sentences from prison to the more common restitution. Sometimes gacaca defendants would work on public works project helping the country rebuild its infrastructure as part of their sentence.

The gacaca system was not developed nor intended to handle such serious crimes. But when Rwanda realized that not every génocidaire could be tried at the ICTR or in their own state courts, they adapted the gacaca system. The informal nature of gacaca meant that there were no lawyers or legally trained judges and there were no rules of evidence.[81] These circumstances led many to criticize gacaca for lacking formal due process requirements.

While Rwanda recognized that gacaca was not the same as a formal legal system, they argued that it was a traditional method used for generations. Also, they argued that those countries trying to tell Rwanda how to prosecute its génocidaires, stood by and did nothing during the genocide. In the end, gacaca was a solution with mixed results. The system may have been far from perfect but for the time it did what Rwandans wanted, which was to hold people responsible for their behavior during the genocide.

What Can You Do

The most often asked question when faced with genocide is "what can I do?" or "I'm only one person, what power do I have?" It is true that as individuals we have less power than the United Nations or a state or other large groups. But individuals do have power, we just have to learn how to exercise it.

Most of us won't know about genocide until it reaches the news. But these events can quickly leave the news during a 24-hour news cycle. So one thing we can do is to encourage our news agencies to follow these stories and support those organizations that do so. We can write or call our local news agency and push them to cover these events.

Most of the nations of the world have a representative at the United Nations. These representatives work for their home country, but in many ways they work for the people of their country. We can contact our UN representatives and ask them to bring evidence forward to the UN to try and prevent or stop genocide.

Our greatest power lies in our voice and how we use it. When we learn about genocide we should educate others. We should talk to our friends and neighbors; we should contact our government representatives and demand action. We can use our social media voice as well to educate others around the world and hold those responsible accountable.

Whatever we decide to do we should do it loud and proud. We must be the voice for the voiceless, the eyes for the blind, and the ears to the deaf. We should never let the promise of "Never Again" be forgotten or ignored. We should take control of our voice and make it heard above the din of everything else to prevent even one death.

Over the years, the world has lost millions of human lives to the barbaric crime of genocide. It must always be remembered that genocide destroys more than just people, it can destroy a culture, a way of life. It may be politically correct to adhere to the idea of "Never Again," but we have all failed to follow through on that promise. As Martin Niemoller, the German Protestant pastor, wrote:

> In Germany they came first for the Communists
> And I did not speak out
> Because I was not a Communist.
> Then they came for the Socialists
> And I did not speak out
> Because I was not a Socialist.
> Then they came for the trade unionists

And I did not speak out
Because I was not a trade unionist.
Then they came for the Jews
And I did not speak out
Because I was not a Jew.
Then they came for me
And there was no one left
To speak out for me.[82]

We may not have the ability to save everyone from the horrors of genocide, but we should feel the obligation to do as much as we can to understand and prevent genocide. The Jewish Talmud tell us that "Whoever destroys a soul, it is considered as if he destroyed an entire world. And whoever saves a life, it is considered as if he saved an entire world."[83]

Conclusion

How we respond to genocide has been limited for many years. In most cases, the international community fails to prevent genocide and merely responds by punishing those most responsible for the genocide. This behavior is a failure under the UN Convention which speak to prevention and punishment. Our failure to prevent genocide has meant that many thousands have died while the world watched.

For nearly 50 years after the UN Convention on Genocide was passed, there was no court to hold génocidaires accountable. The UN established the ICTY and ICTR as a way to provide justice following genocide. These courts though were not permanent and were solely meant to address crimes committed during their respective wars/genocide. Only in the past 18 years has the ICC existed in an attempt to hold any wrongdoer accountable without the need for temporary courts.

The ICC has had limited success so far. Some member countries have criticized the court for targeting African nations in its prosecutions. Burundi withdrew from the ICC becoming the first state to do so.[84] The Philippines declared an interest in withdrawing after the Court began an investigation of the Philippian president.[85] Other countries have also expressed a potential for withdrawal including Gambia, South Africa, and Uganda.[86]

Whether these countries actually leave the Court remains to be seen. But the threat to withdraw shows how the ICC can only function when countries put their faith in the system. Using threats of withdrawal to influence how the Court operates will mean the Court is too weak to accomplish its goals.

At the end of the day, how we respond to genocide is a personal decision. Do we rely on the UN and the ICC to act? Do we support the Security Council and NATO in intervening when necessary? Or do we turn away and wait for genocide to end on its own? There is no simple answer and no single correct response, but the way we have responded to genocide so far has done little to prevent it in the future. That fact alone should indicate that we have not yet found the best response when faced with genocide.

Discussion Questions

1. Do you think NATO's bombing in Kosovo was legal? How does this action relate to the responsibility to protect?
2. What will you do when you hear about genocide happening? You should make a list of actions that you are going to take and compare with others.

Notes

1. Wilkens, Carl (2011). *I'm not leaving*. Spokane, WA: World Outside My Shoes.
2. Ibid. at 13.
3. United Nations Convention on Genocide, available at https://www.un.org/en/genocideprevention/documents/atrocity-crimes/Doc.1_Convention%20on%20the%20Prevention%20and%20Punishment%20of%20the%20Crime%20of%20Genocide.pdf
4. Ibid.
5. Guichaoua, André [translated by Don E. Webster] (2015). *From war to genocide: Criminal politics in Rwanda 1990–1994*. Madison, WI: The University of Wisconsin Press.
6. Ibid.
7. Ibid.
8. Ibid.
9. PBS (2004, April 1). *Ghosts of Rwanda*. PBS Frontline. https://www.pbs.org/wgbh/pages/frontline/shows/ghosts/etc/crontext.html
10. Des Forges, Alison (1999). *Leave none to tell the story: Genocide in Rwanda*. New York: Human Rights Watch.
11. Supra note 9.
12. Supra note 10 at 628.
13. Supra note 5.
14. Ibid. at xlv.
15. Supra note 5.
16. Ibid.
17. Ibid.
18. Ibid.
19. Supra note 9.

20. Ibid.
21. Yoshihara, Susan F. (2006). Kosovo. In Derek S. Reveron and Jeffrey S. Murer (eds.), *Flashpoints in the war on terrorism.* (pp. 65–86). New York: Routledge.
22. Mincheva, Lyubov G. and Gurr, Ted R. (2013). *Crime-terror alliances and the state: Ethnonationalist and Islamist challenges to regional security.* New York: Routledge.
23. Supra note 20.
24. NATO (n.d.). *What is NATO?* Available at https://www.nato.int/nato-welcome/index.html
25. Ibid.
26. Thorpe, Nick (2004, March 24). *UN Kosovo mission walks tightrope.* BBC News. http://news.bbc.co.uk/2/hi/europe/3565799.stm
27. CNN. (1999, April 24). *NATO reaffirms power to take action without UN approval.* Archived: https://web.archive.org/web/20150128045422/http://www.cnn.com/WORLD/europe/9904/24/nato.un/
28. United Nations (n.d.). *Responsibility to protect.* United Nations Office on Genocide Prevention and the Responsibility to Protect. https://www.un.org/en/genocideprevention/about-responsibility-to-protect.shtml
29. Ibid.
30. Ibid.
31. Ibid.
32. Global Centre for the Responsibility to Protect (n.d.). *What is R2P?* https://www.globalr2p.org/what-is-r2p/
33. Ibid.
34. Ibid.
35. Evans, Gareth (2008). The responsibility to protect: An idea whose time has come . . . and gone? *International Relations,* 22(3), 283–298.
36. Ibid.
37. Ibid.
38. Ibid.
39. Ibid.
40. United Nations (2011). Security Council Resolution 1973. Available at: https://www.undocs.org/S/RES/1973%20(2011)
41. International Coalition for the Responsibility to Protect (n.d.) The crisis in Libya. Available at: http://responsibilitytoprotect.org/index.php/crises/crisis-in-libya#violence
42. United Nations (1993). Security Council Resolution 827. Available at: file:///C:/Users/wpruitt/AppData/Local/Temp/S_RES_827(1993)-EN.pdf; United Nations (1994). Security Council Resolution 955. Available at: http://unscr.com/en/resolutions/doc/955
43. Ibid.
44. Ibid.
45. International Criminal Tribunal for Yugoslavia (August 2019). Key figures of the cases. Available at: https://www.icty.org/en/cases/key-figures-cases
46. Ibid.
47. Ibid.
48. ICTY (February 2012). War crimes opinion poll discussed in Serbia. Available at: https://www.icty.org/en/outreach/activities/war-crimes-opinion-poll-discussed-serbia
49. Skilbeck, Rupert (2008). Finding justice: The price of war crimes trials. *Human Rights*

Brief, 15(3), 6–10.
50. International Criminal Tribunal for Rwanda. (n.d.). The ICTR in Brief. Available at: https://unictr.irmct.org/en/tribunal
51. Ibid.
52. Pruitt, William R. (2014). Aggravating and mitigating sentencing factors at the ICTR—An exploratory analysis. *International Criminal Law Review*, 14, 148–176.
53. Ibid.
54. Human Rights Watch (December 23, 2015). Rwanda: International tribunal closing its doors. Available at: https://www.hrw.org/news/2015/12/23/rwanda-international-tribunal-closing-its-doors
55. Ibid.
56. Ibid.
57. Supra note 52.
58. See Schabas, William A. (2009). *Genocide in international law: The crime of crimes*. (2nd Ed.), Cambridge: Cambridge University Press, 101–112 for a discussion of the Rome Statute.
59. International Criminal Court (n.d.). The States Parties to the Rome Statute. Available at: https://asp.icc-cpi.int/en_menus/asp/states%20parties/Pages/the%20states%20parties%20to%20the%20rome%20statute.aspx
60. Novak, Andrew (2015). *The International Criminal Court: An Introduction*. New York: Springer.
61. International Criminal Court (n.d.). How the Court works. Available at: https://www.icc-cpi.int/about/how-the-court-works
62. Ibid.
63. Ibid.
64. Ibid.
65. Ibid.
66. Ibid.
67. Supra note 60.
68. Bazyler, Michael (2016). *Holocaust, genocide, and the law: A quest for justice in a post-Holocaust world*. Oxford: Oxford University Press.
69. Ibid.
70. Ibid.
71. Ibid.
72. Ibid.
73. Ibid.
74. Lipstadt, Deborah E. (2011). *The Eichmann trial*. New York: Shocken Books.
75. Ibid.
76. Ibid.
77. Watkins, Jr. John C. and Weber, John Paul (2006). *War crimes and war crime trials: From Leipzig to the ICC and beyond*. Durham, North Carolina: Carolina Academic Press.
78. Ibid.
79. Ibid.
80. BBC (18 June 2012). Rwanda 'gacaca' genocide courts finish work. Available at: https://www.bbc.com/news/world-africa-18490348

81. See ibid.; Human Rights Watch (31 May 2011). Justice compromised: The legacy of Rwanda's community-based gacaca courts. Available at: https://www.hrw.org/report/2011/05/31/justice-compromised/legacy-rwandas-community-based-gacaca-courts
82. Niemoller, Martin (n.d.). First they came. Available at: https://www.amnesty.org.uk/files/2019-01/First%20They%20Came%20by%20Martin%20Niem%C3%B6ller_0.pdf?l6HOtWW1N8umC_ELxnQI6NpaAYbxRCJj=
83. Babylonian Talmud, Sanhedrin 4:8 (37a).
84. Duerr, Benjamin (3 May 2018). Facing withdrawals, ICC must now rely on greater Security Council action. Global Observatory. Available at: https://theglobalobservatory.org/2018/05/withdrawals-icc-must-rely-security-council/
85. Ibid.
86. Ibid.

Useful Websites

You can visit the websites for the ICTY and ICTR to view their cases.
ICTY: https://www.icty.org/
ICTR: https://unictr.irmct.org/
You can also visit the ICC website to see the ongoing cases there: https://www.icc-cpi.int/

7 What Happens When Genocide Is Denied?

In Deborah Lipstadt's book Denying the Holocaust, *she called David Irving a Holocaust denier. Irving took offense to this label and sued her for damages in England. English libel laws state that the defendant (Lipstadt) must prove that her allegations were true. In the United States, however, the plaintiff (Irvinig) would have to prove that the statement was false.*

This legal maneuver may seem slight but it carries great consequences. Lipstadt was burdened with proving that Irving was a Holocaust denier and thus her statement was true. A trial was conducted which brought attention to both the issue of Holocaust denial and Irving's role in perpetuating it.

Ultimately, Lipstadt won in court and Irving was denounced as a Holocaust denier. But this case shows how difficult it can be to deal with genocide denial. We may never convince deniers that they are wrong. But our role may be instead to educate about the Holocaust and genocide in general to make denial even harder.

As we go through the laws on genocide denial, we will also cover some cases where the law has been put into practice. Some cases have been positive but other have had negative consequences. Are we prepared to deal with denial when we are confronted with it? If not, what should we do about that fact?

W. R. Pruitt, *An Introduction to the Criminology of Genocide*,
https://doi.org/10.1007/978-3-030-65211-1_7

Introduction

We have explored the horrors of genocide, the why, the who, the when, and the where. But one aspect that is often overlooked is the survivors. How do survivors continue their life and live with their losses after genocide? There are many ways that survivors might pursue in order to live with their experiences.

One way to help survivors is to create memorials and a history to share with others to serve as memory of what happened. The oft-quoted idea is that those who fail to learn from history are doomed to repeat it. If we fail to learn from genocide of the past are we doomed to repeat it in the future? Our examination of genocide over time shows that perhaps it is not quite so simple.

Genocide has continued, not because we failed to remember history, but for so many other reasons. This does not mean that we should forget the history of genocide but we should not rely on memory alone to act as prevention in the future.

Genocide denial carries with it a multitude of dangers. Denial alleges that something did not happen, did not exist, or is not true.[1] There are many ways to deny genocide from denying the event outright to attempting to change the way to view the genocide—not as genocide but as something else entirely.[2] But however denial occurs, at its most basic level, denial is an attempt to kill the truth.[3] The effects of denying the truth include impunity for perpetrators and a lack of awareness to recognize the reemergence of threatening behavior.[4] Denial perpetrates silence and if it is not confronted raises doubts about victims, survivors, and their descendants.[5]

When genocide is denied, the victims and survivors are being marginalized and rejected. They are being denied their status as a victim (remember the techniques of neutralization). Denying victims status can make it easier for future re-victimization including a repeat genocide.[6] Victim and survivor denial can also have the effect of shifting blame from the perpetrators to the victims. Denial of victim implies that the victims deserved what happened to them. If that were true, then the victims are transformed into instigators and agitators instead.

The Germans were able to turn the Jewish people into the enemy and then the Holocaust became self-defense.[7] Use of violence in self-defense is not abhorred but often condoned. Genocide denial can lead to victim denial which can lead to the reemergence of extermination. In the ten stages of genocide denial is the final stage.[8] Denial following a genocide is one of the "surest indicators of further genocidal massacres."[9]

Genocide denial is lying. Lying is dangerous because it contributes to creating a false consciousness. Genocide denial ignores facts, attempts to reduce or shift responsibility, and encourage impunity. These types of behavior lay the path for future genocides to be committed. Denial causes many negative consequences but perhaps the worst is the promotion of further genocide.

Holocaust Awareness

When considering genocide memory much research has been done on the Holocaust. The Holocaust represents a genocide which has been proven beyond a reasonable doubt. This does not mean that people have not questioned or denied the Holocaust. Research has shown that Holocaust awareness has been slipping recently.

Holocaust denial is not a new phenomenon. Denial was the reaction of many countries during World War II when word began to spread of the mass killings.[10] From world leaders to journalists to the average citizen, the attempted extermination of an entire race was unbelievable. Holocaust survivors testified to German troops taunting them saying that no one would believe their claims even before the end of the war.[11]

While Holocaust denial is not new it takes on a different dimension in a time when survivors and eyewitnesses are becoming harder to find. Soon the memory of the Holocaust will be left to be told by history alone. The disappearing first-hand accounts of the Holocaust provides an area for denial to flourish. A time will come when society will know of the Holocaust only through museums and memorials. Without first-hand accounts of the horrors history may turn an international tragedy into a localized memory.

In a survey of over 100 countries the Anti-Defamation League found that over one-third of respondents (35%) had never heard of the Holocaust.[12] Awareness of the Holocaust was below 50% in Asia, the Middle East and North Africa, and Sub-Saharan Africa.[13] Those same regions were also less likely to believe the historical account of the Holocaust.

Awareness of the Holocaust is only one step in the process of education. Deniers find space to grow when there is any chance to exploit perceived inconsistencies or confusion. So being aware of the Holocaust does not mean that respondents fully believed in the atrocities that happened.

Outside of Oceania (Australia and New Zealand), Western Europe had the lowest rate of respondents who believed the Holocaust was a myth or an exaggeration; only 11% of people surveyed believed this to be true.[14] North and South America (21%) and Eastern Europe (24%) saw lower rates than Asia (41%) and the Middle East and North Africa (63%). These statistics may reflect a political ideology that opposes Israel which thus extends to the Holocaust. The numbers may also reflect available education on the Holocaust in different regions.

In 2020, a study of the United States focused on younger individuals was released. The findings were disturbing to many. Across the United States, nearly half of millennials (born between 1981 and 1996) and generation Z (born between 1996 and 2015) could not name a single concentration or work camp.[15] Fifty-six percent were unable to identify Auschwitz-Birkenau.[16] Nationally, 63% of young people did not know 6 million Jews were murdered during the Holocaust.[17]

Regarding denial of the Holocaust, 49% have seen Holocaust denial or distortion posts on social media.[18] Fifty-six percent of respondents reported seeing Nazi symbols on social media or in their community.[19] Perhaps recognizing their own ignorance on certain elements of the Holocaust, 64% of millennials and generation Z believed that Holocaust education should be mandatory in school.[20]

But one should also ask whether the manner in which these nations, including the United States, treat Holocaust denial has any effect on these findings. Can a country help in spreading awareness of the Holocaust by taking a strong stance against denial and deniers? If the spread of denial can be contained perhaps the future of Holocaust awareness will not be a downward slide but instead serve to create a conscious knowledge of one of the world's most notorious crimes.

Denying History

Some countries have chosen to take a strong stand against denial. In many cases this is done to protect the memory of victims and survivors. The route taken by some countries to prevent the spread of genocide denial and to protect the memory of victims is to criminalize the act of denying. The criminal law and a criminal conviction thus place a stigma on the individual denier. Criminalizing genocide denial has been favored by many European nations. Of the 21 countries that criminalize denial, 18 of them are located in Europe.[21]

European countries interpretation of free speech versus human dignity might help explain their choice to criminalize denial. European countries tend to be more open to prohibiting speech when it reaches the level of hate speech. By doing so these countries are protecting the rights of individuals and groups to human dignity.[22]

Most European nations are based on the Civil Law system. In general, civil law nations tend to support protection of human dignity over free speech. Common law countries tend to favor free speech over human dignity.[23] But in both common law and civil law jurisdictions, the right of free speech has never been seen as absolute.[24]

Even the United States with the most expansive free speech protection places certain limits on speech. Certain types of speech including obscenity, defamation, fighting words, incitement, and threats are not protected by the First Amendment under freedom of speech.[25]

Predating the First Amendment in the United States Constitution, Article IV of the 1789 Declaration of the Rights of Man and of the Citizen states that "liberty consists in the freedom to do everything which injures no one else."[26] France used this limitation as the basis for its Holocaust denial law.[27] From the early recognition of individual rights, there have been some limitations on these rights. In that way one's rights only extend as far as the next person and cannot violate the next person's rights.

Beyond specific laws on genocide denial, some nations have laws on hate speech that are designed to protect group dignity. In Canada, section 319 of the criminal code forbids hate propaganda; this law has been used to punish genocide deniers. The Supreme Court of Canada found that this law was a permissible limitation on speech given the right of minority groups to protection against vilifying speech.[28] The court found that outlawing promotion of hatred was a justifiable limit on free expression since hate speech serves to harm the dignity of others and society as a whole.[29]

Constitutional interpretation and belief about free speech are important, but there are practical matters to legislation as well. The majority of countries with Holocaust/genocide denial laws were involved in the World War II and have a deep connection to the atrocities committed by the German regime.[30] This close connection may be one reason these countries have decided upon criminalizing denial of the Holocaust/genocide. A national memory scarred by the crime of genocide and other crimes of the German regime almost certainly prompted many countries to outlaw denial in hopes of avoiding reoccurrence.

Preserving national memory based on factual information is the right of every nation. Choosing to preserve the truth may justify the limitation on speech in certain circumstances.[31] When the nation's memory is composed of genocide and atrocity crimes there is valid reason to see preservation as a means to address previous wrongs and to move forward. In addition to addressing previous wrongs, protecting national memory also protects the vulnerable who could be swayed by the lies of genocide deniers. Those most vulnerable—the young, naïve, and misinformed—are shielded when deniers are labeled as liars and criminals [32]

The protection of institutional memory is not without controversy though. Through genocide denial laws, when deniers are tried and punished for their lies the collective memory is reaffirmed.[33] This intervention by the state can be perceived as being overbearing where the state is forcing people to remember in a certain way.[34] However, every country should at least acknowledge that the criminal law carries with it symbolic power to reinforce the nation's priorities and values. For those nations compelled to criminalize denial then, they must view genocide to be worthy of collectively remembering. This decision is important to many nations in order to protect the dignity and memory of those lost.

Genocide Denial Legislation

Criminalizing genocide denial is not something every country can do or is willing to do. This is true especially because a nation must balance free speech interests with protecting the dignity of others. This is not an easy balancing act to accomplish. Infringement on free speech can be overturned by most national and even **supranational courts**. If these laws are found to violate free speech protections then we are left with the freedom to deny genocide.

Supranational Courts

Supranational courts are those that have jurisdiction beyond one country but do not have international jurisdiction. The European Court of Human Rights is a supranational court with jurisdiction in the European Union but not beyond that area. ◄

Many countries treat genocide denial as hate speech, which allows for some limitations. But hate speech is treated differently around the world based on many factors.[35] On one end of the spectrum is the United States which has few, if any, limitations on hate speech. The US shows great deference to all speech in order to secure broad free speech protections. However, European countries like Germany and France have been shown to be more willing to criminalize hate speech. These proscriptions serve to protect a person's human dignity.[36] The European Convention on Human Rights protects free speech but does carve out an exception for the "protection of the reputation or rights of others."[37]

Balancing the protection of free speech with respect for human dignity, 21 countries currently criminalize genocide denial. The majority of these countries are in Europe: Andorra, Austria, Belgium, Czech Republic, France, Germany, Hungary, Latvia Liechtenstein, Luxembourg, Macedonia, Malta, Poland, Romania, Portugal, Slovakia, Slovenia, and Switzerland.[38] The majority of these countries also represent nations attacked and/or conquered by Hitler during the Second World War. This fact might supply a special incentive to protect the memory of the Holocaust and other crimes of the Nazi Socialist government.

Only three non-European countries currently ban genocide denial: Colombia, Israel, and Rwanda.[39] These countries too have had a deep and personal connection to genocide. The FARC in Colombia has used terroristic tactics to gain attention. While Israel did not exist during the Holocaust, as the nation-state for the Jewish people, the country has a special connection to the Holocaust. Finally, Rwanda experienced its own genocide in 1994 that left nearly one million dead. These reasons may have spurred legislation on denial to protect memory as well.

The main focus on these laws is on the act of denying genocide, but most countries with these laws have a broader emphasis. Of the 21 national laws, there are those that are very broad prohibiting many types of actions and those that are more narrowly written. Actions beyond denial that are also criminalized include minimization of a genocide, justification of a genocide, approval of genocide, and doubting a genocide.

The scope of these laws is also different from country to country. There are some laws that cover only the Holocaust of WWII, while other laws cover genocide in general, crimes against humanity, and war crimes. How one goes about performing the act is also important as most laws refer only to publicly made denials. However, the method in which the denial occurs can include writing, speech, publication, or other form of media such as images.

Criminal prosecutions for acts like minimizing, justifying, or approving a genocide are rare, but many countries still retain the right to prosecute individuals for such behavior. While a majority of denial occurs via writing or speech the other modes of communication mentioned above can bring liability in one country but not another.[40]

The principle of legality holds that a law must exist before a crime can occur. Also, all people must have fair notice so that they know what behavior is forbidden and what is allowed. Genocide denial laws can be broader that the name implies. If the public does not understand what the law covers they could violate the law even if they think their actions are protected.

Then there is the possibility that many people will not understand the true extent of these laws.[41]

Better knowledge of these laws and what behavior is outlawed should reduce confusion. These laws could assist other nations in writing domestic law to outlaw genocide denial. What actions one country wants to criminalize will depend on many things, but knowledge of what acts have been criminalized elsewhere is of use.

Denying

The common element of all genocide denial laws is the focus on denying a genocide—a historical fact. To deny genocide is to claim that it did not happen. In legal parlance, a denial is a rejection of an allegation of fact.[42] When evidence shows that a genocide has occurred and that fact is denied, the deniers are simply engaged in lying.[43] Lies often have negative consequences and genocide denial can result in negating victims and encouraging re-victimization.[44] For these reasons, some states have found it proper to criminally punish those who would deny history and attempt to reignite genocidal behavior.

However, not every country with denial laws agree on what cannot be denied. In general, there are four types of international crimes that are covered by these laws: the Holocaust specifically, genocide in general, crimes against humanity, and war crimes.[45] Among the countries criminalizing genocide denial, it may be more accurate to call them Holocaust denial laws. Eleven of the twenty-one nations (52.3%) restrict their denial legislation to the Holocaust (see Table 7.1).

Therefore, while these countries criminalize denial of the Holocaust they do not outlaw denial of other genocides like Armenia or Rwanda. The majority of countries restricting prohibition to the Holocaust do so because they had direct experience with the Holocaust.[46] This history could explain why they have limited their denial laws to cover only the Holocaust as it is the most salient memory they seek

Table 7.1 States criminalizing denial

	Holocaust	Genocide	Crimes against humanity	War crimes
Deny	Austria Belgium Czech Republic France Germany Israel Luxembourg Poland Romania Slovakia Slovenia	Andorra Hungary (Nazi) Latvia Liechtenstein Macedonia Malta Portugal Slovakia Slovenia Switzerland Rwanda	Austria (Nazi) Czech Republic (Nazi) France (Nazi) Germany (Nazi) Israel (Nazi) Latvia Liechtenstein Luxembourg (Nazi) Macedonia Malta Poland (Nazi) Portugal Slovakia Slovenia Switzerland	Czech Republic (Nazi) Germany (Nazi) Latvia Luxembourg (Nazi) Macedonia Malta Poland (Nazi) Portugal Slovakia Slovenia

to retain. But it means that denying other genocides is legal and sends a contradictory message.

Nine of the twenty-one nations with denial laws (42.8%) criminalize denying genocide in general.[47] (Table 7.1). These countries do not limit themselves to the Holocaust alone. This number could rise to ten depending on the interpretation of Portugal's law. The somewhat vague statute criminalizes "denial of war crimes or against peace and humanity."[48] It seems reasonable to assume that genocide is a crime against humanity and therefore covered by Portugal's law. Interestingly, Portugal is the only country banning denial that does not use the word genocide.

These countries have also experienced first-hand the consequences of the Holocaust. But they have chosen to criminalize genocide denial of any genocide. One possible explanation for this broader protection is due to what other behavior the country is seeking to outlaw at the same time. In addition to outlawing denial of fact, some countries may be attempting to limit racial hatred. Genocide denial is too often motivated by animus and hatred based on race, ethnicity, or religion.[49] There are at least five countries that criminalize genocide denial as a way to prevent discrimination.[50]

For example, Switzerland's denial law can be found under the heading of racial discrimination. Their law forbids denying genocide when it is done as a way to racially, ethnically, or religiously demean or discriminate.[51] Slovenia also outlaws denial when done to "provoke[ ] or stir[ ] up ethnic, racial, religious or other hatred."[52] Similarly, Malta, Portugal, and Slovakia prohibit genocide denial when the intent is to discriminate or to incite violence.[53] Macedonia increases the punishment for genocide denial when done to discriminate or incite violence.[54] Denying genocide without intent to discriminate results in a punishment of one to five years, but if the denial is done to discriminate then the punishment is at least four years.[55]

The remaining countries criminalize denial of genocide regardless of intent. Our question from Chap. 1 remerges here as to what qualifies as genocide for denial purposes. There is no specific or common limiting principle on what qualifies as genocide. There is no requirement that a legal judgment of genocide exists. Language found in the laws includes "facts described as genocide," "implemented genocide," "stating or explaining that genocide is not genocide."[56] If we cannot define genocide, how can we know what we cannot deny?

So what remains unclear is whether denying the Armenian genocide would qualify under these laws since there was never a legal determination of genocide but scholarly opinion calls it genocide. A more difficult example might be the Native indigenous population in the United States, Canada, or Australia. Scholarly opinion is not as unified in these cases but many believe the eradication of this population to qualify as genocide. Whether these countries outlaw denying the indigenous population as genocide is not obvious. It may have seemed less likely that these nations would face this question because these examples are farther removed from them personally.

Many countries criminalize denial of crimes against humanity in addition to denial of the Holocaust/genocide. Currently 15 nations prohibit denial of crimes against humanity. Seven of these countries limit the law to crimes against humanity committed by the Nazi regime. The countries choosing to limit the scope of their laws to Nazi crimes against humanity were all touched by those crimes (see Table 7.1). The remaining eight nations forbid denying any crimes against humanity in a much broader sense.

Common language in these laws refer to "genocide or other crimes against humanity."[57] Slovakia specifically references both crimes against humanity in general and those committed by the Nazi regime. Slovakia considers any crime that satisfies the definition set forth by the International Criminal Court as a crime against humanity.[58] Malta only proscribes denying crimes against humanity when it is done to incite violence based on race, nationality, origin, or religion.[59] The scope of Malta's law is narrowed significantly by adding this limitation. This specific intent requirement could act as a safeguard for those who fear government overreach.

One more commonality among denial laws is that ten countries prohibited denial of war crimes in addition to other acts. Four counties limit the war crimes committed by the Nazi regime.[60]

While the name genocide denial implies that these laws cover only genocide, they in fact cover much more than simply denial. Many laws carry the same punishment for denying crimes against humanity or war crimes as they do for genocide denial, contrast to those broader laws with the laws of nation that limit their legislation to cover only Nazi-related crimes and genocide. Why would some countries want to criminalize genocide and crime against humanity denial while others would limit that scope to Nazi-related crimes?

As an example, in Austria a person is prohibited from denying the Holocaust or other Nazi-related crimes against humanity. The likely goal of Austria's laws is the prevention of the resurgence of Nazism, so the limiting factor may be logical. Conversely, across the border in Liechtenstein, a person is forbidden from denying any genocide or any crime against humanity. This prohibition covers a much broader scope of acts including the Armenian genocide, the Rwandan genocide, the massacres of Srebrenica, and more. This coverage appears to be more concerned with protection of human dignity in general. Are there any reasons why Liechtenstein might have gone for broader coverage?

Public Versus Private Denial

It may seem obvious that criminal activity usually occurs in public, but there are times when it can occur in private and thus may not be punishable. There was a well-known debate in the 1960s between Patrick Devlin and H.L.A. Hart. They argued over whether criminal behavior had to occur in public in order to be criminalized or if it could also occur in private. Devlin strongly believed our behavior in both public and private could violate the law.[61] His reasoning relied on the theory that private conduct could offend the morals of society equally as public conduct.[62]

On the other side of the debate, Hart disagreed with this position and aligned himself with John Stuart Mill's harm principle. Mill's argument was that society should only be concerned with behavior that poses a direct harm to others.[63] This direct harm to others implies that private conduct does not always have a direct impact on others. In those cases, the law should not concern itself with private behavior not causing harm. Most nations have followed the harm principle. In doing so they have required genocide denial behavior to occur in public and thus have a greater likelihood of harming others before criminal liability attaches. There would likely be few occurrences where denial in private would directly harm someone.

The vast majority of the states require the denial to occur in public. Twenty of the states with denial legislation restrict coverage to publicly occurring acts.[64] The only exceptions being Israel and Colombia. Israel covers denial occurring in writing, by word of mouth, or publication but nowhere in the law is it required that these acts occur in public.[65] We could assume that a publication or act in writing would very likely be public. However, the law could also conceivably cover speech in private situations as it is written now.

An example of public and private behavior may be helpful. In 2005, the United States Congress passed the Stolen Valor Act which made it a criminal act to falsely claim to have won a military medal. This law is an example of limiting free speech to preserve the memory of fallen soldiers. The law was also silent on whether the act had to occur in public or private. At a public meeting, Xavier Alvarez claimed to have won the Congressional Medal of Honor.[66] As a result of his speech, he was convicted of violating the Stolen Valor Act. Alvarez successfully challenged the law as a violation of his free speech rights. In finding the law unconstitutional, the United States Supreme Court mentioned, among other reasons, that there was no distinction made between public and private speech in the law.[67] If the law were upheld, it could have penalized speech that occurred within one's own home without proof of harm. The Supreme Court did not believe this was a proper use of the criminal law.

Unlike most other countries with denial legislation, Israel's denial law appears to allow denial to be punished whether it is done in public or private. This broad scope of coverage would certainly concern those who see denial legislation as a violation of free speech. Both Amnesty International and Human Rights Watch have criticized Rwanda's genocide denial law based on the fear of inappropriate prosecution as we will see below.[68] In response, Rwanda amended the law to include that acts must be done in public—a way of ensuring that harm exists prior to prosecution.[69] For those countries considering denial legislation, the requirement of a public act may assuage some concerns over the reach of the government in private conduct.

The denial law in Colombia does not appear to recognize a distinction between acts done in private and public. However, Colombia's law is relatively vague and interpretation is important. Colombia criminalizes spreading ideas or doctrines by any means.[70] One possible interpretation here is that the law applies to publicly done acts because to spread usually means to make widely known; making something widely known would imply that it was or became public. Though to avoid such ambiguity, the law's language should be made clearer.

Removing Israel and Colombia, the remaining countries with denial legislation clearly and unambiguous require that the act be done in public. Many of the laws begin with language stating "whoever publicly." Eight countries begin with the "whoever publicly" language including Germany, Hungary, Liechtenstein, Malta, Poland, Slovakia, Slovenia, and Switzerland.[71] This opening clearly requires the action to be done publicly. This type of clear language is important for the criminal law so that we know what behavior is punishable.

Those countries not using the "whoever publicly" language do explicitly state somewhere in the law that the act must be in public before liability attaches. This requirement protects against prosecution for people who commit genocide denial in private. But since most private denial will not cause harm to someone the limitation makes sense.

Genocide denial laws, however, are only as good as the use made of them. Over the years there have been examples of court cases which some would call proper uses and other cases that would be deemed inappropriate uses. We will look at example from both categories to analyze how denial laws are used in operation.

Effective Uses of Denial Laws

Ernst Zündel is a German publisher known for his Holocaust denial. In 2005 he was charged by German prosecutors with 14 counts of inciting racial hatred. He faced up to five years in prison. The indictment claimed that Zündel denied the Holocaust and said the deaths in Auschwitz and Treblinka were an invention of the Jewish people.

The prosecutor presented Zündel's own writings to prove his Holocaust denial calling him a political con man. The court found Zündel guilty under the German law prohibiting incitement of hatred against a minority population. Zündel's Holocaust denial was viewed as causing incitement of hatred against the Jewish population in Germany; he was sentenced to five years in prison.

While this prosecution did not change Zündel's mind about the Holocaust, it showed the public that Holocaust denial would not be tolerated. The case also made a clear connection between Holocaust denial and racial hatred. A precedent had been set that denying the Holocaust was equivalent to racial hatred against the Jewish people. This case may be seen has a positive use of denial laws to act as a **general deterrence** for others.

General Deterrence

General deterrence is a criminal justice purpose of punishing people. In general deterrence we hope to deter other people from committing the same offense because they saw someone else get punished for it. ◄

In France the Gayssot Act was passed in 1990 which bans Holocaust denial. Robert Faurisson, a French academic, was a Holocaust denier. In 1991, Faurisson was removed from his position as university chair because of his denial claims under the Gayssot Act.

After his conviction under the Gayssot Act, Faurisson challenged the law as a violation of his free speech rights. The United Nations Human Rights Committee upheld the Gayssot Act because it served to protect the respect of the Jewish community "to live free from fear."[72] Having upheld the law, the UN Human Rights Commission gave its permission to limit some speech when done to protect a minority group.

In 2005, Faurisson did an interview with Sahar 1—an Iranian television station. During the interview he reiterated his Holocaust denial beliefs. As a result he was charged with Holocaust denial again. After being convicted, he was given a three-month probationary sentence and fined 7500 euros. As can be seen with Faurisson, convicting him of Holocaust denial did not change his views, but it did give the Human Rights Commission the opportunity to explain when denial laws would be permitted to restrict some speech.

David Irving denied the Holocaust in two speeches given in 1989 in Austria. The Austrian government issued an arrest warrant for him and prohibited him from entering the country. The warrant went unenforced for 16 years. Then in 2005, Irving was arrested based on the 1989 warrant.

In court Irving pled guilty to the charge of trivializing and denying the Holocaust. He was sentenced to three years' imprisonment. Irving was also charged with Holocaust denial in Germany in 1992. He was barred from entering the country after his conviction. In 2007, he was expelled from the Warsaw International Book Fair due to his materials which were deemed to promote Nazism and anti-Semitism. Promotion of Nazism and anti-Semitism violates Polish law similar to its denial law.

What these cases share in common is denial of proven historical facts. Each offender was sentenced according to the country's law at the time and none of the offenders changed their viewpoints. But the goal of these laws has been to protect memory and respect for the dead and survivors. With those goals in mind, these prosecutions could be said to have accomplished what they set out to do.

By punishing Holocaust/genocide denial the public is further reminded of the horrors of the event. This reinforces the memory of the events and does not allow for the public to ignore or forget what happened. Punishing deniers also shows survivors and victims that they are not forgotten. Protection of victims and survivors is important to prevent reoccurrence of genocide.

Problematic Uses of Denial Laws

Unfortunately, while there have been cases where use of denial laws has served its purpose, the law can be misused by unscrupulous individuals. The following cases show that genocide denial laws can also not serve the purpose they were intended to. And instead be sued as a weapon against those not in favor with the government.

Following the Rwandan genocide, Victoire Ingabire returned to the country to run for president. During a visit to a genocide memorial, Ingabire noted that the memorial did not acknowledge the Hutus who died during the genocide. While Tutsis were the primary target, many moderate Hutus who refused to participate were also killed. Her speech was labeled genocide denial and revisionism.

As a result, she was charged with genocide denial under Rwanda's stringent denial legislation. In 2012, she was sentenced to eight years' imprisonment. In

2013, the Rwandan Supreme Court upheld her conviction and increased the sentence to 15 years. In 2018, **President Paul Kagame** granted her early release after spending at least six years in prison.

Paul Kagame

Paul Kagame was leader of the Rwandan Patriotic Front (RPF) in 1994 during the genocide. The RPF was the force that stopped the genocide when no one else would intervene. Kagame was seen as a national hero for his work stopping the genocide.

He became president following the end of the genocide. Since then he has become an authoritarian ruler expanding his power to control almost every aspect of life in Rwanda. The Rwandan constitution was rewritten a few years ago to permit Kagame to stay in power for three more decades. ◄

Many observers believe that Ingabire was targeted for prosecution not because of her genocide denial but because of her attempt to run for president. In fact, her statement about Hutu victims was not denial of what happened but recognition of all victims who died in the genocide. The decision to prosecute Ingabire was less about genocide denial and more about protecting the then-president from having to face opposition in the election.

Ingabire was represented in her genocide denial case by Peter Erlinder. Erlinder had served as defense counsel at the International Criminal Tribunal for Rwanda. When Erlinder entered Rwanda to serve as counsel for Ingabire, he was arrested for genocide denial. The government claimed that Erlinder had engaged in conspiracy theories and denial about the circumstances of the genocide.

After his arrest, it was claimed that Erlinder had said that no Tutsis were killed by Hutus. After three weeks of international pressure, Erlinder was released on bail. No trial was ever conducted. Again, the goal here appeared to be less about protect of memory and survivors and more about frightening Erlinder away from defending Ingabire.

The attempted prosecution of Peter Erlinder was seen as an abuse of power by most nations. The right to counsel is a fundamental right in almost every country in the world. Trying to intimidate defense counsel from doing their job violates the rights of the defendant and her counsel. Even though the prosecution never occurred, the optic of the arrest and imprisonment of Erlinder was not good for Rwanda. It gave further evidence of improper use of genocide denial laws to target those not favored by the government.

The final example of a bad use of genocide denial laws is Turkey's Article 301. Turkish law makes it a crime to insult the Turkish people or state. This has been interpreted to mean that recognizing the Armenian genocide violates the law. In some ways, this law does not prohibit denial as much as require denial of the Armenian genocide.

The law has been used to prosecute 60 writers and journalists. Nobel prize-winning author Orhan Pamuk was charged under Article 301 after telling a Swiss newspaper that no one in Turkey dared to mention the Armenian genocide. An Armenian parliament member gave a speech about the Armenian, Christian, and Greek lives lost to genocide. He was censured by the Parliament, barred from three sessions, and fined for his speech.

Again we see denial laws being used to target dissents and government opponents. These prosecutions do nothing to protect the memory of the event or the survivors or victims. These cases are examples of how law can be abused by those in power. The question though is whether some abuse of power should stop countries from passing genocide denial laws.

The positives of denial legislation include prevention of reoccurrence by maintaining memory of the event and its horrors. Also, by remembering these events we honor the victims and survivors and their struggle to return to a "normal" life. Finally, as time goes on, first-hand accounts of genocide will cease to exist, denial laws help retain historical accuracy by reinforcing the facts.

On the other hand, there are drawbacks to denial legislation. The primary issue is the restriction of free speech. While free speech is very important, the Human Rights Commission recognized that protection of minority populations is so important that it could limit some speech. As we saw in Rwanda, political targeting of enemies is an abuse of the law that could happen.

How can the law draw distinction between the positives and negatives of denial legislation? Should limits be placed on prosecutions? And if so, what are these limits? These questions remain when we discuss genocide denial laws. Exploring the possible answers may be just as useful as settling upon a final decision.

> **Critical Thinking Exercise** Research your country's laws about genocide denial, if any. Should your state criminalize denial? What benefits would your nation obtain by doing so?

Denial Legislation Goals

In 1988, US President Ronald Reagan said that "facts are stupid things."[73] More recently, on National Public Radio, it was said, "There's no such thing, unfortunately, anymore as facts."[74] When high-ranking politicians can claim that facts are stupid or simply don't exist, the need to protect history and memory rises in importance. Genocide denial legislation is one way to protect facts from false attacks and repetition of horrendous acts of cruelty against humankind.

If an event the magnitude of the Holocaust can be denied in its entirety it is not much of a stretch to deny the intentions and motivations of the perpetrators.[75] Once the facts of genocide have been deemed to be false or denied outright, a path to reoccurrence emerges. It should not be forgotten that words have power. Words can have the effects of bullets.[76] The Genocide Convention recognizes this fact by criminalizing the public incitement to genocide as a separate, punishable offense.[77] If words can have this great influence and power then it becomes reasonable to prohibit genocide denial because denial could lead to the re-emergence of the crime in future generations.[78]

There are other reasons to criminalize denial as well; these include protection of human dignity and limiting the scope of hate speech.[79] Any state considering passing denial laws should consider the purpose of the law and the scope. As has been seen, some countries are rather narrow in what actions are prohibited while others are much broader in coverage. Any nation looking to pass such legislation needs to assess both what actions are forbidden and the purposes of outlawing denial.

While it is important to establish the purpose and goals of denial laws, it must be remembered that genocide denial is a blatant lie with the potential to cause serious effects. Often, genocide denial is based on bigotry and hatred. Denial of genocide also attempts to change the role of victim and perpetrator. One goal of denial may be to deny survivors the status as victim. Denial of victim is a technique of neutralization that often permits individuals to continue to victimize others because they actively deny that there is a victim.[80] At the individual level, denial of victim could allow perpetrators to ease their feelings of inhibition enough to commit crime, then this denial may serve as an early indicator of genocide reprisal.

As we saw in Chap. 2, there are other techniques of neutralization involved in denial: denial of responsibility and denial of injury. Genocide denial often involves denial of responsibility (Turkey refuses to acknowledge responsibility for destruction of the Armenian population) or denial of injury (no Jews or fewer than 6 million were killed). By criminalizing denial, states have decided that lying has such negative consequences that it should be prevented by the force of law.

A country may choose to go narrow in coverage like Romania: "Denial of the Holocaust in public, or to the effects thereof is punishable by imprisonment from 6 months to 5 years and the loss of certain rights."[81] Or a country may choose to go broad in coverage like Liechtenstein: "Whoever publicly denies, coarsely trivializes, or tries to justify genocide or other crimes against humanity via word, writing, pictures, electronically transmitted signs, gestures, violent acts or by other means shall by punished with imprisonment for up to two years."[82]

No matter how a state chooses to criminalize denial, the message is the same: public denial of historical fact will not be accepted. The side benefits of such laws include protection of the victims, protection of memory, and ideally prevention of future atrocities.

Conclusion

Denying genocide is but one way to forget history and remove the label of victim from survivors. When done with malice, denial can even permit reoccurrence of genocide in the future. As we have seen, some countries have decided to use their criminal law to punish those who engage in genocide denial.

One goal seems to be remembrance of historical events. This does not allow for individuals to deny what happened or to lie about their responsibility in the acts. Another goal appears to be to protect the memory of victims and survivors. When victims and survivors can be denied the possibility of "othering" can continue. If we forget history and continue to other the victims, it becomes clear how genocide could reoccur.

Following the Holocaust there were cries of "Never Forget." The world promised that they would never forget what happened to powerless victims during World War II. Unfortunately, similar to the cry of "Never Again," the promise of "Never Forget" has had some difficulty in maintaining that goal. But the use of genocide denial laws has been one way in which to attempt to fulfill that promise.

The best way to avoid genocide denial is through education. If people were educated on genocide and its devastating effects, it would be harder, though not impossible, to deny its occurrence. There are many motives that might go into genocide denial (refer back to Chap. 5 and the discussion of Aung San Suu Kyi for one example). But regardless of the motivation, the goal is the same—to deny history and attack memory.

The greater the education on genocide, the more difficult genocide denial becomes to maintain. When memory is preserved, the risk of reoccurrence is lessened because the memory of the horrors remains. Preserving memory also protects the victims and survivors and their stories long after they are gone. History and memory can fade, but we can never let denial allow us to forget the devastation of genocide and its long-lasting effects on everyone involved.

Discussion Questions

1. Should genocide denial be a criminal offense punishable by imprisonment? Why or why not?
2. Do you think denial laws protect the memory of genocide or are an impermissible limitation on free speech?
3. After seeing how genocide denial laws might be used in a negative or persecution way, can you think of ways to limit the use of these laws to ensure they are not used in such ways?

Notes

1. Cohen, Stanley (2001). *States of denial: Knowing about atrocities and suffering.* Cambridge: Polity Press.
2. Ibid.
3. Charny, Israel W. (2000). Innocent denials of known genocide: A further contribution to a psychology of denial of genocide. *Human Rights Review,* 1, 15–39.
4. Ibid.
5. Nash-Marshall, Siobhan and Mahdessian, Rita. (2013). Lies, damned lies, and genocide. *Metaphilosophy*, 44(1–2), 116–144.
6. Etlis, Karen (2008). A Constitutional right to deny and promote genocide? Preempting the usurpation of human rights discourse towards incitement from a Canadian perspective. *Cardozo Journal of Conflict Resolution*, 9, 463–477.
7. Alvarez, Alexander (1997). Adjusting to genocide: The techniques of neutralization and the Holocaust. *Social Science History*, 21(2), 139–178.
8. Stanton, Gregory (2016). The ten stages of genocide. Genocide Watch. Retrieved from https://www.genocidewatch.com/ten-stages-of-genocide
9. Ibid.
10. Power, Samantha (2002). *"A problem from hell": America and the age of genocide.* New York: Harper Perennial.
11. Knechtle, John C. (2008). Papers from the First Amendment discussion group: Holocaust denial and the concept of dignity in the European Union. *Florida State University Law Review*, 36, 41–65.
12. Anti-Defamation League (2014 [2019]). The Holocaust—Global awareness and denial. Retrieved from https://global100.adl.org/map?_ga=2.120615240.1331736242.1592934163-1412535895.1592934163
13. Ibid.
14. Ibid.
15. PRNewswire (September 16, 2020). First-ever 50 state survey on Holocaust knowledge of American Millennials and Gen Z reveals shocking results. Available at: https://www.prnewswire.com/news-releases/first-ever-50-state-survey-on-holocaust-knowledge-of-american-millennials-and-gen-z-reveals-shocking-results-301131874.html

16. Ibid.
17. Ibid.
18. Ibid.
19. Ibid.
20. Ibid.
21. Pruitt, William R. (2017). Understanding genocide denial legislation: A comparative analysis. *International Journal of Criminal Justice Sciences*, 12(2), 270–284.
22. Supra note 11.
23. Smith, Roger (2010). Legislating against genocide denial: Criminalizing denial or preventing free speech? *Journal of Law and Public Policy,* 4(2), 128–137.
24. McGoldrick, Dominic & O'Donnell, Therese (2006). Hate speech laws: Consistency with national and international human rights law. *Legal Studies,* 18(4), 453–485.
25. Supra note 11.
26. Weaver, Russell L., Delpierre, Nicolas, & Boissier, Laurence (2009). Holocaust denial and governmentally declared "truth": French and American perspectives. *Texas Tech Law Review*, 41, 495–517, 506.
27. Ibid.
28. Supra note 6.
29. Ibid.
30. Supra note 21.
31. Smiddy, Linda O. (2006). An essay on Professor Fronza's paper: Should Holocaust denial be criminalized? *Vermont Law Review*, 30, 645–653.
32. Bloch, Pascale (2006). Response to Professor Fronza's "The punishment of negationism." *Vermont Law Review,* 30, 627–643.
33. Fronza, Emanuela (2006). The punishment of negationism: The difficult dialogue between law and memory. *Vermont Law Review*, 30, 609–626.
34. Ibid.
35. Supra note 6.
36. Supra note 26.
37. Supra note 24 at 467.
38. Supra note 21.
39. Ibid.
40. Ibid.
41. Ibid.
42. Black, Henry C. (1968). *Black's Law Dictionary* (4th ed.). St Paul, MN: West Publishing.
43. Supra note 3.
44. Supra note 23.
45. Ibid.
46. Ibid.
47. Ibid.
48. Lechtholz-Zey, Jacqueline (2012). The laws banning Holocaust denial. *Genocide Prevention Now*, 9, 9–10.
49. Gorton, S. (2015). The uncertain future of genocide denial laws in the European Union. *George Washington International Law Review*, 47, 421–445.

50. Supra note 21.
51. Supra note 42.
52. Na'amat, T. and Deutch, I. (n.d.). Legislating against Anti-Semitism and Holocaust denial. *Kantor Center for the study of contemporary European Jewry.*
53. Supra note 48.
54. Supra note 52.
55. Ibid.
56. Supra notes 48 and 52.
57. Supra note 48.
58. Ibid.
59. Supra note 48.
60. Supra note 21.
61. Devlin, Patrick (1977). Moral and the criminal law. In K. Kipnis (ed.), *Philosophical issues in law*. Englewood Cliffs, NJ: Prentice Hall.
62. Ibid.
63. Mill, John S. (1981). On liberty. In M. Curtis (ed.), *The great political theories*. New York: Avon Books.
64. Supra note 21.
65. Supra note 48.
66. United States v. Alvarez, (2012). 567 U.S. 709.
67. Ibid.
68. Uwizeyimana, D. (2014). Aspects and consequences of the Rwandan law of genocide ideology: A comparative analysis. *Mediterranean Journal of Social Sciences*, 5(23), 2370–2379.
69. Ibid.
70. Colombia penal code, Article 102.
71. Supra note 48.
72. Robert Faurisson v. France, Communication No. 550/1993. UN Doc. CCPR/C/58/D/550/1993(1996). Available at: http://hrlibrary.umn.edu/undocs/html/550-1993.html
73. Gey, S. G. (2008). The First Amendment and the dissemination of socially worthless untruths. *Florida State University Law Review*, *36*, 1–22: 1.
74. Huppke, R. (2016). In fact-free America, maybe millions of Trump supporters voted twice. *Chicago Tribune.* Retrieved from https://www.chicagotribune.com/columns/rex-huppke/ct-trump-illegal-votes-huppke-20161205-story.html
75. Charney, I. W. (2000). Innocent denials of known genocides: A further contribution to a psychology of denial of genocide. *Human Rights Review*, 1(3), 15–39.
76. Salomon, T. (2007). Freedom of speech v. hate speech: The jurisdiction of 'direct and public incitement to commit genocide.' In R. Henham and P. Behrens (Eds.), *The criminal law of genocide: International, comparative and contextual aspects*. Burlington, VT: Ashgate.
77. Ibid.
78. Supra note 21.

79. Tsesis, A. (2009). Dignity and speech: The regulation of hate speech in a democracy. *Wake Forest Law Review,* 44, 497–532.
80. Supra note 66.
81. Romania emergency ordinance no. 31, Article 6.
82. Liechtenstein penal code, Article 283.

Further Reading

"Genocide denial concerns us all" available at: https://www.dw.com/en/opinion-genocide-denial-concerns-us-all/a-54089948

You can review a collection of articles on genocide denial here: https://theconversation.com/us/topics/genocide-denial-8088

Bibliography

Adalian, R. P. (2004). The Armenian genocide. In S. Totten, W. S. Parson, & I. W. Charny (Eds.), *Century of genocide* (Critical essays and eyewitness accounts) (2nd ed., pp. 53–92). New York: Routledge.

Agnew, R. (2010). A general strain theory of terrorism. *Theoretical Criminology, 14*(2), 131–153.

Aljazeera. (2019). *Former UN chief says Bangladesh cannot continue hosting Rohingya*. Retrieved at https://www.aljazeera.com/news/2019/07/chief-bangladesh-continue-hosting-rohingya-190710191318011.html

Alonzo-Maizlish, D. (2002). In whole or in part: Group rights, the intent element of genocide, and the 'quantitative criterion'. *New York University Law Review, 77*, 1369–1403.

Alvarez, A. (1997). Adjusting to genocide: The techniques of neutralization and the holocaust. *Social Science History, 21*(2), 139–178.

Alvarez, A. (2010). *Genocidal crimes*. New York: Routledge.

Anderson, K. (2018). *Perpetrating genocide: A criminological account*. London: Routledge.

Anti-Defamation League. (2014 [2019]). *The Holocaust—Global awareness and denial*. Retrieved from https://global100.adl.org/map?_ga=2.120615240.1331736242.1592934163-1412535895.1592934163

Arendt, H. (1963). *Eichmann in Jerusalem: A report on the banality of evil*. New York: Penguin Books.

Barkan, S. E., & Snowden, L. L. (2001). *Collective violence*. Boston: Allyn and Bacon.

Barta, T. (2005). Mr. Darwin's shooters: On natural selection and the naturalizing of genocide. *Patterns of Prejudice, 39*(2), 116–137.

Bazyler, M. (2016). *Holocaust, genocide, and the law: A quest for justice in a post-holocaust world*. Oxford: Oxford University Press.

BBC. (2012, June 18). *Rwanda 'gacaca' genocide courts finish work*. Available at: https://www.bbc.com/news/world-africa-18490348

BBC News. (2018). *Myanmar profile-Timeline*. Retrieved at https://www.bbc.com/news/world-asia-pacific-12992883

W. R. Pruitt, *An Introduction to the Criminology of Genocide*,
https://doi.org/10.1007/978-3-030-65211-1

BBC News. (2020). *Myanmar Rohingya: What you need to know about the crisis*. Retrieved at https://www.bbc.com/news/world-asia-41566561

Beachler, D. (2007). The politics of genocide scholarship: The case of Bangladesh. *Patterns of Prejudice, 41*(5), 467–492.

Black, H. C. (1968). *Black's law dictionary* (4th ed.). St Paul: West Publishing.

Bloch, P. (2006). Response to Professor Fronza's "The punishment of negationism". *Vermont Law Review, 30*, 627–643.

Braithwaite, J. (1989). Criminological theory and organizational crime. *Justice Quarterly, 6*(3), 333–358.

Brannigan, A. (1998). Criminology and the holocaust: Xenophobia, evolution and genocide. *Crime and Delinquency, 44*(2), 257–277.

Brannigan, A. (2013). *Beyond the banality of evil: Criminology and genocide*. Oxford: Oxford University Press.

Brannigan, A., & Hardwick, K. H. (2003). Genocide and general theory. In C. L. Britt & M. R. Gottfredson (Eds.), *Control theories of crime and delinquency* (pp. 109–131). New Brunswick: Transaction.

Brants, C. (2006). Gold-collar crime: The peculiar complexities and ambiguities of war crimes, crimes against humanity, and genocide. In H. N. Pontell & G. Geis (Eds.), *International handbook of white-collar and corporate crime* (pp. 309–326). New York: Springer.

Bridgman, J., & Worley, W. S. (2004). Genocide of the Hereros. In S. Totten, W. S. Parsons, & I. Charney (Eds.), *Century of genocide* (Critical essays and eyewitnesses accounts) (2nd ed., pp. 15–51). New York: Routledge.

Brkic, C. A. (2007). Justice denied in Bosnia. *Dissent, 54*, 19–22.

Brown, C. (1997). Theories of international justice. *British Journal of Political Science, 27*(2), 273–297.

Brown, S. E. (2018). *Gender and the genocide in Rwanda: Women as rescuers and perpetrators*. New York: Routledge.

Browning, C. (1992). *Ordinary men: Reserve police battalion 101 and the final solution in Poland*. New York: Harper Perennial.

Campbell, B. (2015). *The geometry of genocide: A study in pure sociology*. Charlottesville: University of Virginia Press.

Carmichael, C. (2006). Violence and ethnic boundary maintenance in Bosnia in the 1990s. *Journal of Genocide Research, 8*(3), 283–293.

Chalk, F., & Jonassohn, K. (1990). *The history and sociology of genocide: Analyses and case studies*. New Haven: Yale University Press.

Chambliss, W. J. (1989). State-organized crime: The American Society of Criminology, 1988 presidential address. *Criminology, 27*(2), 183–208.

Charny, I. (1994). Toward a generic definition of genocide. In G. A. Andreopoulous (Ed.), *Genocide: Conceptual and historical dimensions* (pp. 64–94). Philadelphia: University of Pennsylvania Press.

Charny, I. W. (2000). Innocent denials of known genocide: A further contribution to a psychology of denial of genocide. *Human Rights Review, 1*, 15–39.

Clark, R. S. (2001). Countering transnational and international crime: Defining the agenda. *Hume Papers on Public Policy, 6*, 20–29.

CNN. (1999, April 24). *NATO reaffirms power to take action without UN approval*. Archived: https://web.archive.org/web/20150128045422/http://www.cnn.com/WORLD/europe/9904/24/nato.un/

Cohen, S. (2001). *States of denial: Knowing about atrocities and suffering*. Cambridge: Polity Press.

Conversi, D. (2006). Demo-skepticism and genocide. *Political Studies Review, 4*, 247–262.

Council on Foreign Relations. (2020). *The Rohingya crisis*. Retrieved at https://www.cfr.org/backgrounder/rohingya-crisis

Cushman, T. (2003). Is genocide preventable? Some theoretical considerations. *Journal of Genocide Research, 5*(4), 523–542.

Dadrian, V. N. (1975). A typology of genocide. *International Review of Modern Sociology, 5*, 201–212.

Day, L. E., & Vandiver, M. (2000). Criminology and genocide studies: Notes on what might have been and what still could be. *Crime, Law, & Social Change, 34*, 43–59.

Devlin, P. (1977). Moral and the criminal law. In K. Kipnis (Ed.), *Philosophical issues in law*. Prentice Hall: Englewood Cliffs.

Drechsler, H. (1990). "Let us die fighting": The struggle of the Herero and the Nama against German imperialism (1884–1915). In F. Chalk & K. Jonassohn (Eds.), *The history and sociology of genocide: Analyses and case studies* (pp. 231–248). New Haven: Yale University Press.

Duerr, B. (2018, May 3). *Facing withdrawals, ICC must now rely on greater security council action. Global observatory*. Available at: https://theglobalobservatory.org/2018/05/withdrawals-icc-must-rely-security-council/

Durkheim, E. ([1895] 1982). *The rules of the sociological method.* Steven Lukes (Ed.) (trans: Halls, W. D.). New York: Free Press.

Dutton, D. G., Boyanowsky, E. O., & Bond, M. H. (2005). Extreme mass homicide: From military massacre to genocide. *Aggression and Violent Behavior, 10*, 437–473.

Ermann, M. D., & Lundman, R. J. (2002). Corporate and governmental deviance. In M. D. Ermann & R. J. Lundman (Eds.), *Corporate and governmental deviance: Problems of organizational behavior in contemporary society* (pp. 3–49). New York: Oxford University Press.

Etlis, K. (2008). A constitutional right to deny and promote genocide? Preempting the usurpation of human rights discourse towards incitement from a Canadian perspective. *Cardozo Journal of Conflict Resolution, 9*, 463–477.

Fein, H. (1990). Genocide: A sociological perspective. *Current Sociology, 38*, 1–126.

Fein, H. (1993). Accounting for genocide after 1945: Theories and some findings. *International Journal on Group Rights, 1*, 79–106.

Forges, D., & Alison. (1999). *Leave none to tell the story*. New York: Human Rights Watch.

Fournet, C. (2007). *The crime of destruction and the law of genocide: Their impact on collective memory*. Hampshire: Ashgate.

Fox, Nicole (2019). *Rwanda, genocide, and gender-based violence. Contexts· Sociology for the public*. Available at: https://contexts.org/blog/rwanda-genocide-and-gender-based-violence/

Fox, N., & Brehm, H. N. (2018). "I decided to save them": Factors that shaped participation in rescue efforts during genocide in Rwanda. *Social Forces, 96*(4), 1625–1648.

Freeman, M. (1991). The theory and prevention of genocide. *Holocaust and Genocide Studies, 6*(2), 185–199.

Friedrichs, D. O. (1996). Governmental crime, Hitler and white collar crime: A problematic relationship. *Caribbean Journal of Criminology and Social Psychology, 1*(2), 44–63.

Fronza, E. (2006). The punishment of negationism: The difficult dialogue between law and memory. *Vermont Law Review, 30*, 609–626.

Gey, S. G. (2008). The first amendment and the dissemination of socially worthless untruths. *Florida State University Law Review, 36*, 1–22.

Global Centre for the Responsibility to Protect. (n.d.). *What Is R2P?* https://www.globalr2p.org/what-is-r2p/

Glueck, S. (1944a). *War criminals: Their prosecution and punishment*. New York: Knopf.

Glueck, S. (1944b). *What shall be done with the war criminals? Pamphlet prepared for the American historical association's G.I.* Roundtable Series. Available at: https://www.historians.org/about-aha-and-membership/aha-history-and-archives/gi-roundtable-series/pamphlets/em-11-what-shall-be-done-with-the-war-criminals-(1944)

Glueck, S. (1946). *The Nuremberg trial and aggressive war*. New York: Knopf.

Goldensohn, L. (2004). *The Nuremberg interviews: An American psychiatrist's conversations with the defendants and witnesses*. New York: Knopf.

Goldhagen, D. J. (1996). *Hitler's willing executioners: Ordinary Germans and the holocaust*. New York: Vintage.

Goldhagen, Daniel J., Browning, Christopher R. (1996). *Symposium: The "willing executioners"/"ordinary men" debate*.. United States holocaust memorial museum. Available at: https://www.ushmm.org/m/pdfs/Publication_OP_1996-01.pdf

Gorton, S. (2015). The uncertain future of genocide denial laws in the European Union. *George Washington International Law Review, 47*, 421–445.

Gould, R. V. (1999). Collective violence and group solidarity: Evidence from a feuding society. *American Sociological Review, 64*, 356–380.

Gourevitch, P. (1998). *We wish to inform you that tomorrow we will be killed with our families*. New York: Picador.

Grimshaw, A. D. (1970). Interpreting collective violence: An argument for the importance of social structure. *Annals of the American Academy of Political and Social Sciences, 391*(1), 9–20.

Gross, E. (1980). Organizational structure and organizational crime. In G. Geis & E. Stotland (Eds.), *White collar crime: Theory and research* (pp. 52–76). Beverley Hills: Sage.

Guichaoua, A. (2015). *From war to genocide: Criminal politics in Rwanda 1990–1994* (trans: Webster, D. E.). Madison: The University of Wisconsin Press.

Hagan, J., & Levi, R. (2005). Crimes of war and the force of law. *Social Forces, 83*(4), 1499–1534.

Hagan, J., & Rymond-Richmond, W. (2008). The collective dynamics of racial dehumanization and genocidal victimization in Darfur. *American Sociological Review, 73*, 875–902.

Hagan, J., & Rymond-Richmond, W. (2009). *Darfur and the crime of genocide*. Cambridge: Cambridge University Press.

Hagan, J., Schoenfled, H., & Palloni, A. (2006). The science of human rights, war crimes, and humanitarian emergencies. *Annual Review of Sociology, 32*(3), 29–49.

Harff, B. (2003). No lessons learned from the holocaust? Assessing risks of genocide and political mass murder since 1945. *American Political Science Review, 97*(1), 57–73.

Hatzfeld, J. (2003). *Machete season: The killers in Rwanda speak*. New York: Picador.

Hiebert, M. S. (2008). Theorizing destruction: Reflections on the state of comparative genocide theory. *Genocide Studies and Prevention, 3*(3), 309–339.

Honig, J. W. (2007). Strategy and genocide: Srebrenica as an analytical challenge. *Southeast European and Black Sea Studies, 7*(3), 399–416.

Human Rights Watch. (1993). *Genocide in Iraq: The Anfal campaign against the Kurds*. New York: Human Rights Watch.

Human Rights Watch. (2011, May 31). *Justice compromised: The legacy of Rwanda's community-based gacaca courts*. Available at: https://www.hrw.org/report/2011/05/31/justice-compromised/legacy-rwandas-community-based-gacaca-courts

Human Rights Watch. (2015, December 23). *Rwanda: International tribunal closing its doors*. Available at: https://www.hrw.org/news/2015/12/23/rwanda-international-tribunal-closing-its-doors

Huppke, R. (2016). In fact-free America, maybe millions of trump supporters voted twice. *Chicago Tribune*. Retrieved from https://www.chicagotribune.com/columns/rex-huppke/ct-trump-illegal-votes-huppke-20161205-story.html

Huttenbach, H. R. (2004). Towards a theory of genocide? Not yet! A caveat. *Journal of Genocide Research, 6*(2), 149–150.

ICTY. (2012, February). *War crimes opinion poll discussed in Serbia*. Available at: https://www.icty.org/en/outreach/activities/war-crimes-opinion-poll-discussed-serbia

International Coalition for the Responsibility to Protect. (n.d.) *The crisis in Libya*. Available at: http://responsibilitytoprotect.org/index.php/crises/crisis-in-libya#violence

International Criminal Court (n.d.-a). *How the court works*. Available at: https://www.icc-cpi.int/about/how-the-court-works

International Criminal Court (n.d.-b). *The states parties to the Rome Statute*. Available at: https://asp.icc-cpi.int/en_menus/asp/states%20parties/Pages/the%20states%20parties%20to%20the%20rome%20statute.aspx

International Criminal Tribunal for Rwanda. (n.d.). *The ICTR in brief*. Available at: https://unictr.irmct.org/en/tribunal

International Criminal Tribunal for Yugoslavia. (2019, August). *Key figures of the cases*. Available at: https://www.icty.org/en/cases/key-figures-cases

Jehljune, D. (1994, June 10). Officials told to avoid calling Rwanda killings 'genocide.' *The New York Times* (p. 8).

Kelly, M. J. (2008). *Ghosts of Halabja: Saddam Hussein and the Kurdish genocide* Westport: Praeger.

Kiernan, B. (2007). *Blood and soil: A world history of genocide and extermination from Sparta to Darfur*. New Haven: Yale University Press.

Klein, J. (2007). Where should we stand to get the best perspective on collective violence? *Critical Sociology, 33*(5–6), 957–980.

Knechtle, J. C. (2008). Papers from the first amendment discussion group: Holocaust denial and the concept of dignity in the European Union. *Florida State University Law Review, 36*, 41–65.

Knowles, C. S. (1998). Life and human dignity, the birthright of all human beings: An analysis of the Iraqi genocide of the Kurds and effective enforcement of human rights. *Naval Law Review, 45*, 152–168.

Koenigsberg, R. A. (2009). *Nations have the right to kill: Hitler, the holocaust, and war*. New York: Library of Social Science.

Kolin, A. (2008). *State structure and genocide*. Lanham: University Press of America.

Krain, M. (1997). State-sponsored mass murder: The onset and severity of genocides and politicides. *Journal of Conflict Resolution, 41*(3), 331–360.

Kramer, R. C., & Michalowski, R. J. (2005). War, aggression and state crime. *British Journal of Criminology, 45*(4), 446–469.

Kressel, N. J. (2002). *Mass hate: The global rise of genocide and terror*. New York: Westview Press.

la Roche, D., & Roberta, S. (2001). Why is collective violence collective? *Sociological Theory, 19*(2), 126–141.

Laufer, W. S. (1999). The forgotten criminology of genocide. In F. Adler & G. O. W. Mueller (Eds.), *The criminology of criminal law* (pp. 71–82). New Brunswick: Transaction Publishers.

Lechtholz-Zey, J. (2012). The laws banning holocaust denial. *Genocide Prevention Now, 9*, 1–10.

Leezenberg, M. (2004). The Anfal operations in Iraqi Kurdistan. In S. Totten, W. S. Parsons, & I. W. Charny (Eds.), *Century of genocide: Critical essays and eyewitnesses accounts* (2nd ed., pp. 375–393). New York: Routledge.

Lemarchand, R. (2004a). The Rwanda genocide. In S. Totten, W. S. Parsons, & I. W. Charny (Eds.), *Century of genocide* (Critical essays and eyewitness accounts) (2nd ed., pp. 394–414). New York: Routledge.

Lemarchand, R. (2004b). The Burundi genocide. In S. Totten, W. S. Parsons, & I. W. Charny (Eds.), *Century of genocide* (Critical essays and eyewitness accounts) (2nd ed., pp. 321–337). New York: Routledge.

Lemkin, R. (1945). Genocide—A modern crime. *Free World, 4*, 39–43.

Lemkin, R. (1946). Genocide. *American Scholar, 15*(2), 227–230.

Lemkin, R. (2012). *Lemkin on genocide*. Steven L. Jacobs (Ed.). Lanham: Lexington Books.

Lemkin, R. (2013). *Totally unofficial: The autobiography of Raphael Lemkin*. Donna-Lee Frieze (Ed.). New Haven: Yale University Press.

Lipstadt, D. E. (2011). *The Eichmann trial*. New York: Shocken Books.

Lynch, M. J., & Michalowski, R. J. (2006). *Primer in radical criminology: Critical perspectives on crime, power and identity*. Monsey: Criminal Justice Press.

Madley, B. (2004). Patterns of frontier genocide 1803–1910: The aboriginal Tasmanians, the Yuki of California, and the Herero of Namibia. *Journal of Genocide Research, 6*(2), 167–192.

Maier-Kitkan, D., Mears, D. P., & Bernard, T. J. (2009). Towards a criminology of crimes against humanity. *Theoretical Criminology, 13*(2), 227–255.

Mattaini, M. A., & Strickland, J. (2006). Challenging collective violence: A scientific strategy. *International Journal of Psychology, 41*(6), 500–513.

McGoldrick, D., & O'Donnell, T. (2006). Hate speech laws: Consistency with national and international human rights law. *Legal Studies, 18*(4), 453–485.

Meredith, M. (2005). *The fate of Africa: A history of fifty years of independence*. New York: Public Affairs.

Mill, J. S. (1981). On liberty. In M. Curtis (Ed.), *The great political theories*. New York: Avon Books.

Mincheva, L. G., & Gurr, T. R. (2013). *Crime-terror alliances and the state: Ethnonationalist and Islamist challenges to regional security*. New York: Routledge.

Morrison, W. (2004). Criminology, genocide, and modernity: Remarks on the companion that criminology ignored. In C. Sumner (Ed.), *The Blackwell companion to criminology* (pp. 68–88). Malden: Blackwell Publishing.

Moses, A. D. (1998). Structure and agency in the holocaust: Danial J. Goldhagen and his critics. *History & Theory, 37*(2), 194–219.

Moses, A. D. (2008). *Toward a theory of critical genocide studies*. Online Encyclopedia of Mass Violence. Available at https://www.sciencespo.fr/mass-violence-war-massacre-resistance/en/document/toward-theory-critical-genocide-studies.html

Na'amat, T. and Deutch, I. (n.d.). *Legislating against anti-Semitism and holocaust denial*. Tel Aviv: Kantor Center for the Study of Contemporary European Jewry.

Nash-Marshall, S., & Mahdessian, R. (2013). Lies, damned lies, and genocide. *Metaphilosophy, 44*(1–2), 116–144.

NATO. (n.d.). *What Is NATO?* Available at https://www.nato.int/nato-welcome/index.html

Novak, A. (2015). *The international criminal court: An introduction*. New York: Springer.

Palmer, A. (1998). Colonial and modern genocide: Explanations and categories. *Ethnic and Racial Studies, 21*(1), 89–115.

PBS. (2004, April 1). *Ghosts of Rwanda*. PBS Frontline. https://www.pbs.org/wgbh/pages/frontline/shows/ghosts/etc/crontext.html

Power, S. (2002). *"A problem from hell": America and the age of genocide*. New York: Harper Perennial.

Pramono, S. (2002, October). *An account of the theory of genocide*. Paper presented at the Jubilee conference of the Australian Political Studies Association, Australian National University, Canberra.

PRNewswire. (2020, September 16). *First-ever 50 state survey on Holocaust knowledge of American Millnials and Gen Z reveals shocking results*. Available at: https://www.prnewswire.com/news-releases/first-ever-50-state-survey-on-holocaust-knowledge-of-american-millennials-and-gen-z-reveals-shocking-results-301131874.html

Pruitt, W. R. (2011). *Toward a modified collective action theory of genocide: A qualitative comparative analysis*. Unpublished doctoral dissertation, Northeastern University

Pruitt, W. R. (2014). Aggravating and mitigating sentencing factors at the ICTR—An exploratory analysis. *International Criminal Law Review, 14*, 148–176.

Pruitt, W. R. (2017). Understanding genocide denial legislation: A comparative analysis. *International Journal of Criminal Justice Sciences, 12*(2), 270–284.

Rafter, N. (2008). *The criminal brain: Understanding biological theories of crime*. New York: New York University Press.

Rafter, N. (2016). *The crime of all crimes: Toward a criminology of genocide*. New York: New York University Press.

Rome Statute of the International Criminal Court, Article 30(2). Available at https://www.icc-cpi.int/resource-library/Documents/RS-Eng.pdf

Rose, N., & Miller, P. (1992). Political power beyond the state: Problematics of government. *British Journal of Sociology, 43*(2), 173–205.

Rothe, D. L. (2009). *State criminality: The crime of all crimes*. Lanham: Lexington Books.

Rothe, D. L., & Friedrichs, D. O. (2006). The state of the criminology of crimes of the state. *Social Justice, 33*(1), 147–161.

Rothe, D. L., & Ross, J. I. (2008). The marginalization of state crime in introductory textbooks on criminology. *Critical Sociology, 34*(5), 741–752.

Rubinstein, W. D. (2004). *Genocide: A history*. Harlow: Pearson.

Rummel, R. J. (1995). Democracy, power, genocide, and mass murder. *Journal of Conflict Resolution, 39*(1), 3–26.

Salih, K. (1995). Anfal: The Kurdish genocide in Iraq. *Digest of Middle East Studies, 4*(2), 24–39.

Salomon, T. (2007). Freedom of speech v. hate speech: The jurisdiction of 'direct and public incitement to commit genocide. In R. Henham & P. Behrens (Eds.), *The criminal law of genocide: International, comparative and contextual aspects*. Burlington: Ashgate.

Saul, B. (2001). Was the conflict in East Timor 'genocide' and why does it matter? *Melbourne Journal of International Law, 2*, 477–522.

Savelsberg, J. J. (2009). Genocide, criminology, and Darfur. *Theoretical Criminology, 13*(4), 477–480.

Savelsberg, J. J. (2010). *Crime and human rights*. Los Angeles: Sage.

Schabas, W. A. (2009). *Genocide in international law: The crime of crimes* (2nd ed.). Cambridge: Cambridge University Press.

Scherrer, C. P. (1999). Towards a theory of modern genocide. Comparative genocide research: Definitions, criteria, typologies, cases, key elements, patterns, and voids. *Journal of Genocide Research, 1*(1), 13–23.

Schrager, L. S., Short, J., & James, F. (1977). Toward a sociology of organizational crime. *Social Problems, 25*, 407–419.

Shaw, M. (2007). *What is genocide?* Cambridge: Polity Press.

Sidell, S. (1981). The United States and genocide in East Timor. *Journal of Contemporary Asia, 11*(1), 44–61.

Silove, D. (2000). Conflict in East Timor: Genocide or expansionist occupation? *Human Rights Review, 1*, 62–79.

Skilbeck, R. (2008). Finding justice: The price of war crimes trials. *Human Rights Brief, 15*(3), 6–10.

Smiddy, L. O. (2006). An essay on professor Fronza's paper: Should holocaust denial be criminalized? *Vermont Law Review, 30*, 645–653.

Smith, R. (2010). Legislating against genocide denial: Criminalizing denial or preventing free speech? *Journal of Law and Public Policy, 4*(2), 128–137.

Spencer, P. (2012). *Genocide since 1945*. New York: Routledge.

Stanton, G. (2016). The ten stages of genocide. *Genocide Watch*. Retrieved from https://www.genocidewatch.com/ten-stages-of-genocide

Staub, E. (1989). *The roots of evil: The origins of genocide and other group violence*. Cambridge: Cambridge University Press.

Sternberg, R. J. (2003). A duplex theory of hate: Development and application to terrorism, massacres, and genocide. *Review of General Psychology, 7*(3), 299–328.

Stone, D. (2004). Genocide as transgression. *European Journal of Social Theory, 7*(1), 45–65.

Straus, S. (2012). "Destroy them to save us": Theories of genocide and the logics of political violence. *Terrorism and Political Violence, 24*(4), 544–560.

Sutherland, E. H. (1947). *Principles of criminology* (4th ed.). Philadelphia: J.B. Lippincott.

TheHistoryTV. (2016, March 23). *Genocide and the world response (State Department Rwanda 1994)*. Retrieved from https://www.youtube.com/watch?v=DFgLA2tE7_o

Thorpe, N. (2004, March 24). UN Kosovo mission walks tightrope. *BBC News*. http://news.bbc.co.uk/2/hi/europe/3565799.stm

Tittle, C. R. (1995). *Control balance*. Boulder: Westview Press.

Tittle, C. R. (2004). Refining control balance theory. *Theoretical Criminology, 8*(4), 395–428.

Tsesis, A. (2009). Dignity and speech: The regulation of hate speech in a democracy *Wake Forest Law Review, 44*, 497–532.

United Nations. (1948). *Convention on the prevention and punishment of the crime of genocide*. Available at: https://www.un.org/en/genocideprevention/documents/atrocity-crimes/Doc.1_Convention%20on%20the%20Prevention%20and%20Punishment%20of%20the%20Crime%20of%20Genocide.pdf

United Nations. (1993). *Security council resolution 827*. Available at: http://unscr.com/en/resolutions/827

United Nations. (1994). *Security council resolution 955*. Available at: http://unscr.com/en/resolutions/doc/955

United Nations. (1999). *The fall of Srebrenica*. www.un.org/peace/srebrenica.pdf. Accessed 24 Nov 2010.

United Nations. (2011). *Security council resolution 1973*. Available at: https://www.undocs.org/S/RES/1973%20(2011)

United Nations. (n.d.). *Responsibility to protect. United Nations Office on genocide prevention and the responsibility to protect*. https://www.un.org/en/genocideprevention/about-responsibility-to-protect.shtml

United States Department of State. (1994). *Action memorandum from assistant secretary of state for African affairs George E. Moose to secretary of state Warren Christopher "Has genocide occurred in Rwanda?"* George Washington University: The National Security Archive.

United States Holocaust Memorial Museum. (2017). *"They tried to kill us all": Atrocity crimes against Rohingya Muslims in Rakhine state, Myanmar.* Retrieved at https://www.ushmm.org/m/pdfs/201711-atrocity-crimes-rohingya-muslims.pdf

Uwizeyimana, D. (2014). Aspects and consequences of the Rwandan law of genocide ideology: A comparative analysis. *Mediterranean Journal of Social Sciences, 5*(23), 2370–2379.

Verdeja, E. (2002). On genocide: Five contributing factors. *Contemporary Politics, 8*(1), 37–54.

Watkins, J. C., Jr., & Weber, J. P. (2006). *War crimes and war crime trials: From Leipzig to the ICC and beyond.* Durham: Carolina Academic Press.

Weaver, R. L., Delpierre, N., & Boissier, L. (2009). Holocaust denial and governmentally declared "truth": French and American perspectives. *Texas Tech Law Review, 41*. 495–517, 506.

Williams, J., & Robin, W. (1994). The sociology of ethnic conflicts: Comparative international perspectives. *Annual Review of Sociology, 20*, 49–79.

World without genocide. (2017). *Myanmar—Genocide of the Rohingya*. Retrieved at https://worldwithoutgenocide.org/genocides-and-conflicts/myanmar

Yacoubian, Jr. George S. (2000). The (in)significance of genocidal behavior to the discipline of criminology. *Crime, Law, & Social Change, 34*, 7–19.

Yoshihara, S. F. (2006). Kosovo. In D. S. Reveron & J. S. Murer (Eds.), *Flashpoints in the war on terrorism* (pp. 65–86). New York: Routledge.

Index[1]

[1] Note: Page numbers followed by 'n' refer to notes.

W. R. Pruitt, *An Introduction to the Criminology of Genocide*,
https://doi.org/10.1007/978-3-030-65211-1

CPSIA information can be obtained
at www.ICGtesting.com
Printed in the USA
LVHW111905090123
736772LV00002B/219

9 783030 652104